Profitable Product Management

The Institute of Marketing

Marketing means Business

The Institute of Marketing was founded in 1911. It is now the largest and most successful marketing management organisation in Europe with over 20,000 members and 16,000 students throughout the world. The Institute is a democratic organisation and is run for the members by the members with the assistance of a permanent staff headed by the Director General. The Headquarters of the Institute are at Moor Hall, Cookham, near Maidenhead, in Berkshire.

Objectives: The objectives of the Institute are to develop knowledge about marketing, to provide services for members and registered students and to make the principles and practices of marketing more widely known and used throughout industry and commerce.

Range of activities: The Institute's activities are divided into four main areas:
    Membership and membership activities
    Corporate activities
    Marketing education
    Marketing training

OTHER TITLES IN THE SERIES

Profitable Product Management

JOHN WARD
MInstM, DipM, DipCAM
Course Director, College of Marketing

Published on behalf of the Institute of Marketing

HEINEMANN PROFESSIONAL PUBLISHING

Heinemann Professional Publishing
Halley Court, Jordan Hill, Oxford OX2 8EJ

OXFORD LONDON MELBOURNE AUCKLAND

First published 1984
Reprinted 1986, 1988
© John Ward and Institute of Marketing 1984

ISBN 0 434 92215 3

Filmset by Deltatype, Ellesmere Port
Printed in England by
Redwood Burn Ltd, Trowbridge

Preface

This book is intended as an aid to

- those very many Product Managers who have been given the job of managing a product range with little formal knowledge of the role of Product Management, what it is, or how to go about it;
- those who are actively practising the role but recognize the deep need for outside, objective advice even it if confirms that they are on the right track;
- those aspiring Product Managers who have an excellent academic background but little or no practical experience;
- and to the increasing number of students of business subjects whom colleges and universities are sending on to the market.

It is concerned with coherent, sensible, logical, and above all practical methods of creating and directing the destiny of a group of products or services on which the fortunes of organisations and employees depend and on which, in the aggregate, the fortunes of our country depend.

In step with the widening spread of marketing as a practical business function strides the expansion of the role of Product Manager. The harsh realities of international competitive pressures, in home markets as well as abroad, and of stringent economic conditions, force companies to market their products and services with much greater sophistication of technique and awareness of customer needs than ever before. The young, dynamic profession of marketing, very much in the growth phase of its product life cycle, is no longer the prerogative of fast-moving consumer good companies. It is expanding fast in industrial companies, service organizations, and specialist operations. In all these fields, Product Management is being introduced and widened as a vehicle for expanding profitable business, related to a carefully chosen customer market.

This book has been written to be of value to Product Managers of companies and organisations of all sizes, large and small, in consumer repeat, consumer durable, industrial, commercial, service, and professional markets. Whilst it is primarily written from the standpoint of the UK, the principles and techniques expounded should have great relevance to many overseas countries.

Titles of job functions frequently vary. The title of Product Manager seems to be very much on the increase; but in some companies, where for instance branding is of paramount importance, the title of Brand Manager is more sensible. In others, different markets may be important, such as frozen foods as compared with canned or fresh or dried, when the title of Market Manager may be more relevant. In still others, the tremendous concentration of buying power might make trades more appropriate: the educational market, the catering market, electricity boards, and so on. Occasionally one comes across Commercial Manager, and of course Product Group Manager. Sometimes the word Manager is replaced by Supervisor or Executive. In this book, the title Product Manager is intended to cover all these variants.

To avoid unnecessary repetition of the male and female gender throughout the text I have simply used the male gender. This should however be read as the female gender wherever applicable and is used for the sake of convenience only.

Finally, there are many good books about every single aspect of marketing. This book is about the management of all the elements of marketing, to further the profitable sales of a product or service, tangible or intangible, existing or still to be produced – about profitable Product Management in action. It is an awesome task with heavy responsibilities. As such it must be done well. But it is also exciting and creative. To make things happen releases the adrenalin, is egotistical, often enjoyable, at times frustrating, but deeply satisfying.

Contents

Acknowledgements

It is not only right but a pleasure to say 'thank you' to a number of skilled practitioners in marketing for their substantial help in vetting various parts of this book.

Marketing is far from being an exact science so that the contribution of very experienced marketing men, who are also friends and colleagues over many years, is both of practical value and comforting.

Ray Willsmer was appointed by the Institute of Marketing as the official reader for the Institute. His thoughtful examination and constructive comments on each chapter as it appeared were invaluable, as was his advice based on his own experience as author of several excellent books on aspects of marketing management.

Alan Wolfe, Marketing Services Director of Ogilvy & Mather, is probably the foremost expert on the application of the computer to marketing requirements. There is no shortage of expertise on the general use of the computer, but it is overtly scarce as far as its role for specifically marketing purposes. His research background and the effect of both subjects on forecasting made his comments trebly useful.

John Boddy is one of the few financial experts who not only really understand marketing and the effect of money matters on marketing decisions and vice versa but is himself a skilled entrepreneurial practical applier of what he preaches.

John Wilmshurst is probably already well known to readers of this book as the author of *The Fundamentals and Practice of Marketing*, a 'must' for all students studying for the diploma in marketing or for the CAM examinations. His wide experience, including a period as Managing Director of an advertising agency, gave a vital steer right at the beginning of writing this book.

Tony Yeshin, as Managing Director of Stowcastle Promotions, has a vast practical experience of all facets of sales promoting. No one could give more expert or more practical advice on this subject and his summary of various types of promotion will prove a useful check list for all marketing men.

Peter Kraushar, Chairman of KAE, Kraushar and Eassie, has a commercial lifetime's experience in product and company development and is also well known for his company's Mintel reports. Since the problem of product development is one which must always be in the forefront of every Product Manager's mind, his help and permission to publish just one of his screens is gratefully acknowledged.

Many other friends too have helped considerably through discussion from time to time, among them John Strafford, Chairman of Intech, a foremost authority on selling and sales forces. I hope that those I have not mentioned by name will accept the limitation of space as well as my thanks.

There are strings of letters after the names of those whom I have mentioned by name. These have not been included because I wanted to make this a very personal acknowledgement for all their help and for their friendship over the years.

Finally it must be said that all the views expressed in this book are my responsibility.

1 Responsibilities

*Line authority – Product range – Price –
Communication mix – Fact finding – Field
research – Strategic planning – Profitability
– Non-line authority liaison*

That wise old adage of not accepting responsibility without being given authority cannot unfortunately apply to Product Managers. They have to accept responsibility for everything to do with their product, yet many of the directly influencing factors which can shape its destiny do not come under their authority.

Since Product Management is a function of middle management it follows that top management must delegate responsibility and authority for certain aspects of the business to the Product Manager. Within different companies and organisations such delegation will vary significantly. Consider the responsibility for profit, for example. In theory this must be the responsibility of the Product Manager, but how can it be so in practice when the responsibility for many costs such as production, warehousing, distribution, personnel, administration, can in no way be transferred to Product Managers?

Line Authority

It will help to consider responsibility in two ways: those functions for which the Product Manager generally has direct line authority, such as advertising and promotion, and those which the Product Manager affects very substantially and is in turn affected by, such as production or finance, but over which others have direct authority. Direct authority represents a power base within a company and usually goes hand in hand with control of a budget.

As far as company departments are concerned it is usually the case that marketing has direct line authority over:

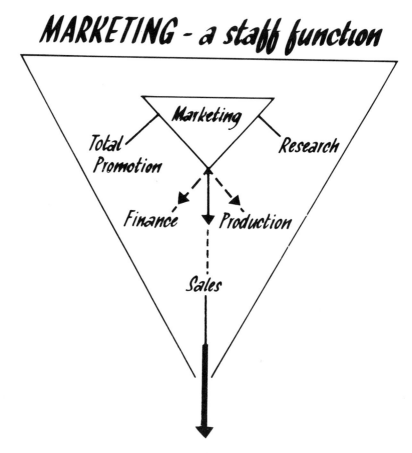

Figure 1.1 The role of marketing is to push everyone in the organization in the same direction. Usually marketing has direct line authority only over promotional activity and market research; sometimes over the sales force; never over finance or production but affecting both and being affected by them. Thus marketing action can only be achieved by persuasion.

(a) external communications – advertising, sales promotion, PR;

(b) market research (not including technical research such as R & D);

(c) product development.

Sales force control   According to research (ADP Network Services Ltd, July 1980) in 44% of companies with a marketing presence (75% of all in the sample) the top marketing person, whatever his title, did have direct line authority over the sales force. This facet of control had increased from 27% some three years earlier. But that is the situation at top management level. The Product Manager, of course, will have no direct control over the sales force. However, even if the Marketing Director has direct line authority he is not likely to get total commitment from them by dictatorship; he still has to persuade hard-nosed Sales Managers to accept a particular course of action. So in practice it makes little difference whether line authority exists on paper or not.

The Product Range

Let us begin the study of the Product Manager's direct responsibilities with the product range itself. In most cases it will have been inherited by the Product Manager, so his first duty must be to ensure that it is still right for the market as it now exists. This must obviously be based on an assessment of customer requirements through research or feedback from those customers, received either direct or through intermediaries such as salesmen or sales agents. This reading of the market must occur on a regular basis since trends are almost always more important than absolute figures. Not only ought this information to reflect reaction to one's own product but to competing products as well, so that one can keep up to date and, hopefully, maintain that strategic product difference which is so essential in any competitive market. This 'product positioning' is discussed in a later chapter but *if there is no communicable reason why your customer should come to you rather than to your competition, you have no reason for being on the market at all.*

So much for the present but what about the future?   Awareness of trends is all important to enable one to keep ahead of competition, let alone beside them with simply a name difference. Constant forward forecasting is necessary based on an appraisal of all possible market data, from the broad usage of the 'product life cycle' concept to an extrapolation of existing trends; from events in other countries to the latest technology. Laser scanners for detecting flaws in metal are in decline, for use in surgical operations in maturity, for cash tills in shops and libraries fast growing, for display and demonstration purposes just beginning. The changes that lasers have brought to very many industries are legion.

It is worth remembering that new products hardly ever occur. The first ball point pen, the first soya bean roast beef, the first microchip pocket calculator, the first liquid quartz movement does not happen often. The vast majority of new products launched every day are essentially variations on existing themes. The Product Manager has responsibility not only for ensuring that his product is right for the market now but also for the foreseeable future by setting in train any changes he believes necessary, for a new size, for a companion product, for a new quality, for a new market sector. *His product's future is his company's future.*

Company Involvement   Whether or not there is within his organization a separate New Product Development Manager, the husbanding of his product range within the constantly changing market environment is the Product Manager's responsibility. Whilst this is so and whilst he should be the prime originator of any development, any major change must represent a company involvement for which approval must be sought from higher authority. This may be particularly relevant in some sectors of the service industries. The development of a new service, whilst perhaps sparked off by the Product Manager, may sometimes require full company involvement. A Product Manager in a package tour company, for example, may well wish to expand his venues from summer holidays to include winter holidays too and thus maximize his market. Such an expansion obviously represents a major company decision rather than that of one Product Manager. Similarly in some industrial companies, particularly those involved with capital equipment, product changes and development have wide ramifications, not least of investment, which often require top management approval.

In high technology companies   marketing is often not competent to advise scientists on points of detail but increasingly they are asked to advise on market sectors most likely to represent profitable opportunities. No longer can one afford to allow pure scientists to work for ten years on a project, only to find, when it does at last see the light of day, that someone else has marketed the idea two years ago.

To summarise   the Product Manager should be responsible for ensuring that his product range is at all times attractive to that part of the total market from which he derives his prime business. Chapters 9 and 10 deal in detail with Product Range Management and New Product Development.

Price

Setting and maintaining a price structure is undoubtedly one of the most difficult facets of a Product Manager's direct responsibilities. To juggle the needs of his company with the reactions of customers, the trade and competition, often within the confines of tax requirements, monopolies commission findings, strictures from the Office of Fair Trading, codes of practice, legislation, and sometimes within the pernicious framework of tendering, requires the judgement of Solomon.

To sell on price   usually meaning a low price rather than added value or customer benefits, can often be detrimental to both market and product development. In the retail market, for example, the demand from multiple grocer's for 'own label' aluminium foil at low prices, with the inevitable shrinking of manufacturers' margins that ensued, is generally believed to have delayed market development by some five years since manufacturers did not have enough money left to spend on creating a strong consumer awareness, trial and momentum. In the printing industry, cut-throat competition, with little or no branding, has forced many out of business.

In essence, one must price in relation to market demand   In practice, however, very many companies, especially in industrial markets, do a 'cost plus' calculation: what are my costs, add on the company's required profit margin, and the selling price is the result. Astonishingly this method is even applied to companies which export; not only is this wholly wrong from the marketing viewpoint but it is not logical, as even a small consideration of such markets as cosmetics or spa water or supersonic travel will show. In exporting, such a 'cost plus' method fails to take account of both fluctuating exchange rates and major differences between countries. There is no greater misnomer than 'the Common Market'.

The correct way to price   must be to decide what customers are likely to pay within the various market-influencing factors, within the strategy for one's product, and within the minimum requirements of one's own company, then deduct costs, and if the margin of profit remaining is sufficient one is in business. If it is not, one must charge more, possibly in conjunction with a small product change, or reduce costs. If neither can be done there is no point in proceeding.

Many questions arise, of course. How to find out what the market *will* bear; can one be reasonably sure of costings; can one afford to gamble on substantial volume increases in the future with, hopefully, lower unit costs; might not 'contribution' be more relevant than profit; and so on. These are discussed in the Chapters 4, 5 and 6 on Marketing Strategy and Financial Control.

Standard trade margins   are coupled with pricing responsibility for the Product Manager. These must again be related to one's own strategy and company requirements but, almost inevitably, they will need to be very much in line with trade practice for the market. Whilst standard trade margins are the direct responsibility of the Product Manager, other margins may not be. For example responsibility for cash discounts will almost certainly rest with the Financial Controller, as will taxes such as VAT. Often special discounts for bulk purchase are a divided responsibility between sales and finance. In all these discounts, however, the Product Manager must be involved, and be prepared to make recommendations and really sell those recommendations. The same can be said for promulgating a 'Recommended Retail Selling Price' which should be a company rather than a product policy.

Communication Mix

Direct responsibility for all forms of communication with one's chosen audience and with the distribution outlets through which one sells, should be part of the Product Manager's portfolio. It naturally follows that this embraces total responsibility for the image of the product held by the public at large.

The natural starting point is the product   its naming, its packaging and any literature concerning it, such as instruction leaflets, warranty cards, and so on. It is just as important for the paint used on a fork lift truck to be aesthetically pleasing, functional and distinctive, as for the surface design of an instant snack. Hospital ward instructions for the use of a surgical chair should be eye catching as well as readable, and in keeping with the product image. The brochure for an office cleaning service or a specification sheet for an architect have just as great a need for good creative design as have car accessory components in a supermarket.

If one's own company does not possess a design department then it is often sensible to commission an outside design company. Many packaging manufacturers have a design department or offer a design service; some are good, and some are suspect to say the least.

Hand in hand with surface design goes naming   indeed in many cases the name must come first. Whether this is to be a company name such as Massey-Ferguson, or a brand name such as 'Save and Prosper' unit trust or 'Daz', is the responsibility of the Product Manager although within the confines of any relevant corporate strategy. As examples, all Heinz products must be Heinz; all Procter & Gamble products must have a predominant brand name, with P & G almost as a legal afterthought; all Johnson & Johnson products must have J & J but can also have a brand name such as 'Bandaid'. There are many differing corporate requirements which relate to the corporation's belief about the importance of a corporate identity.

Media advertising ranging from specialist technical publications to television, almost inevitably involves control through an advertising agency. For marketing people even to attempt to write their own copy, choose an appropriate type face and size, provide their own visuals, decide on and book their own media space or time, is pointless when they are not trained in these skills and when they have many other things to do with their valuable time. Yet extraordinarily there are people who struggle on, attempting to do all these things with conspicuous lack of success. Often the motive is expressed as 'We just need to keep our name in front of our customers', as if the customers' reactions and the money spent are of no importance and expertise is not needed in such cases.

Usually an advertising agency is used in a much wider context than purely for good advertising. Research tells us that clients use an agency as a sounding board for a wide range of discussion and advice. Certainly all product naming, product design, packaging and display material should be discussed with them at the very least. After all, on many occasions they are the only people talking directly to the end user about one's product. Since they talk to that same end user on behalf of a number of their clients, they often have a wider understanding of the user's motivations and actions than has one's own company. In this way the agency has a significant contribution to make.

Advertising agency liaison is, or should be, maintained at several levels including top management. But liaison between Product Manager and agency account executive should be the level at which executive control is exercised, subject to any overriding corporate image requirements or clashes with other company product advertising which must involve top marketing management.

As a general rule, it is better for the Product Manager to control the advertising through the advertising (or copy) strategy, his budget commitments, regular agency reports of 'Opportunities to See' and 'Cost per Thousand' and research studies, and to let the agency be concerned with 'creativity' unless the company has a qualified advertising manager overseeing all product advertising, in which case he can exercise competent creative control. This is examined in greater detail in Chapter 12.

Display material and all that is embraced by the phrase, such as price lists, window bills, posters, educational tracts, competition entry forms, and the whole plethora of pieces of paper, plastic, board, and other materials that are required from time to time, can often be designed and bought more cheaply from a display printer than through an advertising or design agency. Whilst recognising that tight budgets may demand such direct involvement, the Product Manager should always be conscious that this may be false economy because the creative involvement of printers, for example, in one's total marketing planning is minimal. The creative input and control that an agency can exercise over display material, in order to reflect an agreed common image in everything used for customer persuasion, often outweighs the extra cost of their fee for creative management control. On the other hand, agencies are likely to go to quality printers who charge top prices, simply to safeguard their own image. Consideration of cost of extra agency input, which of course must be paid for, is always a problem for Product Managers.

Direct mail   and all similar forms of direct communication with customers should be the prerogative of Product Management. It can often be more efficacious for pinpointing individual decision makers than media advertising. This is especially so when the potential customers may be few, or widely scattered, or require a longer message than is sensible in an advertisement. Of the many advantages of direct mail, the most pertinent is that it is a direct communication from one individual to another. To take advantage of this major benefit a letter should always be enclosed, whether or not with other literature such as price lists or order forms. But a direct mail letter is an advertisement; it is not the same as writing a sales letter to one's sales force; it must follow the rules of advertising. Consequently, whilst many of us do write our own direct mail 'shots' it is better for an expert to do so. In any case, very frequently one needs to hire or buy access to a mailing list through a direct mail specialist, either an agency which acts in the same way as an advertising agency, or a direct mail house; the British Direct Marketing Association can advise.

Because of all these factors, direct mail must be the responsibility of the Product Manager but all such communications strongly affect the sales force, assuming the company has one. Even if none exists, as in many service companies, there will certainly be some members who are responsible for gaining new business or for maintaining existing business, and close liaison with them is a necessity.

There remains the day to day communication with customers, primarily by the sales office but sometimes by accountants or others direct. These cannot be the responsibility of Product Management.

Sales promotion   as with so many other marketing actions, directly affects salesmen. There are occasions, usually very short term and tactical, where part of the sales force programme might include some customer sales promotions, but usually responsibility should devolve upon Product Management.

In fast moving consumer goods particularly, but in many other markets such as hotels and banks, buying power is concentrated in fewer and fewer hands. Increasingly, sales force structures must include key accounts salesmen or sales managers to be responsible for major buying offices. These salesmen have to be well-rounded business negotiators, able to negotiate quantities, prices, deliveries, advertising support and sales promotions. Marketing departments are often in a state of flux trying out various ways of handling this increasingly complex situation to best effect. In Beechams, for example, one element of the management in the Toiletries Division is a Trade Development and Relations Manager whose job it is to provide the back-up marketing information to the Key Account Sales Manager. In addition, there is a Sales Promotion Manager straddling all product groups and brands in the Division. In Whitbread London Ltd there is one Sales Promotion Manager responsible for all forms of sales promotion for some 1,000 public houses in his region. With such changes there is an increasing need for 'tailor making' promotions for special customers and a decreasing tendency towards national or regional promotions. Even in small companies and those with very specialised products this is the case.

In such a dynamic marketing environment, it is still necessary for the Product Manager to retain overall control of all forms of sales promotion affecting his product, for the very substantial cost will be debited to his budget. Whilst, with very few exceptions, all sales promotions are short term, in total they can have a very profound effect on brand image – adversely, if the standard of promotion and its administration is not in keeping with the image. In this context, while it is easy to give money away, this form of promoting, whether disguised as special discounts, advertising allowances, coupons, extra credit, introductory offers or whatever, can be very damaging to a good quality image. It is always difficult to justify a lower price than the customer expects to pay. Creative promotions can take more time and effort but are frequently better in maintaining an image, and also cheaper.

Public relations   With such a controversial and emotive subject an attempt at definition may be helpful. The relationship of the company with various defined 'publics', such as the financial community, one's employees, the townsfolk around one's factories or offices, is generally a corporate responsibility and should have its own corporate budget. Its effects can very seldom be measured in sales terms and it is not a Product Manager's responsibility.

Public Relations as applied to a product might better be called 'Product Publicity' and *is* the legitimate responsibility of the Product Manager. It may embrace anything from a poster for schools, a wine tasting or other in-store demonstration, support for an important customer's golf tournament, to that highly charged topic: sponsorship. Generally speaking, Product Publicity should be capable of measurement in sales terms although that can definitely not be said of sponsorship.

Such a neat division between Public Relations and Product Publicity is patently not possible in some organisations, particularly in the industrial and service sectors. In a company such as Datasolve Ltd, for example, the Product Manager for one package of computer services is inevitably affected by the actions of another Product Manager for a different package being sold to the same customer.

Both P.R. and Product Publicity should be considered for inclusion in any marketing action plan, if for no other reason than the altruistic belief that business should be, and should be seen to be, integrated into society.

Exhibitions and trade fairs   For the high cost of stage appearances to be at least amortised, definite objectives ought to be set. The number of new enquiries, number of follow-up appointments made, or even orders taken, are seen as sales objectives, and in consequence, exhibitions and trade fairs tend to be the province of Sales Management rather than Product Management. Obviously, the decoration of the stand, the face that it projects to the passing throngs, should represent the company. Thus the image elements should require and obtain marketing involvement. If one product or product category is predominant on the stand, then that involvement is the concern of the Product Manager, but the main responsibility rests with sales. This is also the case with the very many exhibitions of lesser importance: a surgical instrument company holding an exhibition in a hospital ward or lecture room; a shirt company showing their autumn range in an hotel room; an electronics firm presenting new technology to a group of overseas buyers in a conference hall.

In general   the most effective choice and mixture of all the communication methods available to the Product Manager test his skill and business acumen to the full. Constant checking, testing, analysing and adjusting is necessary to ensure that stated communication objectives are achieved. The driving school notice which said 'Special crash course for beginners' is not likely to be applicable to the Product Manager faced with the task of deciding the 'best' communications mix.

Fact Finding

Within most organisations it is true to say that the marketing man is the only person who sets out to gather and collate all pieces of data which could possibly affect the profitable sales of his product. Factual data is essential for all planning. Objectivity must be the watchword, not wishful thinking. *Obtain the facts not the folklore.* Always, think wider than the 'box': wider than the box of one's own office, one's own product, one's own company, or

Communications mix

Figure 1.2 A consistent image towards one's customers is a necessity whatever methods of communication are used. On the assumption that no company can afford every possible method, the 'best' mix to achieve concentration of effort is always a key decision for Product Managers.

even of one's own market. Learn to recognise connections which are not immediately apparent; for example, it is the case that the failure of the annual movement of anchovies down the Pacific coast of America directly affected the price of bread in the United Kingdom, since they are widely used for cereal fertilizer, particularly in Canada and the U.S.A. To take another case, the world's five hundred or so serious earthquakes every year, in well documented areas where the earth's plates move against each other, can profoundly affect the sale of tents.

There is so much data available if one searches deeply enough. This is especially so in the U.K. where we are singularly fortunate in possessing one of the best government information services in the world, primarily in the

Central Statistical Office but through many other ministries and offices also. There is a wealth of information available from trade and private sources too. Often the problem is to choose the data which are relevant and which have low degree of statistical error. Information sources are dealt with in a later chapter but essentially there are five major types:

(a) own company;
(b) government;
(c) private industry;
(d) regular audits;
(e) ad hoc research.

It is the Product Manager's direct responsibility to be constantly aware of and to collect all relevant data, and to circulate it within his company and to his agencies, wherever it can be of benefit. It is generally the case that the marketing department circulates more external data within the company than any other department, and this is as it should be. The Product Manager must be the fount of all knowledge about his product.

At the same time he cannot do without data from others within the company; such information as costings from accounts, work in process from production, finished goods stocks from warehousing, customer sales analyses, ex factory despatches and a host of others. The sales force can be an excellent source of immediate practical data about the market place. Beware, however, of placing too much reliance on an individual salesman's report. Salesmen are the very best eyes and ears of the world but sometimes the worst researchers. They can often warn of price changes, competing product changes, new introductions, new accounts and so on with great accuracy and usefulness, but to reflect attitudes, motivations, usage even, is far more difficult. This is partly because of the often subjective way in which the salesman considers his customers or prospects. He must react in a subjective manner to moods and words and actions, even though this may be the result of objective study. Partly the salesman may have his own personal reason for lobbying for a particular product change, a reason based perhaps on his ability to reach his targets or an excuse for not doing so; partly perhaps because of his own relationship with management: after all, he will not relay back anything that may be construed as detrimental to his own efforts; but perhaps mainly because of the relationship between the two, the interface between salesman and customer, in the sense of different motivations, different criteria. If the buyer likes the salesman he may give him a rosy picture rather than an adverse report, 'We're all colleagues together, let's be careful what we say to head office'. If he dislikes the salesman he may give him an answer much worse than is actually the case. The buyer may not want the salesman to know the whole truth for competitive reasons, afraid perhaps that the salesman will relay his information to his competitors.

These reasons are often just as applicable in industrial and service markets as in consumer markets, although it is probably fair to say that the more technical the product or service, the more accurately the salesman may reflect customer reactions. In industrial, professional, and service markets, customers generally are fewer, both buyers and sellers are more technically trained and sellers are perhaps geared more to being professionals of the industry than professional salesmen. The sale in these cases tends to be over a longer period of time and often encompasses more than one decision maker at more than one level and with different motivations; from production foreman to full Board presentation is by no means unusual in a 'Decision Making Unit'. In such markets the information required is often of a technical nature which can be given on an objective, quantifiable basis, and thus less subjectivity creeps in.

Field Research

Commissioning outside research is part of the day to day business of fact finding. If the company has its own research department then they must be involved and perhaps initiate projects of their own volition. But very many companies are not so endowed. In any case it is the Product Manager's responsibility to originate research projects which he believes necessary to supply more up-to-date information or to fill in gaps in knowledge and usually the cost must come from his product marketing budget. It is worth remembering that *research companies do not sell research, they sell management control information*. Costs can only be justified if the research data that results can actively be used in the control of marketing action for the product, and is not simply interesting information to have.

Because an understanding of some of the techniques of research can require a scientific training, such as sample validation, statistical significance and so on, these are best left to the expert. The Product Manager's responsibility is to find and to brief properly the best research company in all the circumstances. If he has his own company Research Manager to turn to then there is no problem, one hopes. If not, he could do worse than to ask the Market Research Society or the Industrial Market Research Association for advice, which will be freely and willingly given.

It should be recognised, however, that the report from the research company can only be of a technical nature and that the application of the research data to the market place must be the job of the Product Manager. A. C. Nielsen Co. Ltd recognise this necessity very clearly and in spite of their presenter's undoubted knowledge of, and familiarity with, a market situation, quite correctly insist that they cannot give market advice.

Industrial and service organisations often seem hesitant at using outside research companies, appearing to believe that such research is only for consumer goods companies. It is to be hoped that this is not a prevalent attitude since very great assistance in decision making can be obtained through market research. The fact that, for example, many such markets have relatively few customers and therefore statistically significant samples are often not possible, is no real problem for competent research companies.

Strategic Planning

All the data in the world is useless if nothing is done with it but *planning of any sort is not possible without good data* on which to base plans. Further, as far as Product Managers are concerned, all marketing plans have to be 'sold' to others within the company. Acceptance is necessary from hard-nosed Production Managers, Accountants, Sales Managers, and so on. It is much easier to 'sell' a forward plan if it is based on irrefutable fact. There are still some entrepreneurs who can ride by the seat of their pants and we cannot help but admire them. Further, every marketing plan worth the name requires an element of flair, of unpredictive action, of throwing oneself into the future based on feel, intuition, hunch. But planning does take as much of the gamble as possible out of the future. To reduce business risk must be cost effective and generally more profitable than riding blindly along on pants which tend to get shinier and less reactive with every year that passes.

The marketing strategy

There are three planning vehicles by which Product Managers control the future of their products. The first is the marketing strategy which distills the commercial policy for the product group into a succinct, coherent statement covering all actions. It should ensure that everyone within the organisation, from packaging to sales to agency, is working to maximum effect within the same parameters. Such a strategy should be long term, not changing with every wind that blows; for to change any part of it is to change a policy, and to be continually changing policies ensures that eventually no-one knows what the correct policy is, and consequently each goes his own way.

It is self-evident that such a marketing strategy requires deep thought, discussion, and time to prepare. It is so important that a whole chapter in this book is devoted to it (Chapter 4). From it stems the advertising strategy, sometimes called the copy strategy if significant sums of money are spent on advertising, and a sales promotion strategy if significant sums are spent in this direction.

When writing the marketing strategy, which may well take three months if no strategy exists and which should take up no more than one side of an A4 sheet of paper, the Product Manager must obviously have regard to an existing corporate strategy. Most companies have one and usually such strategies are more all-embracing, more general, less specific than a product marketing strategy.

Marketing objectives

The second planning vehicle which is the province of the Product Manager is the setting of objectives. Essentially these must be specific and numerate. 'To aspire to brand leadership in two years time' is not an objective: it is a pious hope. 'To achieve a turnover of one million pounds' is a specific aim against which progress can readily be measured. Objectives must be attainable and realistic. To set higher objectives than are reasonably attainable in the fond belief that employees will work harder is both unfair and self-defeating. Objectives are a valid management tool only if people are stimulated to their achievement.

As for a strategy, in well-regulated companies there will be corporate objectives included in the long range corporate plan, which often covers five or seven years: longer can only really be called star gazing. Within it will be annual objectives, usually updated every six months. The objectives set by the Product Manager should be more up to date, based on much more evidence and therefore more realistic than the comparable figures incorporated in the long range plan. Thus the Product Manager's numerate objectives should supersede those in the corporate long range plan, rather than the other way round.

Unfortunately, if the long range objectives are higher than those in the latest product plan, there are some Chief Executives who will insist that the figures in the long range corporate plan are sacrosanct and that the latest product objectives must be changed to conform. The Product Manager must then change the third control vehicle under his command, the 'Action Plan', so that the higher figures required can be achieved. Inevitably this will mean a greater marketing expenditure which may be the cause of much argument, but the Product Manager is making a very stiff rod for his own back if he meekly accepts a higher objective than he honestly believes possible to attain.

The annual marketing plan of action

This is the third control vehicle of the Product Manager and gives in great detail the exact methods by which the objectives will be achieved. If the objectives change, so must the plan. Unlike the marketing strategy, which should be unchanging, marketing objectives and marketing action plans must obviously change each year depending on the market and own product changes.

Ideally, the Marketing Plan of Action should cover a year at a time. If it covers two or three years there is less of a feeling of immediacy, in all likelihood it is less definite because of the probability of market changes, and so others have less commitment than to the more immediate annual plan. Other key executives must be committed to the plan of action because they will have to carry it out: Finance, Production, Sales, and others must all be consulted and in agreement, otherwise the plan is just a piece of paper with no force. To obtain commitment, the Product Manager's persuasive powers must be utilised to their utmost: he needs to be flexible on small points and win all the major actions. At the end of the day, when the plan has been agreed by other executives and top management and put to bed, it must be not just a plan but an executive document, which heads of departments keep in their top drawers to refer to frequently because they want to, rather than in their bottom drawer because they have to.

That plan now becomes a control document for the Product Manager to progress his planning through the year. In addition, if he is wise and annotates it through the year it is not only an action plan, an execution document, and a control vehicle, but also an historical record which he can use in preparing the following year's Action Plan which becomes far less of a traumatic chore than was the first.

Because the Annual marketing plan of action is a very detailed document, the Product Manager must constantly check that it remains realistic. Probably monthly meetings are necessary to check progress but certainly at quarterly intervals there should be a review with other key executives. Anything which is no longer tenable should be changed; there is no point in perpetuating action requirements or objectives if market fluctuations render them obsolete. If too many significant changes have to be made through the year, however, the plan was not sufficiently well thought out and discussed.

Each of the three control vehicles of marketing strategy, marketing objectives and marketing plan require a great deal of forecasting for each to be realistically based. Forecasting of all types is an integral part of a Product Manager's life and a separate chapter is devoted to it (Chapter 8).

Profitability

At the beginning of this chapter it was said that the Product Manager should consider the profitability of his product firmly his responsibility. But for a very large part of total costs, he can only try to persuade others to be cost conscious; in the purchasing of raw materials and packaging materials, for instance. With administration costs, for example, he can only accept the cost accountant's apportionment, which is usually a percentage worked out in the Finance Office or in the Organisation and Methods department. Obviously the Product Manager cannot be held to account for total profitability.

Contribution

In some companies the Product Manager is held to account only for the financial contribution of his products to the total company overheads. This approach certainly eliminates fixed costs from his responsibilities and is perhaps fairer; but profit as a responsibility then becomes no part of his stewardship. This seems unrealistic and tends to support the often justifiable criticism of marketing people, that their eyes are too often fixed on volume targets to the detriment of profit. In service companies, working on contribution is even less relevant since a high proportion of total costs is that of people and their time.

Accountancy terms

From the marketing point of view, one may well ask the question 'What is profit?' It is frequently the case within the accountancy world that different terminology is used for the same thing: even 'profit before tax' can mean different things to different accountants, and certainly there are many interpretations of 'gross profit'. It seems to be generally accepted that the only true measure of profit is on capital employed. But what is capital employed? Even with inflation accounting, people's views differ.

Financial ratios

For the Product Manager to control his products he needs two, or perhaps three, financial ratios. A financial ratio is the relationship between two different statistics; for example, profit to sales, or sales to stocks, or fee income per consultant. If the Product Manager has two such ratios which are really keys to his circumstances, he should have little difficulty in knowing whether or not his action plan is on course. This may be a better way of judging the effectiveness of a Product Manager than placing sole reliance on profit, however it is measured. At the end of the financial year, however, the company's profit will be an amalgam of individual product profits, even if costs have not been apportioned exactly, or if no attempt is made to do so.

Increasing profit

Whilst all this may seem somewhat academic and remote from marketing it is nevertheless very relevant indeed, and should be resolved in each organisation so that the Product Manager can consider ways of increasing profitability. Examples of available options are:

(a) Increasing sales volume – in a static market, often the most difficult;
(b) sales concentration on the more profitable outlets – salesman tend to concentrate on those from whom they receive a welcome;

(c) increasing emphasis on higher-volume lines in the range – changing the mix;

(d) Increasing minimum order size – often not keeping pace with inflation;

(e) charging for formerly free services – deliveries over a certain radius or below a certain quantity; charging for a speculative presentation; preparation of speculative plans;

(f) increasing prices – unfortunately, in these inflationary times, often the easiest way to increase profits;

(g) reducing costs – getting estimates; watching every element like a hawk;

(h) tightening up on credit and bad debts – little point in selling to customers who do not pay;

(i) sharpening the cost effectiveness of the communications mix – constant testing; pinpointing the potential customer who really matters

(j) being more professional in the handling of significant marketing budgets – watching the pennies.

Profits are of course the difference between income and expenditure, both of which are so important that further discussion can be found in Chapter 6.

Non-line Authority Liaison

Marketing decisions affect every department within the organisation, particularly production, sales, finance, warehousing, and distribution. Whereas stock control for example, is not generally a responsibility of marketing, the failure to have products available at the right depot at the right time can badly affect the implementation of the marketing action plan. This may be a result of poor forecasting leading to wrong purchasing, leading to wrong production scheduling, leading to wrong production, leading to wrong distribution, leading to a dissatisfied customer. But of course the forecasting could have been good and any other link in the chain at fault. Consequently the Product Manager must involve himself in all stages of the operation, not simply at the beginning and at the end. Any bottle neck, any hold up, can adversely affect the end result to the Product Manager's detriment.

The elements of control are awareness and persuasion. Awareness must be based on up-to-date and relevant reports, such as production schedules, work-in-process reports, or finished goods stocks, combined with personal discussions by telephone or in meetings. Perhaps the increasing use of video can combine the two and cut out a lot of wasted time. But be careful that personal rapport is not wholly mechanical or electronic. Persuasiveness is not based on a glib tongue; it is a result of mutual respect, which is sensed rather than overtly displayed; a sound grasp of facts concerning the situation; a real understanding of the other person's viewpoint, and an ability to present an argument in an interesting way.

Sales force

Throughout this book, the importance for Product Management of gaining the respect and cooperation of Sales Management and of the sales force in the field is stressed. Without it the annual marketing plan of action cannot be achieved. The basic function of Sales Managers, at whatever level, is to so motivate and control the sales people under their command that they gain the orders which create the profits to keep the company healthy and prosperous. This is true whether one is selling through distributors, agents, wholesalers, retailers, or brokers, or whether one is selling direct, by personal calling, on the telephone, or direct marketing. It applies whether you use professional sales people or others who may be professionals of their industry or specialism.

Product Managers must constantly be in touch, with a constant two-way communication existing between them.

From sales force
Sales statistics
Customer statistics and personal appraisals of buying changes
Sales force structure and changes to personnel, territories,
    journey routes, calling patterns
Sales incentives, achievements
Dealer incentives and achievements
Sales forecasts, breakdowns, and achievements
Product pluses and negatives, range problems, new product ideas
Advertising reflections and feedback
Sales promotions, operational problems, results, trade reactions
Distribution and delivery activities, packaging acceptance
Competitive activities, products, prices
Market trends and changes apparent or threatened.

To sales force:
Market statistics and analysis
Analysis of own and competitive sales, brand shares,
    regionality, seasonality
Research results
Customer analysis
Forecasts, objectives, targets
Advertising schedules and effectiveness
Sales promotion schemes, incentives, P.R. product publicity

Literature, display, brochures, leaflets
Tests proposed, operated and results
Product development, own and competitors
Special data for key accounts
Tenders, contracts, proposals, presentations
Strategies and plans.

Each requires the other: marketing cannot live in ivory towers. Product Managers should be seen to be involved with the 'sharp end' by going out with salesmen and into the trade by themselves, by attending sales conferences, by recognising the old dictum that we have twice as many ears as mouths so that we should listen more than talk. If there is a sales office, close contact will provide an invaluable first reaction to plans and personal feelings. As well as informal contact, formal meetings are necessary, perhaps monthly and with a preset agenda, of which the minutes can be given a wider circulation.

Production

We exist on the company's products, in service as well as in manufacturing organisations. Our future lies in constantly keeping that product range up to date. Product Managers are responsible for telling Production what to make, how much, and when it will be required. Production Managers are responsible for the way they make it, in what quantities at a time, and when they make it, provided it is available when and where required. As a profit centre in its own right, Production Management also has a right to a say in the marketing person's responsibilities as they affect Production.

Whilst marketing can only work by providing the customers with what they want, there is always likely to be a practical balance between cost effective production and market requirements. A case in point was Dairy Crest's problem at the launch of their 'Lymeswold' cheese, the first new cheese for some two hundred years, when demand was five times greater than supply because of tremendous publicity. The fact that production was more in the hands of the Milk Marketing Board than of Dairy Crest did not help the problem. It illustrates the vital need of Marketing and Production to liaise constantly and also for Product Managers to really understand the manufacturing process, to know and understand the snags and problems, so that marketing plans are rational and sensible.

On one particular issue Production may well have problems which seldom beset marketing, and that is with trade unions. Further, it is Production who must order through the Buying Office raw and packaging materials, based on marketing forecasts, so that often they are very much in the hands of outside suppliers.

Product Managers have a duty to supply Production with any information that may have a bearing on the production process. For example:

Forecasts of sales by time period
Anything which affects those forecasts on an on-going basis, such as the start date of a major advertising campaign
Product development ideas as soon as they start to affect Production, particularly if technical R & D come under them
Packaging changes envisaged similarly
Sales promotional schemes that will involve production or packaging
Costing problems that may be helped by Production
Marketing strategy and annual plans
Market data and trends.

Product Managers need information from Production similarly. For example:

Production schedules
Work in progress
Finished goods
Manufacturing problems that could affect availability of product
Cost breakdowns of advertising material, such as labels, stickers, etc.
Special orders progress
Changes in lead times, batch quantities, manufacturing processes.

The Product Manager should sit in on weekly production meetings, be seen to visit production plants, and generally attempt to be as knowledgeable and co-operative as possible, whilst maintaining authority over the total product marketing operation. He is the General Manager for his product.

Distribution

Distribution, in the sense of the physical transport of the product to the point of sale and in terms of the choice of distribution point, affects Product Management control. Stock control can make or severely mar sales. Excess stocks can adversely affect profitability and lead to panic measures such as price cutting, and similarly, shortages can lead to lost sales on a long-term as well as a short-term basis. What does the Product Manager need to know from Distribution?

Finished goods stocks with all normal breakdowns
Orders-delivered analyses, with delivery times
Changes in delivery methods, use of outside transport
Stock condition including packaging material
Stocks and condition of merchandising or advertising material
Special order positions
Any feedback on customer relations from drivers.

While in many instances Distribution can obtain details of goods being received by them from Production and of orders for delivery from Sales, it is sensible of Product Managers to send to Distribution copies of anything which could eventually affect them so that they are in the picture. This is particularly necessary for things like special promotional packs, special contracts or orders, and for annual sales forecasts by time period. Again, Product Managers would do well to visit depots and warehouses from time to time to ensure on-the-spot attention to detail and awareness.

Chipboard manufacture epitomises the sort of distribution pattern that causes innumerable problems of stock control, of delivering orders within a reasonable time, and of customer satisfaction, which Product Management should keep constantly under review. Chipboard is widely used in many industries but particularly in furniture, building construction, ship building and D.I.Y.

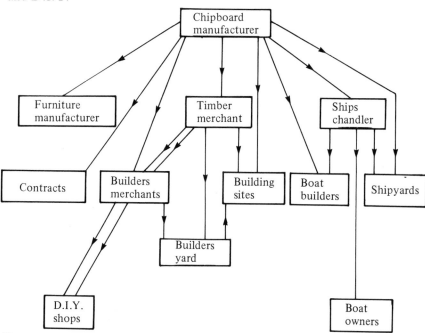

Figure 1.3

It is obvious that such a complex distribution pattern could very easily become a costly nightmare. Requests from the sales force for direct delivery to a particular building site or shipyard if acceded to, could easily become the norm, involving extra transport, extra stocks, extra paperwork, extra selling time and so on. On the other hand, one full lorry load delivered to one building site at the request of a timber merchant who is a good customer, has obvious attractions.

2   Organisation and Control

The four functions: Finance, Marketing, Production, Personnel – Especially Marketing – Product management action chain – Marketing department structures – Control at the top – Product Manager's position – Constant review – The ideal – Attitude to people – Attitude to responsibility – Attitude to customers – Attitude to self

The Four Functions

In the broadest sense, there are only four functions in any company or organisation:

Finance   From payroll to bought ledger to company accounts

Marketing   Including sales, market research and all forms of communication.

Production   With distribution, warehousing, depot structure, transport. Applicable to service operators for such things as architects' drawings, insurance proposals, brokerage agents.

Personnel   The right people properly motivated and trained, in the right place, at the right time.

No matter what the title of the head of each function, such as Finance

Director, Marketing Manager, Factories Controller, Administration Manager, each is on a par with the other in terms of importance within a company. Each must plan, put those plans into execution, and ensure, through detailed control, that they work in practice. Each requires information from the other to carry out these operations effectively.

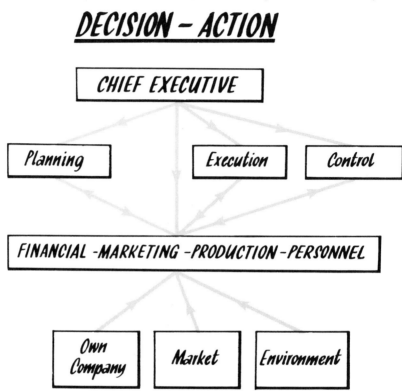

DECISION - ACTION

CHIEF EXECUTIVE

Planning   **Execution**   **Control**

FINANCIAL - MARKETING - PRODUCTION - PERSONNEL

Own Company   **Market**   **Environment**

Figure 2.1

Especially Marketing

Since Marketing, perhaps more than any of the other three functions, is vitally concerned with the outside world and its effects upon the company's total marketing operation, such as government action, social change, new techniques, international market trends and changes, as well as the more immediately relevant market intelligence, there should be a greater flow of information emanating from Marketing than from any other function.

A reasoning interface

This internal relationship is an extremely delicate one. It must be based on reasoned argument, persuasion, and diplomacy. Marketing plans will only be actioned effectively if others carry them out with commitment. Whenever Marketing is newly incorporated into an existing structure, entrenched positions and understandable jealousies will inevitably make life difficult for the ambitious Product Manager. He can succeed when the people who are affected realise the great help that sensible marketing decisions can be to their own operations. Thus a conscious effort on the part of the Product Manager is required, aimed at winning respect, not affection. Product Managers cannot impose their will. They must gain co-operation.

Top management outlook

Marketing must permeate a company. It cannot be practised by a few individuals in isolation. If top management support a marketing-oriented outlook the Product Manager will have, and will be seen to have, greater authority. A contrary or negative attitude however, will result in the Product Manager banging his head against so many brick walls that he will either give in or get out.

Product Manager's Action Chain

The start point must be the chosen customer: to find out everything possible about them and their market environment, through information gained from every possible source both outside and inside the Product Manager's own organisation. This leads to the formation of a marketing strategy and plan of action. Whilst this is the job of the Product Manager, top management involvement is necessary to ensure conformity with corporate plans and to provide any necessary funding.

Such plans need to be actioned through some form of selling operation and campaign of communication, often through a distributor network, in order to reach the consumer. This is not the end of the chain since a constant feedback of data must be maintained because nothing is static and change is occurring constantly at every level. Thus it is a chain which is endless and the structure of the Marketing Department must be able to take account of all these factors.

Marketing Department Structures

Very many marketing departments originate and grow like Topsy, often with little coherence or future direction. Consequently they vary widely, and sometimes wildly, not only between industries but between companies within the same industry. There is evidence now of more rational structuring and some trends are emerging. But marketing is a dynamic discipline which

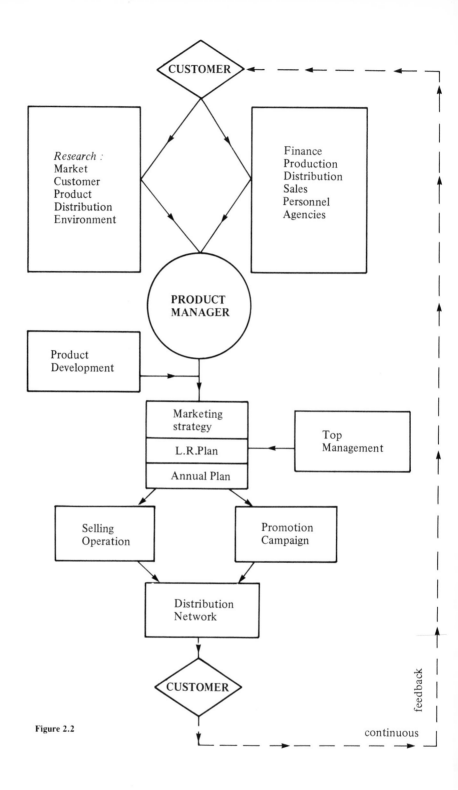

Figure 2.2

not only initiates change but must also reflect change, and companies are often very different one from another. Any guidelines, therefore, must not be considered as rigid and dogmatic, but simply as reasonable in often fluid situations.

Control at the Top

Marketing probably has a closer affinity with sales than with any other department. At its most basic, no marketing plan of action can ever succeed if the sales organisation is not committed to it, since they are the only ones who can obtain orders. Furthermore, every part of the marketing plan affects every salesman directly often where it matters most – in his pocket. To many Chief Executives it therefore makes sense for the top marketing person, whatever his title, to have direct line authority over the sales force. Increasingly this is the case as in the following example.

Figure 2.3   International Paint Co. Ltd: Vehicle Refinishing Division

The Product Manager's Position

So where does this place the Product Manager, and is that a sensible title for him anyway? There are many influencing factors which can help to determine his role in differing situations.

1 Is the Product Manager responsible for a group of products, such as commercial and industrial paints as in I.C.I., or is he responsible for an individual brand such as Daz for Procter & Gamble? Obviously in the latter case 'Brand Manager' would be a better title.

2 Does the market breakdown make it sensible to have *Market* Managers, such as for Heinz Salad Varieties?

3 Can the total market sensibly be broken down into recognisable sectors,

Figure 2.4 ICI Paints Division (primarily Dulux)

such as catering, or franchise, or hotels, or duty free, all sectors which Trust House Forte cover?

4 What does the company policy require? A single paramount company name such as Cadburys; individual brand names for a company such as Rowntree Mackintosh, or a bit of both, such as Johnson & Johnson for baby products and Band-Aid (By J & J) for first aid dressings?

Figure 2.5 Johnson and Johnson Ltd

5 How does the concentration of buying power into fewer and fewer hands affect overall marketing? Is there an increasing need for a marketing backup for Key Accounts sales executives, such as in Beecham's Toiletries Division where there is a Trade Development Executive.?

6 Can there be justification for separate marketing service people to back Product Managers, with statistical data as for the Marketing Controller in Reckitt & Colman Household Division, or in the Regional Offices of Tarmac Civil Engineering? Increasingly the computer is a very useful adjunct to a Product Manager's existence but often the vagaries of programming, of modelling, of statistical analysis, require the help of an

expert in these fields. Similarly with advertising where media buying agencies, so-called creative hot shops, and production companies may separately be used instead of the full service advertising agency, or where several agencies are used by a large company. Co-ordination is necessary for maximum buying and creative effectiveness. Research can also be seen as a service operation to Product Management for both regular audit data as well as for ad hoc research.

Figure 2.6   Reckitt and Colman Household Division

7 Is the total turnover for any one brand or product category so vast that the sheer size requires it to be broken down into manageable portions, as for Dulux paint?

8 Should the Product Manager have product development responsibilities or should he be left to look after his own existing products lest they be neglected?

9 How technical is the product or market? Does it require qualified biochemists or horticulturists such as in Fisons fertiliser division, or actuaries as in some insurance companies?

10 To what extent is export a separate function or part of the U.K. Product Manager's job, as is too often the case?

11 Has the company newly embraced marketing, and to what extent is formal marketing planning practised? Is the first executive the only one, and should he be called Marketing Manager, as in A. E. Edmunds Walker, the distributor of car components?

12 Is one restricted to a finite distribution chain but with hundreds of products, as in Unipart where responsibility for say, clutch and allied products is a substantial job?

13 How large is the company overall? Is it vast requiring a large number of responsible marketing executives, like Unilever, or is it comparatively small?

14 How competitive is the market? Is it highly competitive, like video, or is it very specialist, such as water purification?

15 What are the relevant profit centres within the company? Each Product or Brand Manager must have a budget and access to detailed costings, and be a profit centre. Hence, in Tarmac marketing is allied to regional offices, which are the profit centres.

16 To what extent is top management able and willing to delegate decision making? A dictator feeds on 'yes' men.

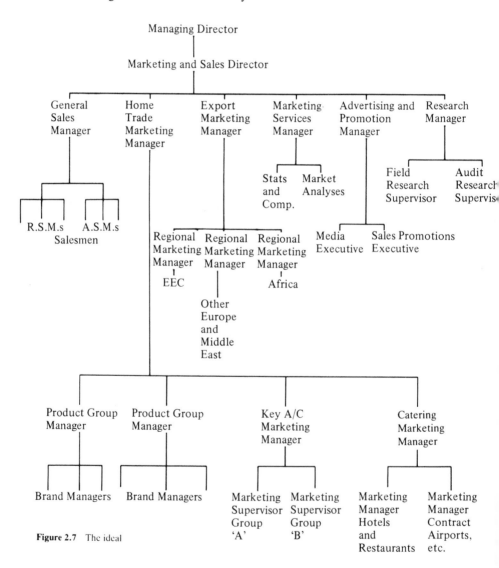

Figure 2.7   The ideal

Constant Review

All these considerations inevitably lead to a plethora of structures, each of which can be perfectly sensible for individual companies. There is a constant need to review responsibilities in light of the ever-changing patterns of markets and the speed at which product development and innovation occurs. An ever-present organisational danger in such a fluid situation is the overlapping of responsibilities. This must be avoided like the plague: divided responsibility is no responsibility.

The Ideal

If one took a mythical large company and endeavoured to create a suitable marketing structure, perhaps it might look like figure 2.7, with suitable scaling down by size and type of company.

Attitude To People

Marketing deals with human beings at all levels and with all their foibles and idiosyncrasies; with customers, traders, own staff; with internal politics, preconceived ideas, traditional ways of thinking, antagonism to change. Thus the profession of marketing cannot be an exact science.

In the final analysis the Product Manager's decisions will be based on his belief that a particular course of action is best in all the circumstances to achieve set objectives, based on peoples' motivations, on their doing things.

Any and every decision actioned by a Product Manager affects others. Indeed, it can be argued that a Product Manager does not *do* anything himself, except think. He must persuade others to action the doing: producers to produce, salesmen to sell, printers to print, advertising agencies to create advertisements.

Understanding

The attitude to adopt is one of understanding with genuine sympathy – of empathy. Such an attitude requires a real liking of people. To recognise that, for good and sufficient reasons, others often think and act differently from ourselves. For instance that:
  (i) women do think and act differently from men:
  (ii) professional buyers are often unadventurous for what, to them, are perfectly sound reasons;
  (iii) retailers act in certain ways based on their front line dealings with often recalcitrant customers;
  (iv) Managing Directors have different constraints from Managers;

(v) Production Managers, who live in the world of machines and trades unions, have special problems;

(vi) sales forces must often react subjectively, since their success is bound up with being accepted as individuals by a widely diverse range of buying types.

Objectivity

In contrast, the Product Manager must be wholly objective at all times, whilst recognising all the varying subjective influences affecting those from whom he must obtain commitment. His statements and actions must be based on fact, or as much fact as possible, or rational deductions from factual evidence. These are less argumentative, more likely to be accepted as reasonable, easier to communicate and usually more palatable. Constantly being objective does not often lead to being loved by those around one but it should engender respect. But to be respected requires us to respect others.

Attitude to Responsibility

Authority

Product Management is a middle management position and therefore must report to higher authority as well as be responsible for others. But whilst this is so, the Product Manager must act as responsibly as if he alone were responsible for his product. This requires a commitment and a maturity which, age for age, tends to be greater than for any other management function. It is the reason why Product Managers are called Managers. They must manage people and events for the benefit of the whole company, not simply for one product or product group, even though all their endeavours revolve around one product group.

Expertise

At whatever organisational level the Product Manager is, he must be *the* expert on his products. A constantly up-to-date knowledge of product, competition, and market is a natural prerequisite for good planning and decision making. Knowledge in depth of product does, however, beg certain questions. For a very technical product or service, for example, is the Product Manager likely to be sufficiently technically competent to understand all its ramifications? Must he be as expert on, say, streptomycin or financial exchange regulations as a research chemist or banker? Can he be expected to understand the financial ramifications and accountancy jargon of costing detail? Is it possible, without being a medical representative, to understand what makes a hospital consultant or nursing officer tick? The answer must be 'Yes' as far as humanly possible. Certainly sufficient understanding is necessary to be able to talk on the same wavelength to an accountant, a chemist, a nursing officer, without pretending the same degree of expertise, so that they respect as reasonable any action the Product Manager takes.

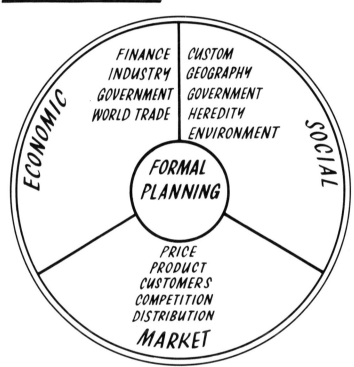

Figure 2.8 The product manager must be *the* expert on every conceivable factor which could influence his product. This is a vital prerequisite for good planning and decision making.

Practicality

It is very easy to be general and not specific. Whilst a good Product Manager must be a good thinker he must also be essentially practical, a difficult combination when the day-to-day affairs leave little time for wider thought. To this end, mental discipline is essential for without it there is the danger of living only from day to day, taking fire brigade action, panicking, extemporising. There is no excuse for woolly thinking, half baked ideas naively executed. To maintain overall control and yet to have a total grasp of detail requires both a good thinker and a good practitioner.

Attitude To Customers

'The desire to protect the consumer is today gaining ground in many quarters. It is rooted in the idea that in the modern economy, a seller's interest tends to override the buyer's interest. The knack of earning money has received far more attention than that of spending it.' That statement could easily have been written today. In fact it was written 22 years ago in an OEEC report entitled *Better buying through consumer information*.

> 'The unscrupulous deceive the unwary
> and
> The innocent deceive themselves.'

Judging by the opprobrium which often seems to be heaped on the heads of business men and women, by pressure groups, by politicians, by the media from time to time, the above statement encapsulates the general public's attitude to 'those nasty commercial people'. How can such an attitude be justified when 90% of the working population is employed in organisations for which the end result of their efforts is the selling of goods or services to others? Perhaps many of them are unhappy at the way in which their own managers behave. Perhaps it originates from some of our educational establishments, since the commercial world has never been the first choice of graduates en masse, even though many of them finish up in business. Or perhaps it is justified, at least in part. Perhaps some of us in executive positions are different people when we run our businesses from the sort of people we are when we and our families buy things.

Monopolies

One can argue that although we have a Monopolies Commission in the UK there are no monopolies. Take London Transport: there is plenty of competition from the car. Take the water boards: one of the fastest growing markets is bottled water. Tasting the chlorine and thinking of all the other chemicals there might be in tap water, one has a certain amount of sympathy for the bottler of 'Scotch Mist'. Private medicine is fast growing since the National Health Service does not seem to perform sufficiently well for very many people.

However, there are many customers who have no alternative to London Transport, or the water boards, or the NHS and for them these services are most certainly monopolies. Whatever the monopoly does, these people must accept it. Since they are a totally captive audience, those responsible for decisions ought to be especially careful and aware of moral considerations, without the necessity for those customers to have recourse to an ombudsman.

Cause and effect

Let us make no mistake, we in business have brought down on our own heads much of the consumerism to which we are subjected: the Consumer Affairs Officers, codes of practice, such a maze of legislation from the EEC as well as our own parliament; that no Product Manager cannot but plead ignorance of the law.

Businessmen in the past have been responsible for selling unsafe space heaters, children's nighties that catch fire, infant milk overseas where it is quite impossible to expect the right conditions for sterilisation, and so on. There are many examples of such insensate acts in industrial and service markets too; the insurance policy that is not all it seems to be when the accident happens, the high rise building that can be unsafe in certain circumstances, the river pollution through untreated effluent. Not infrequently, such acts are compounded by insensitive reactions to accusations, more concerned with avoiding lost sales than with righting a wrong.

The buck stops

What is responsible for such anti-social activity? Is it unthinking innocence? Is it simply bad marketing through ineffective testing or no testing at all? Is it the mad rush to keep up with competition (and ahead if possible) that blinds one to the normal cautions? Is it the fast buck from a plastic duck syndrome? Is it sheer callousness? *Who* is responsible? At the end of the chain it is inevitably top management of course. But someone starts the ball rolling. Someone makes a decision to go ahead without knowing all the facts or deliberately ignoring them. Someone actually puts the product or service on the market. Product Managers cannot shake off their own responsibilities by pointing the finger at someone higher up. This is about as pointless as moving a deckchair to a better position on the Titanic's boat deck.

Morals and ethics

Let us be positive. All Product Managers have a duty to ensure that their products are fit for the job to be done, and that communication with the recipients is 'Legal, truthful, honest and decent'. This duty is one of morals and ethics, morality being concerned with the distinction between right and wrong and ethics being the way in which the moral question is treated. So this duty is a personal one. Honestly carried out, it is also in the best interest of one's own company. The chaos which might be caused by marketing a product or service unfit or unsuitable for the job to be done, must rub off

HONEST

TRUTHFUL

LEGAL

DECENT

Figure 2.9

uncomfortably on *all* the company's products and its name. It takes many years to create a strong company or brand image but it can be quickly killed by one false move. People's memories can be long and irrational, as corned beef suppliers can testify after a typhoid scare.

The end result

Since the Product Manager is responsible for the total image of his product and since it is so important that this image should be favourable, he must think through the use of the product to the end of the chain. What happens to plastic milk bottles, for example, if local authorities do not possess incinerators capable of burning their chemical constituents? If BP does have to cross beauty spots with pipelines, how can they overcome the howls of anguish from environmentalists which could adversely affect product sales? If a particular type of detergent does cause dermatitis to some people, however small a minority they may be, should they not be warned?

Finally, think of one's own staff. Many of them must be sceptical of the morality of some company executives, otherwise the myriad consumer organisations would not be so well supported and financed. From the point of view of internal productivity, pride in working for a fine company, and the fact that Product Managers must work among them, Product Managers should be seen to be whiter than white.

DECEIVE YOURSELF AND YOU DECEIVE OTHERS!

Attitude to Self

So what sort of person makes a good Product Manager?
- Someone able to size up a situation quickly, realistically;
- who can sense the possible effects of external actions on his own plans;
- who has that all-important 'feel' of the market place;
- who can see the various courses of action in the circumstances, can gather all the options and take positive action to exploit the situation;
- who has the presence and commands the respect of his colleagues for obtaining commitment to his measures;
- who is logical, numerate, clear, and mature in thought as well as incisive and decisive in action;
- someone not easily panicked, who is a good thinker and a good practitioner;
- knowledgeable to the point of being an expert on his or her products: to an extent, a Jack of all trades but a master of marketing:
- who can systematically and single mindedly attack and attain the objectives set, with overall control and a grasp of detail;

– who, with all his logicality, can exercise an entrepreneurial flair when the occasion demands;

– who can communicate with and sell to top management, as well as to his colleagues, associates, equals and peers.

But any generalisation would be wide of the mark in specific industries. One can imagine that a Product Manager for heavy earth-moving machinery, such as Blaw Knox, would be very different from a Product Manager for Helena Rubinstein cosmetics, and that a Product Manager in a service industry, say a computer bureau such as Datasolve, would be very different from a Product Manager for surgical instruments such as Thackray or Allen & Hanbury.

The more technical the product, the more technical the Product Manager needs to be, in order to be able to command respect and understand the real benefits of his product in the market place. A Product Manager responsible for laboratory techniques concerning the effects of tides on harbour installations, would not stand much chance if he knew virtually nothing about the sea and hydrography. A Product Manager in a veterinary pharmaceutical company responsible for pills which literally have to be blown down the throats of cows, must have a good knowledge of biology and biochemistry. Such people exist and do a good job. No one can put a rubber stamp on them as a type. Indeed one of the joys of marketing is that it is very difficult to be type cast.

3 The Marketing Audit

A new appointment – Product history manual – Time period – Check lists: Own company; the market; product range; finance; production; distribution; purchasing; export; sales; sales force; communication; research – Services

A New Appointment

Planning must be based on fact. What is our history, our achievements? What is our image among trade and customers? What is our expertise? What are our strengths on which to base future action? What are our weaknesses which we must avoid exacerbating? What are our problems and opportunities and how do they compare with competitors? How are we suited to the market and to what sectors in particular? Where can we best exploit the market? Where do we want to go; is that a sensible direction and does it require radical change? These, and many more questions must be answered before we can plan rationally.

Let us start from the position of a Product Manager newly appointed to take over responsibility for an existing product range – of services, of industrial goods, of consumer products. He may have been in the company concerned for some time or have recently joined; it is immaterial. Even if the Product Manager has been employed in that company for some years, perhaps as a Product Manager on other products, he must look at the total marketing situation afresh, just as a Product Manager who is a new employee.

The 'Product History' Manual

To gather all the information that one needs to know will take a great deal of probing, of asking questions, of searching for and scrutinising past reports, of examining research reports and perhaps even of carrying out extra research. And all the information *must* be written down.

The most sensible way is to originate and maintain a 'Product History' manual to which extra sheets can be added from time to time. Of course, such a task takes time, which can often be ill-afforded. But it will save endless time in many directions, not least in preparing the annual marketing plan and in avoiding arguments and winning arguments. In a busy career, it is extraordinary how easy it is to forget things and to become ensnared in the trap of giving a subjective reply to an important question, because it is too difficult to find the real answer. It is rather like taking up Pelmanism and then forgetting why one took it up in the first place!

Time Period

How far back should one go if no product history exists? Five years at least for detailed data if at all possible, and as far back as one can go for more general data. In well regulated companies much of the data required already exists in computer data banks and all that is necessary is to retrieve it. Increasingly product histories will be kept as separate entities in computers' memories for retrieval at any time.

Check Lists

There are very many good marketing check lists in existence, some exhaustive, some particular to an industry. Let us list all the factors which must be audited, that are important to know before we can plan, execute and control effectively. There will be a host of other factors that it would be nice to know in certain circumstances, but let us stick to essentials. For the sake of clarity, they will be grouped under specific headings.

Own company

   1 Corporate objectives
       – Markets in which a major presence is required
       – Allied markets which may represent a profitable opportunity for expansion from an existing small base

- New markets to be exploited
- Plans for merger, acquisition or joint venture which could affect Product Manager's responsibilities
- Plans for future manufacture, factoring, or acting as selling agents
- Financial objectives, profit, turnover, R.O.I., etc.

2 Corporate strategy
- Policy on corporate image required
- On naming, design, presentation to the various publics specified as important
- Financial control, funding, stringencies, reports
- Product development and diversification
- Use of existing assets within the group, company, division, etc.
- Personnel management, hiring and firing, training and incentives.

3 Corporate long range operating plan
- Broad methods by which the corporate objectives will be achieved in terms of production, distribution, marketing, sales, administration and finance.

4 Procedure for controlling and updating Corporate Operating Plans and the anticipated involvement of Product Managers.

The Market

5 Size, make up by market sectors, by product groups, by company or brand shares, by sizes and other market distinctions.
6 Trends based on past history, changes brought about by technical advances, movements dictated by raw material availability and prices, by distribution changes, etc.
7 Consumer and other customer attitudes and usage habits; decision makers and influencers.
8 Effects of government actions, social changes, economic factors.
9 Pricing structures and levels through the market history.
10 Major communication methods and changes.
11 Product life cycle curves: position, duration before change, limiting factors.

Product range

12 Specification: original and any subsequent changes by formulation, recipe, size, type, market sector, etc.
13 Research and development programmes for future changes.
14 New product introductions, launches, innovations, withdrawals.
15 Patents, warranties, trade marks, licences, guarantees involved, legal constraints.

16 Product tests which have not been proceeded with, with reasons.
17 Sources of raw materials, fluctuations, seasonalities.
18 Sources and types of packaging materials.
19 Own packaging changes: historically, under consideration.
20 Brand name, method of presentation, relationship to other company names. Printing specifications: name, logo, contents, legality.
21 Source of design work, of product, packaging and surface design.
22 Trade and consumer awareness, attitude, image, usage of product and packaging. Ease of handling, opening, keeping, protection.
23 All the above for competitors together with comparative data.
24 Sources of data for own range and competition with degree of accuracy, frequency and up-to-dateness.

Finance

25 Turnover history of product range at 'current' and 'stable' prices, in total, and by major product type and market sector breakdowns.
26 Profit history, gross and net before tax, relative to turnover, investment or capital employed, in total, and by main product type, customer type and relevant market sector breakdowns.
27 Financial contribution history similarly.
28 Relevant financial ratios for marketing, such as profit to turnover, turnover to stocks, turnover to marketing budgets.
29 Reasons for changes in above records.
30 Source of funding expansion; availability of working capital.
31 Internal bookkeeping transactions across profit centres.
32 Price history in terms of average selling price less tax with relationship to inflation, competitors prices, product development, with reasons for change.
33 Price structures, standard trade prices, quantity discounts, other standard discounts such as multiple head office overriders, trade advertising allowances, increases on preceding year, etc.
34 Costs records in terms of raw materials, packaging materials, manufacturing costs, administration, selling, distribution, servicing, R & D, marketing.
35 Marketing budget breakdowns in total and separately for such relevant items as advertising, sales promotion, printing, research, etc.

Production

36 Capacity for manufacturing product range, in relation to other products, by time of year. How flexible is this?
37 How labour intensive is this capacity, what degree of skills are required,

what are trade union relations, how important are they?

38 Production times, speeds, lead time required.

39 Problems involved in shifting production within the range and to other products.

40 Requirements if product shape, size, specification, etc. are changed.

41 Possibilities and problems of adding promotional messages or literature.

42 What happens to produced goods, finished goods stores, warehouses, depots?

43 Method of production scheduling, progress chasing, setting targets.

44 Quality control methods and standards.

45 Reports of scheduled production, work in process, finished goods, warehouse stocks. Accuracy standards.

46 Any subcontracting, reliance on other group companies, overseas branches.

47 Methods of liaison between production and new product development, design, sales, finance, distribution, marketing.

48 System of costing, relationship with purchasing, method of apportioning manufacturing costs among various products.

Distribution

49 Stock locations, factory finished goods stores, depots, warehouses.

50 Physical methods of moving stocks, type of transport, travelling times, flexibility; to other store houses and to customers.

51 Handling methods at various locations; degree of mechanisation, palletization, handling.

52 Packaging requirements for ease of handling, size, shape, coding, protection, reading of product type and destination.

53 Stock levels, methods of deciding and of arranging change, reports and checks, up-to-dateness, rotation, out-of-stock.

54 Order processing methods and times; split deliveries action, notification and checking.

55 Relationship of distribution points to customers, and of delivery people to customers.

56 Distribution reports, analysis, accuracy.

57 Liaison with marketing, sales, production, finance.

Purchasing

58 Methods of ordering raw and packaging materials, machinery replacements, additions and maintenance.

59 Methods of ordering design work and print work and any other allied

purchase such as outside promotional services, legal clearances, etc.

60 Lead times required for all these.

61 Relationship between sales forecast, production requirements and purchasing. Methods of deciding on quantities.

62 Duration of purchase contracts, relationships with suppliers.

63 Quality control of goods inward, methods and action.

64 Basis of decision making concerning supplier, home and overseas.

65 Procedure on cost control, ability to keep up-to-date with prices, technological innovation, suppliers.

66 Methods of advising problems on delivery, price, quality, etc.

67 Liaison with marketing, production, distribution, finance.

Export

68 In which countries of the world is the product range sold?

69 Which are important sources of sale and for what parts of the range?

70 Any product changes for specific countries?

71 List of packaging changes, particularly of surface design.

72 Trade mark differences, licences, quotas, guarantees.

73 Sales methods, own company offices and sales forces, associated companies, distributor network, sales agents, joint ventures.

74 Physical distribution methods to reach overseas markets.

75 History of sales by product, by geographical area, in sterling equivalent turnover, sterling profit, and, where possible, market shares.

76 Total market data by country including competition, seasonality, etc.

77 Methods of communication by country, advertising, sales promotion, exhibitions, trade fairs, conferences, etc.

78 Marketing budget history by country, related to sales.

79 Costing breakdowns by country.

80 Any major problems of shipping documentation, with shipping and forwarding agents, with production, with quality control particularly in different climates, with different cultures and standards of living.

81 Prospective expansion areas.

Sales

82 Unit sales with breakdowns for market sector, geographical region, customer type, by size, product type, etc. (NB: sterling sales are recorded under 'Finance' at no.25.)

83 Relationship of sales to forecasts and targets. Method of forecasting, bases used, accuracy expected.

84 Establishing targets: of sales, distribution, order size, etc. Methods of origination, control, notification. Are targets based on forecasts and

are both the same as objectives? Are there separate forecasts for sales, production, and finance?

85 Methods and accuracy of sales analyses, orders received, returns, additions and errors, ex-factory, own production, or subcontracted, factored, acting as agency, etc.

86 Order analysis by number, size, customer type, area, split deliveries, time from original order to actual final delivery.

87 Order processing procedure, checks, action with enquiries and complaints.

88 Order to call ratios or to quotations, proposals or tenders submitted. Major reasons for success and failure. Cost of ordering.

89 Sales to call ratios, average order size, minimum order size.

90 Market shares by company, product group, brand, self and competition, in units and sterling, by type, area, etc.

91 Trends and responsibilites.

Sales force

92 Structure and organisation with changes in operation, responsibilities, calling patterns. Use of telephone selling, agents, distributors, etc.

93 Personnel, with changes in numbers, location, job specification.

94 Methods of incentive, commission, bonuses, promotions, in cash, in 'perks', and in kind.

95 Journey cycles, routing methods, time spent selling related to administration, research, merchandising, travelling, etc.

96 After sales service organisation and reputation.

97 Merchandising methods, personnel, effectiveness, including demonstration.

98 Sales reports, method, frequency, content, new product ideas.

99 Method of selling, use of call cards, hand held computers, transfer ordering.

100 Use of price lists, brochures, literature, display material, samples, audiovisual aids.

101 Cost to the marketing budget, as opposed to the sales budget, of printed material, aids, samples, promotions, joint trade advertising, exhibitions etc.

102 Customer correspondence and personal communication, handling and reporting procedure. Access to legal advice.

103 Recording of inter-group, or inter-division sales.

104 System for provision of quotations, specifications, tenders, proposals; of providing drawings, speculative presentations, examples, costs, etc. Drawing up conditions of contract.

105 Sales conferences: where, when, why, modus operandi, contribution

required from marketing.

106 Training both in company and external, method, frequency, effectiveness, progression, cost.

Communication

107 Media advertising history, customer, trade, public relations, corporate. Media used and media tested, in season and out of season. Weights, measurements, costs, effectiveness.

108 Relationship of media advertising to sales, to attitude changes, to distribution, to market shifts.

109 Relationship to competitive advertising.

110 Media production costs, original artwork, copyright, relationship between 'above' and 'below-the-line'.

111 Media budgets, method of origination, past history at constant prices, relationship to sales.

112 Sales promotion history, successes and failures, methods of measurement. Promotional activity against trade, customer, and middle men.

113 The extent to which promotional pricing activity has affected recognised standard trade or consumer prices.

114 Cost effectiveness of sales promotions against various customer types.

115 Relationship to competitive promotional activity.

116 Direct mail, use, cost and effectiveness against various 'publics'.

117 Public relations activity, rarely measurable in sales terms.

118 Product publicity, more specifically against product group and more measurable.

119 Use of direct mail lists, list management, response rates.

120 Display material, purpose, use, effectiveness, for special promotional activity or regular business, exhibitions, conferences, etc.

121 Literature such as price lists, brochures, specification sheets, notices, promotional activity. Costs and usefulness.

122 Exhibitions, trade fairs, conferences, seminars, usage, usefulness, costs.

123 Integration of own total communications programmes with trade or special customer requirements.

124 Use of outside agencies, advertising, sales promotion, research, design, media buying, creative, public relations, marketing, commando sales, demonstration, merchandising, exhibitions, direct mail, etc. Responsibilities and costs.

125 Origination of strategies, particularly advertising and, often, sales promotion. Who originates, how controlled, what changes and why.

126 Overall integration of all communications, are they projecting the same image?

127 Measurement on continuous basis, methods, responsibilities.
128 Comparison with competition on a continuous basis, methods and costs.
129 Legal constraints and controls, responsibilites and monitoring methods.
130 Constant relationship of all forms of communication in whatever 'mix' to sales.

Market research

131 Regular data provision for market assessment from government sources, primarily the Central Statistical Office but many others: from retail audits, consumer audits, Customs & Excise, trade associations. History, method, and costs.
132 Specially commissioned studies with limited or general circulation. Reports, analyses, costs.
133 Overseas research reports with relevance to own markets.
134 Research reports on specific aspects such as usage and attitude, motivation, psychology, preference, advertising effectiveness.
135 Marketing 'steers' to technical research in suggesting lines of enquiry relative to perceived market trends.
136 Test market reports by self and of competitors actions.
137 Research budgets, relationship to overall marketing budgets and, where possible, to turnover.

Services

The vast majority of these facts are just as applicable to service organisations as they are to manufacturing companies. Many service organisations also manufacture, or have products manufactured for them, such as some software computer houses. Others, such as banks and building societies, manufacture 'products' such as ledger accounts which are specific things. Still others, like auctioneers, are concerned with making products available.

But there are some who provide 'pure' services, like assessors and consultants, to whom the section under 'Production' may less readily be applicable. In general, therefore, for service operators, this checklist is directly applicable. If it is not so in every aspect, then look for analogies for your own business.

General

As we said at the beginning of this chapter, the first time that all these facts are sought, collected, collated and analysed, it is a long job, a chore. But no

Product Manager can possibly be the single expert on his products without them. All these facts are *essential* for the efficient handling of a group of products: they are not just nice to know. Product Managers must know what happened in the past, what worked, and what was a waste of time, effort and money: what was cost effective, and what created a stir but was not worth it; what aroused interest without raising sales. One cannot plan ahead without a knowledge of the past, all the time remembering that the data represent past history, not the future. It is the trends of the past which are so important for the future. Since the origination of the Product History is such a task, once it exists it is almost criminal not to keep it up-to-date, for oneself and for one's successors.

4 Strategic Planning

*Purpose – Longevity – The corporate
strategy – Marketing strategy composition
– Market sector definition – Prime
customer profile – Product positioning –
Source of business – Location of sales –
Geographical area – Seasonality – Pricing
structure – Budgetary control – Example*

The first, most important and most difficult necessity for any Product
Manager is to create a formal marketing strategy for his or her group of
products. In essence it is the commercial policy which provides a set of
guidelines between which every operation carried out by any individual or
department in the company must be contained. A 'strategy' is a policy,
whereas a 'plan' is the action that will be taken, within the confines of the
policy, to achieve objectives.

1 Purpose

The marketing strategy is a positive document designed to ensure that
everyone is pushing in the same direction, that the right hand does know
what the left hand is doing, that every part of the total marketing effort
dovetails with the rest. For example, that the design department or agency is
not trying to appeal to men if women are the purchasers, that salesmen are
not striving for deep penetration and volume if exclusivity is a prime
requirement, that packaging is suitable for the instore position that it is

hoped to occupy, that the distribution chain is suitable for reaching the prime customer, and so on.

This is as vital a necessity for industrial and service products as it is for consumer goods. The strategy must be tight enough to ensure that everyone is very clear as to the direction of their involvement, no equivocation, no 'ifs and buts', no escape holes. However, it must be recognised that it is a series of policies designed to last for a long time. It is not a list of 'dos and don'ts'. Nor does it contain any numbers since numbers change from time to time, therefore no statement has finite limits. It consists of a series of tramlines which are not so restrictive as to cramp all entrepreneurial flair and not so wide that it allows anyone to do as they wish. In consequence, the definition of each element of the marketing strategy requires great skill and verbal discipline.

2 Longevity

Three things follow   First, it requires deep, careful thought, analysis of all relevant data and of all possible policies. Secondly, it is vital to have discussions with many other people in executive positions in order to gain their commitment to the strategy. Thus there is a recognition that it will become the *company*'s marketing strategy and not the sole property of an individual Product Manager. Thirdly, it must be long lasting. To change any part of the marketing strategy for any crosswind that might blow is to change a policy. And if one is continually changing policies then no-one, not oneself, or one's colleagues, one's employees, one's customers, or the end-consumer, knows where he stands, what is required of him, what he can expect. All coherence, all consistency is gone. The marketing strategy should last for years. Strategies for household names such as Persil, Mars, Coca Cola, Smirnoff, are essentially the same as they were ten or twenty years ago.

But major changes in markets do occur   OPEC does quadruple the price of oil, video does open up many new avenues of communication, changes in money markets do give new opportunities to banks, consumer tastes do change, particularly when exposed to product developments based on new technology. So occasionally elements of a marketing strategy should change.

In retailing one can think of a number of groups who might have benefited by a change in direction: Woolworths, Barkers, the Co-op among them. Mothercare did see the problems looming for them as a result of the declining birthrate, and changed the appeal statement of their strategy from 'Mothers of children from minus one to plus five' to 'minus one to plus ten' in

very good time. They changed their merchandise and layouts and promotional activity accordingly.

Some industrial companies seem more prone to ossify than to progress.
Shipbuilding, cutlery, heavy engineering, constructional cladding spring to
mind. In the service sector the microchip has caused many a computer
bureau to think hard about its future direction. So one must be sensible and
recognise that deep rooted market changes must inevitably require changes
in the marketing strategy. If, however, the strategy was well thought out in
the first place, foreseable changes ought to have been taken into account so
that any change to any part of the strategy is a rare event.

3 Corporate strategy

In larger companies there will be a number of different Marketing
Strategies relating to groups of products or services which have different
market requirements. Obviously a company like Gillette will have separate
strategies for razor blades, Papermate writing instruments, and toiletries.
Toiletries themselves represent a diverse range of products and it would
probably be necessary to have different strategies for Badedas bath products
and Rightguard male toiletries, among others, since they are in different
markets, even though the same customers may buy in several of those
different markets.

All the individual strategies will collectively result in a general image of
the company by different 'publics' such as customers, traders, employees,
shareholders, the financial community. It is important, therefore, that each
individual strategy conforms to an overall corporate strategy, so that, just as
an individual strategy lays down guidelines for individual product groups, so
the corporate strategy lays down guidelines for the total company.

It is usually true to say that the corporate strategy will be much more
general and less specific than an individual marketing strategy. By its very
nature, it must be so. It is also probably true to say that it is less a marketing
strategy than a general business strategy. The corporate strategy may lay
down policies on criteria such as:

- The method and use of the company name: all-important for such as
  Massey-Ferguson; far less important for Procter & Gamble, as far as
  consumers are concerned, than brand names such as Daz or Crest; ICI
  for one division such as agrochemicals, but Dulux for decorative paints;
- The style within which, whatever name is paramount, its usage must
  conform, from the typeface to the colour of paint;
- Financial requirements: basis of funding R & D, test markets,
  expansion; relationship with banks, financial institutions, shareholders;
  profit requirements, taxes, inflation;

  – Future development: through own devices, aquisition, merger, joint venture; with potential brand leaders requiring substantial investment or where only modest outlays are required;
  – Physical assets: restrictions imposed by existing factories, distribution methods, personnel; contracting out; overseas sources; group resources;
  – Personnel: attitudes of longevity or hire and fire; relationships with trades unions, staff associations; dissemination of information; salary levels: delegation of authority.

Product Manager's involvement   The corporate strategy is not of course the responsibility of the Product Manager. Through his Marketing Manager or Marketing Director he must be aware of it, since the guidelines it contains apply to him just as to other key executives. Top marketing management has a prime responsibility to ensure not only that each individual strategy conforms to corporate requirements but also that they do not clash.

In smaller companies,   in many service companies, and in one market companies, one *marketing* strategy may suffice. It is still sensible to have a separate *corporate* strategy based on the business as a whole, including such points as investment policies, diversification, factoring, overseas links, and so on. The marketing strategy must concentrate on specific marketing factors in the same way as an individual marketing strategy in a multiproduct or multimarket company; but there will be some common elements between the two as for example in image, or product positioning, or distribution.

Marketing strategy composition

As a discipline in cogent, meaningful prose, the strategy should ideally cover no more than one side of an A4 sheet of paper. For this to happen, every word must count, every loose word be tightened, and every superfluous word ruthlessly excised. Whilst in individual companies, headings will undoubtedly vary, short pungent paragraphs will cover the following nine topics as a minimum:

  – Market sector definition;
  – Prime customer profile;
  – Product positioning;
  – Source of business;
  – Location of sales (distribution);
  – Geographical area coverage;
  – Seasonal influences;
  – Pricing structure;
  – Budgetary control.

Figure 4.1

Let us now analyse each of these key factors in turn.

Market Sector Definition

On the certain assumption that no one product group can possibly be 'all things to all men' one must define the market sector that we are in, or wish to be in, from the customers' points of view, that is from the point of view of the end user, then select that part of the market that we can best tackle. This will be largely based on our strengths and weaknesses related to the market audit we have carried out and explained in Chapter 3. We require a clear, concise, and understandable explanation of the market, broken down into the major market segment that is of prime interest to us.

How do we define the market?

The market in which a research company operates is not 'research' but 'management control data'. The buying company is not basically interested in research techniques but in filling in gaps in up-to-date knowledge, in order to take some of the gamble out of decision making. A company selling warehouse shelving is in the market for 'profitable stock control', the shelves are only a means to an end. Housewives buy washing powder because they want 'clean laundry'. Railways are in the market for 'moving goods, livestock and people from A to B', not for the transport of things by wagons on railway lines.

What sort of market sectors might there be?

There are a number of sector definitions common to all markets but most will have breakdowns which are peculiar to them.

Profitability   Many factors influence profitability. Inevitably there will be some types of customer who will be slow payers, or who will demand and expect extra discounts, or who will demand extra service, or who are simply geographically further away so that selling and distribution costs are higher.

Pricing   Within any competitive market there will be a spread of prices, some premium, some middle of the road, and some low. These tend to appeal to different types of customer and for different reasons.

Usage frequency   Some customers will be heavy users, some medium, and some light. This can apply to readers of newspapers, to frequenters of doctors' surgeries, to users of local authority social services, to users of Persil, to holders of conferences. They represent different market sectors, buying or using goods and services in different ways and for different reasons.

Commitment   'Prime' users are those 'sold' on the idea or product, requiring no persuasion except to choose between different brands or suppliers. To these people the product or service is a necessity, not a luxury. If a woman has six children and she goes out to work she must have access to a launderette or her own washine machine, to fast foods, and many other things.

'Potential' users are generally more numerous, are not totally convinced of the merits of the product category, require persuasion, information, even education. If one can persuade them to accept the usefulness of the product category and can capture them for oneself, one often gains strong loyalty.

'Non-users' are often more numerous still and are probably best left to

MARKET POTENTIAL

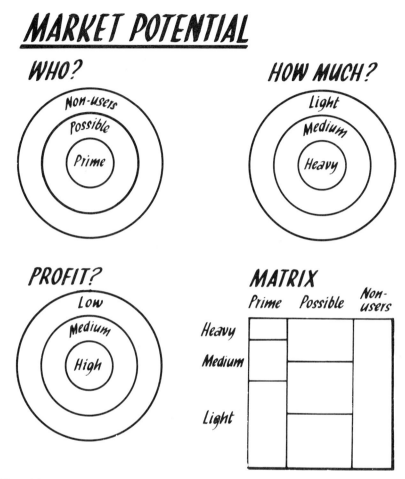

WHO?

Non-users
Possible
Prime

HOW MUCH?

Light
Medium
Heavy

PROFIT?

Low
Medium
High

MATRIX

	Prime	Possible	Non-users
Heavy			
Medium			
Light			

Figure 4.2

major companies or brands to try to motivate. However, if the market is to grow and develop, many from this category must be attracted with cogent reasons.

Quality   Some customers will require the best quality that money can buy, and whilst 'value for money' is an ever present requirement, their prime stress is on top quality. This may be for socio-economic reasons, pride, or just plain snobbery, or it may be that their business requires the very best quality. Others are perfectly satisfied with an average standard quality, whilst still others are only interested in the lowest quality, probably for money reasons.

Design Company	Explanation	Comment
All design work.	We can design anything.	? Believable. ? Affordable. ? Give satisfaction to all from fork lift truck to fashion.
Consumer Products	We can design anything in the consumer world.	From a washing machine to a beer mat?
Fashion.	We have particular skills in fashion design.	Greater concentration of effort, perhaps affordable to reach. But there are fashions in drinks, men's wear, wallpapers.
Ladies' outer wear	We have particular skills in designing ladies' outerwear.	Very believable. Easy to reach few customers. Perhaps narrowed market too much. Can expand later.

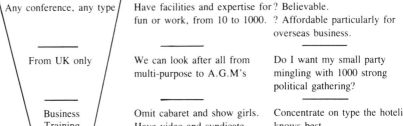

Conference Hotel

	Explanation	Comment
Any conference, any type	Have facilities and expertise for fun or work, from 10 to 1000.	? Believable. ? Affordable particularly for overseas business.
From UK only	We can look after all from multi-purpose to A.G.M's	Do I want my small party mingling with 1000 strong political gathering?
Business Training	Omit cabaret and show girls. Have video and syndicate rooms.	Concentrate on type the hotelier knows best.
Max. 50	Comprises bulk of working conferences.	Realistic, believable and affordable.
50 mls.	Can get good name locally for regular business.	Easy to reach, narrow, perhaps too restrictive.

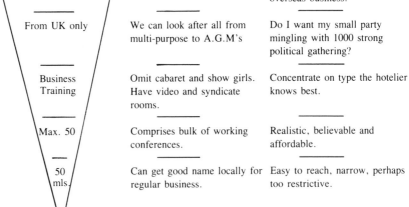

Figure 4.3

Volume   Each of the above will have an effect on sales volume. From the supplier's point of view, he might be equiped with modern production lines and have an absolute requirement for maximum volume, and therefore must opt for deep penetration of the market. Usually this applies to major companies. Those, such as I.C.I., Heinz, N.G.Bailey in the electrical contracting world, have organisations, administrative systems, and financial resources which can more efficiently operate with large volumes of business than with small. Other companies may find that smaller volumes, perhaps for more specialist or more exclusive products, are perfectly acceptable and even desirable.

Fewer customers, more concentration of effort, lower costs, lower volumes can lead to greater profits. Holiday Inns have specialist conference facilities which they must keep busy all the year round. Many smaller hotels can be more flexible and only require conferences in autumn or spring, having no difficulty in maintaining room occupancy in the summer and at Christmas.

Usage methods   Most markets lend themselves naturally to breakdown by type of usage. The markets for lasers cover usage for detecting flaws in metals, for surgical operations, for geological surveys, for retail cash tills, for display and demonstration, among others, each of which is a separate market sector. Rat killers are used by the farming community, by local authority 'rodent operators' as well as by domestic consumers. Financial loans may be for major one-off purchases, for evening out cash flow, or for regular day-to-day trading, in both the business and domestic markets.

Distribution   Sales methods, such as the use of one's own sales force, telephone selling, sales agents, distributors, mail order, or direct response advertising, tend to prescribe the type of outlet through which one sells, and these can represent different market sectors. For example, cut flowers and dry bulbs have a natural chain through the fresh fruit and vegetable markets to the shops, but many major multiples now require and receive direct service and special packing from producers such as Geest and Selected Growers.

Estée Lauder in the up-market cosmetic world is only interested in some five hundred department stores who will accept the company's own 'consultants', whilst Rimmel will sell to whosoever will buy. Other considerations should lead to the choice of distribution method rather than the distribution method leading to the choice of market sector. However, if one already has a selling method for other products or services then these are bound to have an influence on market sector choice for new products being introduced into the range.

Own capabilities One's own capacity, financial structure, technical competence, skills, and other strengths, in conjunction with many of the considerations mentioned above, must have a significant bearing on market sector choice. What can you sensibly achieve?

Consider these two examples from a design company and a conference hotel. At which level will they operate? Which level will be believable and affordable in terms of reaching the various market sectors concerned?

It must be accepted that if one positions oneself as being particularly expert at fashion design, for example, one will also pick up a great deal of other design work. It is simply that to position oneself in the wide market place with some specialisation is both more meaningful to the customer and more affordable for oneself than to be a generalist with no cutting edge whatsoever.

Purchase decision For the potential customer to come to a decision concerning the purchase of our product or service, he, she or they must go through the following steps.

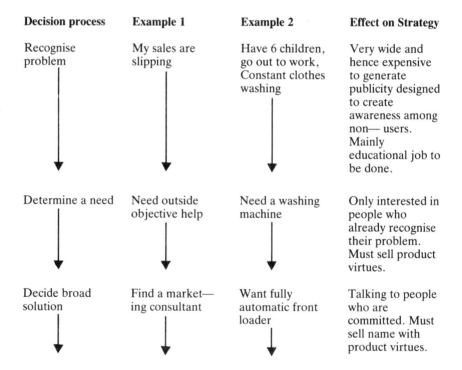

Decision process	Example 1	Example 2	Effect on Strategy
Recognise problem	My sales are slipping	Have 6 children, go out to work, Constant clothes washing	Very wide and hence expensive to generate publicity designed to create awareness among non— users. Mainly educational job to be done.
Determine a need	Need outside objective help	Need a washing machine	Only interested in people who already recognise their problem. Must sell product virtues.
Decide broad solution	Find a market— ing consultant	Want fully automatic front loader	Talking to people who are committed. Must sell name with product virtues.

Search for supply source	Get list from Assn. of Consultants, directories, or business colleagues	Look at advertisements. Go to shops, Get Leaflets	Am in the hands of others. Must ensure they are fully conversant with my wares and motivated.
Call for and evaluate evidence of competence	Decide on short list of 3, brief, and ask for presentation	Talk to 3 stores salesmen and/or showrooms of suppliers on short list	Own staff and publicity are paramount. Personal selling vital.
Place order	Agree contract	Make down payment	Ensure customer satisfaction.

This is an additional and complementary way of concentrating one's marketing effort intowhat is realistic and affordable.

Prime customer profile

Having clearly defined the sector of the market with which we shall be primarily concerned, we can now describe the sort of person who is most likely to be our customer. No doubt many others will be attracted but our prime customers are those to whom we must speak directly by whatever means are available to us. They represent the basis of our business, without them we have no business.

There are obvious differences between domestic customers and businessmen in terms of the decision making process but it should be recognised that we are all domestic consumers as well as being businessmen, we do not cease to become human beings once we enter the office. However, let us separate the two for the sake of clarity.

Domestic consumer

We need to describe an individual so that everyone can clearly understand the type of person we want to attract. Such a description may have many dimensions but three will certainly be required: sex, age, and socio-economic grouping.

Men and women are different, although 3% of housewives are officially male! Obviously an appeal to one is not likely to appeal in the same way to the other. Johnson & Johnson know very well that women will look at the baby in their advertisements whilst the men will look at the mother.

Span of years In somewhat similar vein one would talk with a different voice to a 15-year-old than to a 50-year-old. The strategy will give a sensible span of years, perhaps 25–35 or 35–55, whatever is reasonable.

Socio-economic breakdowns are intended to relate to a life style, to a mental approach to our personal environment and to our purchase decision; for example, a docker may well earn more than a bank clerk but is less likely to shop in Harrods.

The most usual groupings, used for media and research purposes and for most marketing purposes are those as defined by the Institute of Practitioners in Advertising (IPA) and are usually four in number: AB, C1, C2 and DE. However, the government uses slightly different strata for their censuses and research operations, such as the National Family Expenditure Survey, and use A, B, C, D, E_1, E_2, OAP. Acorn, the C.A.C.I. project that has provided a most useful analysis of homes in the country, has thirty-nine breakdowns ranging from 'A1: Agricultural villages to K38: Private flats with single pensioners'. It should be remembered that most of us aspire to a higher echelon in life – perhaps we are all snobs at heart – so that while we may appeal to one group we may have to talk to them as if they were one notch higher.

If possible, we should *add flesh to these bare bones* by some descriptive phrase such as:
- 'Adult males who feel trendy';
- 'Working class boys just being introduced to hard drinks';
- 'The hard-working backbone of all women's organisations who enjoy the prestige of office'.

The DMU or Decision Making Unit

When selling a service or an industrial product there may be as many as nine people involved, each of whom makes some input to the final decision. Indeed, in some cases it may eventuate in a Board presentation with one or two members being the key to the final decision.

Even in the consumer world, when selling a new product to a major multiple buyer, that buyer may have to obtain Merchandise Committee approval to authorise a new 'listing' on his computer. Our strategy must single out the key decision makers by title as well as by as much demographic data as possible. For example, 'Factory Managers responsible for over 50 staff who are likely to be male, over 40 years of age, and with a high degree of technical sophistication'.

Product positioning

Having defined the people who most matter to us, what do we say to them? We must find something to say about our product or service which answers the question 'Why should I buy from you rather than from someone else?' We must find a difference from our competitors. If all we can say is 'me too' we have no cogent reason for being in the market place at all. Very few of us are copywriters and in this statement we are not writing slogans or advertising appeals. But it is from this statement that copy will be written, that packaging will be created, on which display material will be based.

(i) In principle it is best if we position ourselves in the market in relation to *some specific product attribute* that we possess. Sometimes although rarely, advertising 'puffery' can be created that really works: 'Heineken reaches the parts that other beers cannot reach'. But that usually takes much more money for a longer period of time than many companies can afford. Further, the product attribute must be of interest to our 'prime customer profile'. It is no good talking about something that interests us but is of no interest to them. When enzymes were first used in washing powders they were technically a tremendous breakthrough. But from the consumer point of view, they were horrible little wriggling things that were looked at through a microscope. Or to say that we are brand leaders or the biggest in the field may be of considerable pride to us but perhaps of little interest to the end user.

Our positioning really does have to be different from our main competition. Our product development programme should have, as a first consideration the need to introduce something with a difference. It is most often those products with no difference and therefore nothing to commend them, that fail. Often in highly competitive markets, differences are minimal. However, they must exist and further be capable of being discernibly and communicably different from the customers' points of view.

(ii) If we were copywriters, sitting down with a blank sheet in front of us and a wet towel round our heads, how might we think this through to a successful conclusion?

One can consider most products and services in three ways:
– Physically
– Functionally
– In character.

Consider kippers in a boil bag with butter and contrast them with kippers from a wet slab or frozen. They are different:
– *Physically* by most of the senses, sight, feel, smell.
– *Functionally* since with the boil bag it is perhaps not even necessary to clean the saucepan after cooking, particularly if one is a man, but with

the wet kipper one must not only scour the grill or frying pan but clean the air too.

– *In character* because true or not, we all think that the nutrients are trapped in the bag and cannot escape, whereas in grilling or frying they all go up in smoke. Further in the boil bag the butter has permeated the flesh so that it is all succulent and juicy whereas with the grilled kipper, a blob of butter put on the top, skates all over the surface most unappetisingly.

So a good copywriter could take any one of these attributes and make a meal of it. And it is only one difference that he wants because that is all that customers will remember.

The positioning statement for Fairy Liquid took three months to decide but the end result was simply 'Mildness with a strength reassurance'. In

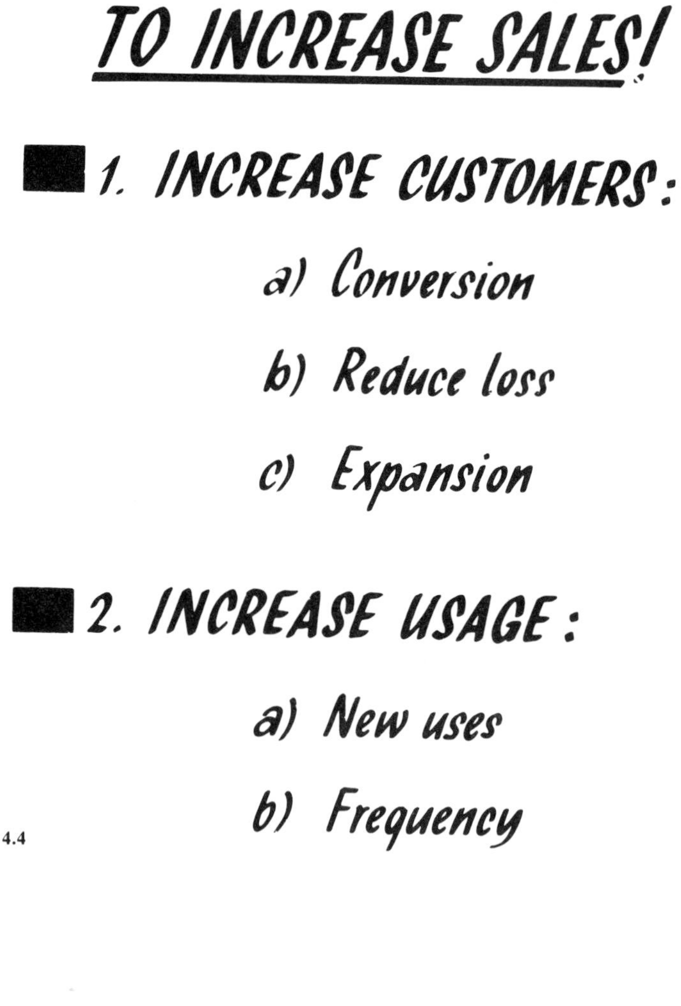

TO INCREASE SALES!

■ 1. INCREASE CUSTOMERS:

a) Conversion

b) Reduce loss

c) Expansion

■ 2. INCREASE USAGE:

a) New uses

b) Frequency

Figure 4.4

other words it was 'kind and gentle to the hands' but also got dirty dishes beautifully clean. As brand leader this has lasted nearly 20 years. Buzby for British Telecom started in 1976 with 'Make someone happy with a cheap rate 'phone call', moved after several years to 'Make someone happy with a 'phone call' omitting the cheap rate, and was eventually shortened further to 'Make someone happy'. This is based on the original research which showed a very low knowledge of the actual cost of a cheap rate trunk call, coupled with the need to stimulate more calls at off-peak periods.

Source of business

With any company or organisation there are only two ways to increase sales: either get more customers, or get those customers you already have to buy more from you, or both. Within each of these, however, there are variations on a theme which represent different marketing policies.

More customers

Take from competition   If the market sector has reached the mature phase of its product life cycle, if it is static with no more non-users left who are willing to enter it, then the only way one can expand one's business is to take it from competitors. This usually requires a hard, aggressive, high spending, branded policy using every marketing tool in the book including all forms of sales promotion since often in such cases one is selling a promotion rather than a product. Life assurance, baked beans, fork lift trucks are possible examples.

Take a share of expansion   If the market sector is in the growth phase of the product life cycle it is dynamic, new entrants are available constantly, both in terms of new customers and new competitors. Everyone in the market is pushing to get new customers, to persuade them that this new product category is for them. It is necessary, at least for the more dynamic suppliers, to sell a concept, to inform, to educate. Small boats, packaged holidays abroad, laser controlled cash tills, frozen foods are perhaps good examples of this category.

Staunch an outflow   Normal business entails a constant process of attrition, of gaining new customers and losing others. If one can staunch any loss one automatically has more customers. This requires a 'loyalty' programme of doing one's utmost to ensure customer satisfaction and repeat purchase in markets where this is possible. Store credit cards are designed for this purpose, as are motoring clubs, tea cards, and the like.

More business from existing customers

Find new uses   A product development programme to extend the usage of the product to other areas by the same customers will increase sales. To use Flash for floors, then paintwork, then all other surfaces; for housewives to use pocket calculators in supermarkets to check on purchases; to use Beanstalk shelving in warehouses and for display purposes.

Greater frequency of use   For repeat purchase products, people often have gaps in their purchases, sometimes called 'Fad and Fatigue' cycles. They may use a product frequently for a time and then tire of it. Later, after a respite, they may return to it. This often happens with indoor games or slot machines. It happens with foods such as custard or salad cream. If one can shorten the 'resting' time, one automatically increases sales. Probably a reminder campaign of some sort will bring it back to the notice of the lapsed customer.

Computer help

For many of these different policies, provided that numerate data can be obtained, there are computer programs that can help one in arriving at the 'best' policy in all the circumstances. There are several programs which should be known by one's own computer staff or advisers.

Location of sales

The dividing lines between different types of distribution outlet get more and more blurred on the one hand, and in fewer and fewer hands on the other. Boots and W.H. Smith move more and more towards being department stores. Department stores get more and more shops within shops. DIY shops expand in all directions. More and more chemists sell gifts. In services, all sorts and conditions of person, shop, and operator become insurance agents. Banks move into the building societies' domain. Computer systems bureaux move into miniature hardware. Yet in virtually every field that one can think of there is constantly increasing concentration of power, in banks, in hotel groups, in grocers, in public houses, in building societies. This constant change makes concentration of effort by suppliers more and more essential and more and more difficult.

Very few suppliers can afford to give equal attention to every type of distributor who might represent an outlet for his goods or services. He must concentrate most sales, advertising, and promotional effort on that distribution sector that will give him the best return relative to the market sector he has chosen. Such consideration as whether he wants volume or exclusivity, to be where purchasing power is greatest among distributors, or where it is less onerous, where after sales service is important or negligible, where he can exercise some control on the end user purchase or none, will loom important. The key is to be available where the prime customer, as profiled above, will reasonably expect to find you or where you can reasonably expect to direct them.

Geographical area

Reasons for difference

There is a saying in marketing which is of great moment – 'Never throw good money after bad'. Every company and organisation will have some weak areas of the country and others which are stronger. Sometimes one knows the reason for a weakness, sometimes not. Lever Brothers cannot claim Newcastle as one of their prime selling areas since it is the home of Procter & Gamble. York is not exactly the best area for Cadburys for obvious reasons. The Citrus Marketing Board of Israel find that small sized Jaffa grapefruit sell better than large ones in the northwest and conversely that large sell better in the southeast. This is a result of the affluence of the southeast over very many years. Ethnic minorities create substantial differences by area, as shops around an American air base can substantiate.

Hereditarily the potteries, textiles, agriculture all create major area differences in the sale of industrial goods. Sometimes a difference can stem from a first class salesman, or conversely a poor salesman, on a particular territory. A salesman who perhaps several years ago created ill will, is remembered by the trade long after the company has forgotten it.

Support strength

Essentially the Product Manager's budget, as it relates to total effort for a product, not simply media advertising expenditure, should be broken down geographically in relation to business. If 10% of his business is in the Midlands, for example, then 10% of his budget should be spent there, even though that area is responsible for 15% of the population. The temptation to boost a weak area should be avoided since any extra money spent there should be capable of working harder for you in a strong area, assuming that the budget is not so great that you are already saturating that area of strength. There are not many Product Managers who could say that they are able to spend all they want in every area, Marketing budgets are never as great as one thinks necessary.

Product and market strength

Total market strengths   However, this basic policy begs four very important points. First, one's own strong areas may not coincide with the total market strengths by area. Plumrose is much stronger for certain canned meats in the north of England contrary to the total market. In the service sector many provincial agencies fairly obviously have greater strengths in their locality as consultancies often do. In such circumstances it might make good sense to try to increase one's business in the better total market areas.

With most 'pros' there is a 'con' however. Major products and brands are always stronger in the best market areas since they comprise such a major part of it. Any attempt by a weaker brand to increase share in a strong area will therefore meet greater competition.

Cash or effort   Secondly, should one spend in *cash* terms in relation to strengths and weaknesses, when the same amount of cash will not buy as much *effort* in, say, London as in Wales? The cost of reaching the same number of people varies substantially by area. Generally it is better to exert *effort* in relation to area strengths and weaknesses and accept that this will not show the same *cash* breakdown. As against this, however, such a policy asks acceptance of the fact that one's best sales area may not be one's most profitable area. One must weigh up all the advantages of volume and total cash profit compared with lower volume and less cash but greater profit per unit of sale.

Minimum necessary   Thirdly, there is little point in spending any money at all in an area where the proportion of the affordable budget based on sales performance, is not sufficient to do a worthwhile job. There is a mimimum for each area below which it is pointless to fall.

Future trends   Finally, very many markets change in terms of area bias. This is particularly so when the market sector is in the growth phase of the product life cycle, when it is evolving and dynamic. It used to be said that a new fashion in ladies' wear took five years to get from Bond Street to Sauchiehall Street. Now, with the same names over the same fascias in all major towns and cities, the availability of new fashions is instantaneous, be they in London or Glasgow. But *still* there is a time lag because of different temperaments, attitudes, feelings that what might be right for the great big city is not necessarily right for us, and so on. Tipped cigarettes started in the south east of England and took many years to become a major factor in Scotland, but Churchman's Tipped were always stronger in Scotland than in England on a per capita basis.

Decision

As with every question of marketing policy, one must weigh up all the advantages and disadvantages, judge where one thinks is the best opportunity for one's own product, short term and long term, and come to a decision.

Seasonality

There are very few products or services not affected by seasonality, even if for no other reason than that many executives are on holiday in July and August so that no one can, or will, give a decision. This is particularly true for service operators. The number of patients in hospital varies substantially by time of the year, as do the reasons for their incarceration. More babies are born in summer based on conception during the cold, long nights and the occasional power cut. A good time for selling Christmas cards is in the summer, but only for shops at seaside resorts. Antifreeze is bought *after* the first frost of the winter and, six weeks later, to all intents and purposes is dead. We tend to wait for the first cold spell before getting our central heating serviced. The lambing and calving season keeps the veterinary surgeons on the go.

Peak or off peak

Since no one can afford to spend money and concentrate effort on one product all the year round, our marketing strategy must state the broad times of the year when greatest effort will be exerted. Apart from knowing when this is for the total market and ourselves, there is only one major question to answer. Should we exert efforts at peak times or save some energy for the off peak times?

One could argue that if you cannot sell at peak times, when can you? At the same time one could argue that if you miss out on sales at peak time, it will hurt substantially more than missing out at off peak times. Generally one must accept the principle that the greatest expenditure of effort must be at peak times. One simply cannot afford to miss the major selling season of the year. This is equally true for industrial and service markets, where gestation time from start to finish of obtaining new business may be many months. As one goes along the decision making chain to final approval, the ability to reach and obtain action from the ultimate decision maker is vital.

Developing markets

However, markets will not evolve unless someone makes that happen. Turkeys have not become year-round sellers by concentrating effort only at Christmas. Ice cream is eaten in winter as well as in summer, albeit in 'take home' packs compared with 'in hand' packs. If one has a large share of a developing market one has a responsibility for making it develop, recognising that any such development must help one's competitors too.

Probably the easiest way of developing a market over time is to extend the 'shoulder' of the peaks, particulariy at the beginning of the seasonal upswing, by bringing people into the market earlier. The shoulders of summer holidays have extended both ways, from May to September. But as a general rule, once the season is over, it is over and done with. Sometimes the mere availability of a product category earlier is sufficient reminder to start the seasonal climb, as with camera film. Sometimes it is the availability of a different pack size, 26oz Lucozade for convalescence in the winter, 6oz bottles in the summer as a refreshing drink. 12oz Ribena for Vitamin C in the winter and diluted in cartons as a refreshing drink in summer, money shops in the tourist season, traditional banks at other times.

Pricing structure

Pricing cannot be divorced from costing and budgeting. It is one of the most difficult of marketing decisions, to such an extent that part of Chapter 6 is devoted to it. Essentially we should price our product at the price the 'market will bear', providing we can make an acceptable profit as a result. This is easy to say but very difficult to assess. It should not be 'cost plus', that is to say, find out the costs, add the company's required profit margin, and the result is the selling price: that way ignores market reaction. We should be able to say 'we know where we want to be in relation to competition based on our name, product and availability. We believe that we can command a price of so much from our chosen market sector. Now if we deduct our costs we are left with a profit of so much, which is acceptable. So:

PRICE = COST + PROFIT is the WRONG way
MARKET PRICE – COSTS = PROFIT is the RIGHT way.

Policy

In our strategy we need a statement as to the pricing policy to adopt. The philosophy behind our considerations will broadly be based on one of the following variations.

Competitive passive   We will follow the market leaders of our sector by consistently being the same as, lower than, or higher than they are. Fairy soap is consistently priced slightly lower than Camay and Palmolive, whatever they do.

Competitive active   We intend to be our own masters and maintain a price level and structure that we think will best develop the market. This implies that we have sufficient muscle in our market sector to be able to maintain such a policy. Abbey National is a good example.

Market penetration   We require a consistently high volume of business and can accept relatively low unit profits. Brand share is important to us. Perhaps Johnson & Johnson Baby Powder is an example which carries along on its coat tails, so to speak, baby oil, baby lotion, and baby soap.

Market exploitation   We wish to be seen to be an exclusive product because of name, quality of product, high technology. Because of our USP (unique selling proposition) we can command a premium price. Estée Lauder is a prime example.

Structure

Today, with buying power concentrated into ever fewer hands, the control we might have on our end price, if we are selling through any middle men, becomes less possible and more problematical. Whilst we may wish to have exclusive distribution in order to exercise total marketing control, the blurring of dividing lines between distribution outlets coupled with legislation which seeks to nullify any restriction of trade, makes such a course less likely and, indeed, less attractive as time goes on.

In the present climate of deep price cuts in very many markets, although there is an increasing recognition that the first customer requirement is 'value for money', which is by no means the same as the lowest price, an encouragement to such price cuts is a high trade margin. This enables the distributor to cut as he requires and gives the supplier little or no control over his end price.

It is of course very necessary to be in line with trade practice, but trade practice in 'white goods', washing machines, refrigerators and the like, which catered for tremendous price cuts, reduced any element of reason in the market place and consequently respect for brand names, and has led to legislation through the Office of Fair Trading. All that can usefully and legally be said on this point is that manufacturers and traders must recognise the ramifications of a *laissez faire* policy.

Budgetary control

The budget with which we are concerned is the marketing budget. As with most factors, particularly when dealing with financial affairs, the definition of what is included under this heading will vary by company and organisation. The following is generally accepted as covering most marketing requirements but obviously, in specialist markets other headings may be required.

– Media advertising expenditure;
– Media production costs;
– Special discounts (not standard trade discounts);
– Sales promotion;
– Public relations and product publicity;
– Exhibitions, trade fairs, conferences;
– Printed material;
– Packaging design;
– Market research;
– Direct mail.

Our marketing strategy should list the basis of arriving at the budget that we need to achieve the objectives set us. These are set out in detail in the chapter on finance (Chapter 6).

Other factors

The above nine commercial policy statements comprise the marketing strategy for the product range, or individual product or brand. There may well be others peculiar to an individual company. It is better not to put in everything that could possibly, under any eventuality, affect the product on the grounds that its omission might affect someone somewhere. Similarly it is better not to proliferate other strategies unless it is absolutely necessary. If one has an advertising agency then one must have an advertising strategy, sometimes called a copy strategy. If very large sums of money are to be spent on sales promotion, then it is sensible to have a promotional strategy. Whatever other strategies are required they must all spring from and not conflict with the marketing strategy.

Example

Here is a marketing strategy for a package tour company marketing a range of overseas, up-market, cultural holiday tours, providing learned lecturers and local guides of high standing.

Market sector This market is primarily one of learning, of history and culture in an interesting and easily assimilable form, by personally visiting sites around which such events are centred.

Customer profile   Appeal will be to highly intelligent men and women who are avid to learn more and to visit locations of which they have read in order to make this knowledge live. Whilst these tours will represent a holiday for them, they are primarily concerned with learning. To this end physical discomfort will not deter them. They may be of any age but, because prices will be high, appeal will be to 35+ in the ABC1 socio-economic groups. They may be academics, professionals, mature students, or fascinated amateurs.

Positioning   This will revolve around the company name as being highly professional with many years experience of requirements of specialist knowledge seekers. As support, the high standing of accompanying lecturers will be stressed. The total image will revolve around the expansion of knowledge.

Source of business   Continued expansion will be based primarily on attracting new people to see and appreciate the wonders of ancient civilisations and cultures within the context of today. This will be based on the widening general education of the population. Secondarily, continuous effort will be made to retain existing customers for future tours.

Distribution   will be based on normal travel agent outlets but constant efforts will be made direct to organisations, such as archeological or musical societies, so that a trained head office and own sales staff is necessary.

Area   effort will be based on university towns and areas where specialist groups are particularly active.

Seasonality   By judicious organisation of different tours in hot countries and colder climates, year round sales will be expected with particular emphasis on academic holidays. It will be anticipated that customers will probably take up to a year from initial exposure to booking.

Pricing   will be based on a premium commensurate with the customers' view of the value they derive and the high standard of tour staff, lecturers, guides, accommodation, and arrangements. Special discounts will be publicly offered to recognised groups.

Budgeting   Each tour will be a profit centre and, once established, budgets will be based on a percentage of the cost of each person travelling (case rate). For new tours budgets will be based on a pay out period of three years and on the job to be done (task).

5 The Annual Marketing Plan

The need for action – Objectives v Action – Setting objectives – Corporate objectives and plan – The marketing plan – Components of the marketing plan; Background; Strategies; Action; Long term development; Summaries – Control – Updating – Summary of headings

The Need for Action

'Action is a mere consequence of thought' wrote the Greek philosopher. Certainly much thought has had to be given to our marketing strategy, beginning with very deep thought about the parts of the market most suitable for exploitation by us, in our circumstances – market segmentation. There is no substitute for the profound study of the market and ourselves as a basis for clearly defined action. But at the end of the day, strategic planning is just that, a springboard from which action must come. All the strategies in the world will not achieve anything of themselves.

The exciting part of a Product Manager's life is in making things happen, in shaping events to the benefit of the products for which we are responsible and of our company. We shall not be judged on our strategies but on our actions, and rightly so.

Objectives v Action

Actions are designed to achieve objectives. We all work better with specific targets to achieve, deadlines to meet. This has reached a fine art in most sports: positions in league tables, bonuses for scoring runs, times to beat for athletic events. It is even prevalent in most cultural events: number of performances of a play, attendance at 'first nights', admissions to a particular exhibition, money collected at charity events.

But which comes first? The chicken or the egg? Can we decide on the action we should take before knowing what -objective to aim for? Or can we decide what our objectives can be before we know, within reason, what action we can reasonably take? It is a little like the MP talking to a friend about another MP: 'There are two things I dislike about him – his face.' The two faces of objectives and action are very much intertwined. Each must complement the other.

Setting Objectives

Sensibly

In practice it is sometimes the case that we are told 'Your sales last year were 100. Next year we shall look for a 10% increase because that is what the corporate plan says.' Or perhaps we say that to ourselves on the assumption that no Product Manager worth his salt could do less, irrespective of market conditions. If we said less we should be considered by our betters to be lacking in moral fibre, in entrepreneureship, or so we might think. On the other hand, if we said more we would be sticking our necks out too far. Such a subjective and arbitrary attitude is not, of course, for the professional Product Manager!

Attainably

Objectives must be sensibly realistic. Of course they must stretch us and everyone else involved with their attainment, but they must also be capable of achievement, given the tools incorporated in the annual marketing plan of action. In order that this may be measurably attainable, and may be seen to be so, objectives must be specific and factual, involved with numbers and not generalities:

- 'To gain 1000 new account customers';
- 'To increase turnover per customer by 10% resulting in a total turnover of £1 million';
- 'To sell 50 Type "B" machines';
- 'To achieve an average 10% share of the market in Year 1'.

They involve statistical methods of extrapolating good past data as well as an appraisal of the likely future activity of the market concerned and its effect on our own products. These are described in the chapter on 'Forecasting' (Chapter 8). Suffice it to say here that the objectives originated by the Product Manager have to be 'sold' to others – to finance, to sales, and to production in particular. Therefore the simpler and more easily explainable the method of arriving at the objectives, the better.

In time

It must be remembered that we are writing our annual marketing plan at least six months before the commencement of the year under consideration. This gives time for discussion, amendment, submission to marketing management, consideration by top management within the corporate framework, the provision of finance for the necessary spending, perhaps head office approval sometimes from overseas, and final Board approval. All these steps must take place in good time before the end of the current fiscal year so that there is a smooth transition from one year to the next. In consequence, whilst we have data for past years, we must estimate results for this year before deciding our objectives for next year.

Looking Ahead

It is generally sensible, therefore, to set objectives for three years ahead, with the first of those years being very firm and the other two less firm, even though we are incorporating them into an *annual* plan. It is particularly necessary to do so if the market is very dynamic, or has fast growth, or if one is entering the market for the first time.

With pay-out

In the latter case, it is often necessary to show a clear 'pay-out' period. If this is acceptable over, say, a three year period it means that one borrows a great deal of money in year one to cover launch costs, breaks even in year two, makes a profit in year three but only enough to pay back, with interest, what was borrowed in year one; so that at the end of year three one is 'all square'. From then on one hopes that profit can accrue to everyone's benefit.

With capital goods such as electric generators, dredgers or other harbour craft, and products such as ethical medical preparations where many clinical trials must take place, a period longer than three years may be necessary. With many repeat purchase consumer goods, however, few companies will wait as long as three years to get their money back. Some services, on the other hand, may take some years to gestate, particularly if related to new industries which are themselves surging into the future, such as programs for hand-held computers for salesmen.

Other services may be capable of recognition very quickly, such as the provision of tank testing facilities for ship construction, but such business is likely to take a long time to convert to positive cash flow. Still other services ought to be profitable very quickly, for instance a new dry cleaning service.

So if the pay-out period is longer than three years, then our annual plan should state the numerate objectives for whatever time period is necessary. It should not be for less than three years.

Seriously

It is as well to remind ourselves that objectives should be set by Product Managers, or if imposed from 'on high', accepted by him, with all possible seriousness for several reasons:

- Together with the objectives for all other company products, they form the company's future course and prosperity;
- From them will stem individual targets, thus setting the scene for many individuals' incomes;
- If they are not treated with respect by others within the company, nor will the plan of action – result: chaos;
- The Product Manager's future may rest on them. Too many objectives not achieved will not exactly endear him to top management.

With parameters

Finally, no matter how seriously objectives are set, to achieve them exactly is simply good luck. It is preferable, of course, to achieve objectives with some margin to spare, rather than to fall short by even 1%. To miss an objective by so much as a hair's breadth is still to miss it, with some consequent stigma, unfair though this may be. This is why silly manoeuvring often goes on. Higher management insists on higher objectives than are sensibly attainable. Product Management tries to gain acceptance of a lower figure than is possible of attainment and so on.

It really is sensible to decide parameters within which objectives are acceptable, perhaps ± 5%. They will depend on the accuracy with which objectives can be set in the first place and the critical nature of the product group within the company's total sales. The marketing plan will show the results of achieving the higher figure and the lower figure. Then, as the objectives are progressed during the year less nail-biting, and calmer, more rational assessments of success or otherwise can be made.

Accepting change

If, through the year, the objectives are clearly no longer possible of attainment, they must be changed, no matter what traumas such action might bring in its chain. There is no sense at all in maintaining impossible objectives on paper, simply because of reluctance to upset 'the best laid plans'. To do so means that the end-of-year reaction may by even more violent. This stricture applies just as much to exceeding objectives as to falling below them. Runaway sales are exciting but can cause immense problems of supply and financial funding, in just the same way as sluggish sales.

So we must set objectives based on trends of ourselves and the market place from past data and on foreseeable future market actions, with the whole melded by what we know are the constraints of our own capabilities, of available finance, sales force time, production capacity, other product priorities, and so on.

Corporate Objectives and Plan

Mention has been made twice of the constraints of corporate objectives as applied to individual product objectives. Often, these are contained within a long range corporate plan, perhaps looking ahead five years, sometimes seven years, and occasionally as far into the misty horizon as ten years.

Numeracy is just as important in setting corporate objectives as for a product's objectives. But these must, of necessity be rather wider and perhaps more all-embracing, such as 'To obtain a return on capital employed of 15% over 5 years'; 'To aim to break into the US market in 1985'; 'To diversify into laser scanners by aquisition within five years'; 'To offer consumer banking services as a major adjunct to insurance'.

Whatever the overall objectives, there will also be a series of annual turnover and profit objectives, perhaps by major product group or company division but often down to an individual Product Manager's responsibilities. These tend to be up-dated every six months which accepts what is, of course, the case: that they cannot be as up-to-date or as detailed as those set by Product Management. Similarly with the corporate operating plan. Corporate action to achieve the required objectives within the corporate strategy will be more general than is necessary for individual product plans. But much of the plan may affect a Product Manager directly and some of it indirectly.

It is a great pity that in many companies, Product Managers never see corporate plans. In some, they do not even know of their existence – assuming that they do exist, of course. In those enlightened companies where Product Managers are allowed and even encouraged to provide an input at the planning stage, the corporate operating plan will inevitably be based on a much more realistic set of assumptions than if their views had not been sought. Additionally, the imposition from on high of targets and budgets which appear quite unrealistic, simply because they are an arithmetical breakdown from larger figures, will be minimised and even eradicated. In any event, it is up to the Product Manager to project his own views into the corporate plan deliberations as forcefully as possible so that he is not faced with seemingly impossible targets with totally inadequate budgets which he is tamely expected to accept.

The Marketing Plan

Let us now set about the task of creating this annual marketing plan of action. First, if we want other people to read it, it must be easy to read. That means two things: length and style. No-one wants to read a tome; twenty pages is ample; brevity is a great discipline against waffle. If a number of reference tables are required they will be better placed as appendices at the back so that interested parties can read them if they want and others need not.

Content should be readable as a whole, not as a series of disjointed contributions from different sources. If, for example, the Sales Manager writes the section detailing his responsibilities with a style which is very different from that of the Product Manager, then the Product Manager should rewrite it, whether the Sales Manager likes it or not, and similarly with other contributors such as the advertising agency, the Sales Promotion Manager, the Contracts Manager, the Service Manager.

Secondly, the plan must be a plan of action, specific, 'nuts and bolts' detail, not a series of generalities or platitudes. At the end of reading the plan, everyone involved must be crystal clear as to what is required of them because they must commit themselves to its operation.

Components of the Marketing Plan

The headings for the constituent parts of the marketing plan which are given below, will be found generally suitable for most companies but, as with the Marketing Strategy, each company or organisation will probably need some changes and additions to suit its own needs.

Introduction

Half a page to detail:

   (i) The products for which the plan has been prepared. In many companies there will be a number of annual plans prepared for different product groups, all of which must be read and accepted by a number of executives. So it is important to start off by clearly stating this, as well as . . .

(ii) The period of the plan. Usually this will be for 'The fiscal year commencing. . .', but it might be for a shorter time or even, for companies with long contracts, for a longer time.

(iii) The relationship to other annual marketing plans. For example, it might be a plan for a part of the XYZ Division of the company which must be added to products Y and Z to complete the division's programme.

(iv) Whether this plan represents the first draft, the second draft or the final document. If the Product Manager is wise, he or she will have discussed his ideas with key executives concerned before putting pen to paper. In spite of this, however, the first draft is bound to receive some objections. Sometimes the Product Manager gives in, sometimes he argues and wins, and sometimes he insists that his ideas must stand. So a second draft is almost invariably necessary. One hopes that there are no objections to this. Nevertheless second thoughts can mature and lead to some changes.

Eventually the final document is circulated and becomes the substantive document for action. In the Introduction it is important to state which version it is, so as to avoid someone working to information from the first draft which was subsequently changed.

(v) Executives or departments committed. This is vital; for the plan to succeed, others must implement it, they must signify acceptance. Perhaps the requirement by one company, of a clear signature from heads of departments on the final document, is the best way of ensuring commitment. Perhaps a round table meeting, properly recorded and minuted is preferable. Perhaps individual memoranda to and from heads of departments is sensible. Whatever method is used, commitment must be obtained. It cannot be stressed too often or too strongly that marketing action will only be achieved through others.

Background

(i) Include just sufficient background information so that anyone reading the annual plan 'cold' without the detailed up-to-date knowledge of the market possessed by the Product Manager, can readily understand the plan without having to ask numerous questions.

If the 'Product History' has been properly maintained as it ought, it is a simple matter to transfer to this section a précis of the more recent events in the market and for the product group. It should not be more than a page in length.

(ii) Almost certainly, however, one will need the last few years' sales history. The last five years' record of turnover, profit, and market share for the products concerned, if available, as well as for the total market and aɪy major market sector or competitor, is a necessary backcloth to a consideration of the proposed plan. Since this will inevitably mean a series of tables, they will be best placed as appendices at the back of the action document for people to refer to as they please. Under the heading of 'Background', a short description with one or two supporting figures will suffice.

(iii) Other factors which may be relevant are:

- Past product or packaging changes for oneself or competitors;
- Seasonal or regional differences in demand and any change in this respect;
- A picture of pre– and post-sales service requirements;
- Mention of major customers, their importance to the company, any changes envisaged bearing in mind the 80/20 rule, that 80% of one's business is likely to result from 20% of one's customers;
- Changes in market factors, such as the effects of recent technology, or social change, or government activity.

It must be stressed that this section is not intended as an exhaustive report on the market. If anything approaching that is required then, again, it should be placed at the back as an appendix. One must assume that the various executives reading the plan *do* know the product and the market, and simply need reminding about certain factors of which they may not be instantly aware in the busy lives they lead.

Strategies

(i) The marketing strategy, assuming that this exists, should be lifted straight from last year's marketing plan, examined to ensure that every clause is still relevant, and slotted straight into the new plan. As has been said at some length in the chapter dealing with the marketing strategy, nothing should be changed unless it is absolutely necessary. If some clause seems wrong in the light of more recent experience, then it must be examined and discussed with all the seriousness needed to consider a policy change, before action is taken.

(ii) If a considerable sum of money is to be spent on advertising in its many forms, especially through an advertising agency, then an advertising strategy will certainly be required. This is discussed further in the chapter dealing with communication (Chapter 12). Again, strategy from last year's plan should be positioned in this year's without change if at all possible.

(iii) Similar comments apply to a promotional strategy if one exists or is necessary. It is only really important to have one if a substantial proportion of marketing funds is to be spent 'below-the-line'. Even then, since sales promotion is essentially a short term activity, a promotional strategy cannot be expected to be as long lasting as a marketing strategy or even as an advertising strategy. There is no need to proliferate strategies for their own sake. Too many can be a positive menace in the sense of inhibiting personal flair and a flexible attitude.

Objectives

The objectives that the plan of action is designed to achieve must be clearly and crisply stated, in unequivocal numerate terms as described earlier in this chapter.

Action

Now follows some fifteen pages comprising in detail the action that it is intended to take. Recognising the need for each company to have headings related to its own needs, the following types of action should be covered.

  (i) *Market development* Any development anticipated as a result of general influences, or as a result of direct action initiated by oneself or competition.

 (ii) *Product development* Any development work that will directly affect this year's action. Products that will be introduced into test areas, or moved from test to expansion areas or national distribution, with details of methods, forecast results, and costs. Any effect on existing product sales must be itemised. Included are any new introductions or changes to products for which one is a factor, distributor, or sales agent.

(iii) *Distribution* Action to be taken to expand or contract physical distribution in the marketing sense, with forecast effects; concentration on certain trades, market sectors, or services.

 (iv) *Sales force* Any changes to size, direction, reward structure, together with specific action to be taken to achieve sales targets. This will form the basis of the sales department's own plan of action.

  (v) *Advertising* A detailed media schedule of all types of advertising, to customers, consumers, and trades, together with advertising objectives, creative work, and measurement criteria.

 (vi) *Sales promotion* A detailed breakdown of planned action is required but this is the only part of the overall plan where perhaps total detail for the year is not possible. This is because sales promotion is essentially short term. Often therefore the ability to be flexible, to be in a position to take advantage of something topical, even local, may be highly desirable. Thus detailed plans for, say, the first quarter of the year are sensible, with the remainder in broad outline only.

(vii) *Product publicity and public relations* There should always be something under this heading but the permutation of possible publicity vehicles is endless, ranging from direct mail to sponsorship, from erudite speakers at seminars to trade press editorial, from taking prospective customers to Lords cricket ground to providing company neckties. Whatever methods are used, there should be some evidence of an attempt to measure results. A great deal of money is often spent on these means to an end and it should be controlled.

(viii) *Research* The affordability of research is directly related to its planning well in advance. There are always gaps in knowledge which research can, and often should, fill. Whatever research is necessary must be stated, with details of method and cost, whether this be regular audit research, obtaining published reports and other desk research, or carrying out ad hoc research for a specific purpose.

(ix) *Test operations* There should always be something under test because that is for 'tomorrow'. We must never stand still. To do so is to fall back. We must constantly be testing things which we believe might help us in the future – new products or packaging, new advertising themes, different monetary weights for elements of the communications mix, different methods of distribution, of payment, different prices, and so on. Those tests we plan for this year must be itemised with detail.

Now we have two pages of figures:

(x) *Targets* At the beginning of our marketing plan we have set out our objectives. Now we need various target breakdowns to make these objectives manageable for the various units which must, together, achieve them. Targets will certainly be of sales, broken down perhaps by geographical area, by sales period, by customer type, by product, by size, flavour or commitment. They may include distribution targets, agency targets, orders to calls, contracts to tenders, and very many others. From these targets will stem those of other departments: finance, sales, production, purchasing, distribution.

(xi) *Budgets* Here should be incorporated all major cost elements, but principally marketing budgets and their relationship to sales and profits in whatever breakdowns seem sensible; certainly by product type and geographical area, perhaps by customer, or communication vehicle, and so on.

(xii) *Timing schedule* This is a chronological statement of actions over time: 'By 1 May this will have happened, at 17 June this will occur, on

25 September this will happen'. It represents an invaluable window on the plan and an excellent element of control.

Longer term development

Finally, in order to ensure that everyone, including the Product Manager, recognises that this year's action plan is not simply a 'one off' but is part of an on-going, long term operation, some evidence is needed that its effect on the future has been thought through. It is not necessary to go into great detail and produce another five year plan; simply one page or so of the likely effects that this year's operations will have on next year and perhaps the year after that. It helps to keep the longer term perspective in everyone's minds when the preceding actions have been forcing consideration for one year only.

Summary

The above completes the annual marketing plan. Some people feel that a summary sheet, either at the beginning or at the end is a good thing, so that those who do not wish to read the whole document need not do so.

If the Marketing Plan has been written crisply, clearly, concisely and cogently, not only should there be no need for a summary, but it is difficult to write a worthwhile summary that is sufficient for everyone to understand clearly, what action is planned. Further, a summary could be misleading. In essence, the whole plan is in as summary a form as possible, with no frills and furbelows.

However, at top management level, it may be necessary for a number of individual marketing plans to be collated and distilled into one summary. There is a limit to the amount of detail that a top manager needs to know, or indeed could know. In multiproduct companies a summary of the salient points of a plan for each product is often required and it were better if the Product Manager provided it rather than anyone else.

Control

The whole purpose of writing the marketing plan in this way is for those executives who actually have to carry it out, to *want* to refer to the document frequently, to keep it in their top drawer for ready reference, and not in their bottom drawer in order to forget it and carry on in their own way.

It must be recognised that it is a highly confidential document. Managers, however, must be trusted with it or they should not be managers. It is useless to state, as one Managing Director did, that there should only be six numbered copies of the original document which must be locked in his safe every night. Such an edict ensures that the plan is never taken out.

If the plan is used as a frequent reference as it should be, then it is an excellent control vehicle for the Product Manager. Everyone knows what he must do and by what date. It is relatively easy for the Product Manager to make sure that each keeps to his commitment. As each week's figures come off the computer, he can continuously monitor events and results against targets. And if he keeps his marketing plan up-to-date all the time, it becomes far easier to write the following year's plan. Further, the annotated plan can be kept as an historical document with future reference value.

Up-dating

Unlike the marketing strategy, the annual marketing plan is full of detail, some of which could be in error as the year progresses. Provided there is time to change during the year, it is pointless to continue with out-of-date material. The Product Manager should constantly be monitoring his action plan. Every month he should make quite certain that remaining future action is still reasonable. Every quarter, it is sensible to call a meeting of affected executives to discuss the plan from each one's point of view, and to confirm, or otherwise, the validity of future action.

At this juncture, any changes that are necessary to the plan should be made. If individual targets need changing, ways should be found to make up any loss in other directions. But if it becomes clear that overall objectives are not likely to be attained within the parameters laid down, then action to warn top management as early as possible is essential.

With increasing experience of initiating, writing, gaining commitment to, and controlling his annual marketing plan of action, the Product Manager will find that fewer changes will have to be made and that the respect accorded his marketing plan by others will mature and grow, to the benefit of all.

The Marketing Plan

Summary of suggested headings for the Annual Marketing Plan of Action

Introduction

    Product description
    Time period
    Relationship to other plans
    Document stage, 1st, 2nd, or final
    Commitment

Background

    Details of market growth
    Details of product growth
    Product and/or packaging changes
    Seasonal and regional factors
    Service requirements
    Major customers

Strategies

    Marketing
    Advertising
    Promotional

Objectives

Action

    Market development
    Product development
    Distribution
    Sales
    Advertising
    Sales promotion
    Product publicity and Public relations
    Research
    Tests
    Targets
    Budgets
    Timing

Long term

Effect of annual plan on future

6 Financial Control

Financial acument – Net sales value – Fixed and variable costs – Marketing costs – Product contribution – Other fixed costs and depreciation – Cash flow – Product management choice – Break even analysis and payout – Service costing – Pricing influences – Service pricing – Marginal cost pricing – Contribution pricing – Discounting – Financial ratios – The marketing budget

Financial Acumen

Finance is such an integral part of a Product Manager's life that there are many references to various aspects of it throughout this book, notably in the first chapter describing the Product Manager's responsibilities, as an aspect of strategic planning, and as part of the annual marketing plan of action.

It has been alleged that some accountants think that the average marketing person's appreciation of the need for financial 'number crunching' is akin to a person who has Van Gogh's ear for music! Perhaps they are right. But it really is not good enough for a Product Manager to admit that he does not understand the management of money, that he would much rather leave it to the accountants whose job it is anyway. The Product Manager is responsible for the profits generated by his products. He cannot shirk this issue and leave it in the hands of cost accountants, financial controllers and the like. He must be able to talk to accountants in their own language, understand their systems, their financial checks and controls, and at the same time acknowledge their expertise in their own discipline. That way ensures their vital co-operation and the Product Manager's ability to control financially the products for which he is responsible.

So this chapter is concerned with gaining sufficient financial acumen to handle the job of Product Manager successfully, without endeavouring to teach finance in all its many ramifications. In order to understand some of the elements of product accounting and in particular the relationship between profit, contribution, and cash flow, let us consider the launch of a new or improved product on to the market. As has already been said in an earlier chapter, accounting terms vary considerably between companies, as do their meanings, so we must be careful to explain exactly what we mean. One further caveat, only major breakdowns are used in the examples. Within accounting departments more details will be used.

Net Sales Value

Our start point must be anticipated sales, since virtually every cost will depend, to a greater or a lesser extent, on the amount we sell. This throws up two problems. How do we measure sales and how do we allow for inflation?

Customer mix

Sales are best measured at 'Net Sales Value' (NSV), which assumes that all standard trade discounts have been deducted but not special promotional discounts; the latter are usually part of the marketing budget. As usual there are grey areas. A special multiple head office 'over-rider', an extra discount for selling minimum quantities in a stated number of outlets, will be given on every sale so that it becomes part of the standard trade discount structure. But this 'over-rider' may be different for different multiples, so that the net value of sales has to assume a specific customer mix. If the actual position differs from that anticipated, then the NSV will change. Further, one multiple may not reach the agreed minimum sales target by the year end, yet his retail pricing policy has assumed your extra discount. Are you to say that he cannot have it now? It would take a strong company to do so.

This problem of the right customer mix also applies to a whole range of customer types; the proportion of sales made through agents or distributors; by telephone or direct; sales by tender or contract; to small customers and large.

Product mix

Similarly it applies to the product mix as well as to the customer mix. Perhaps a company works on mythical 'SUs', statistical units, which are a convenient mathematical way of adding together products of different sizes or types by relating them to one unit. Perhaps one has to do a separate forecast for each different unit, convert each at an average selling price and add all the NSVs together – a mammoth job.

VAT

For most product sales in the U.K. and in many other parts of the world, there is the added complication of VAT to be considered. VAT, being part of the price the customer must pay, should be considered part of the selling price, although often it is positioned as an additional charge at point of sale. From the supplier's point of view, it should be collected and recovered as a separate entity. It obviously is not included in NSV.

Price changes

Estimates of price changes over time must be included, of course. These may be as a result of product innovation, or competitive or market change, as for example with video for which prices are coming down as volume expands with deeper penetration of the market. Or they may change through the ever present inflation simply to keep pace with the value of money, if the market will accept them. Petrol prices are an excellent example of the near impossibility of this happening in times of over-supply.

Rates of exchange

There still remains the overall problem of the change in the value of money relative to some index such as the government's Retail Price Index. For some, there is the problem of exchange rate changes, of particular importance for the subsidiary company of an overseas parent or for overseas sales of a UK based company.

Although the Product Manager should be aware of these problems, the methods by which the company compensates for them must be the province of the accountants and be left to them. However each company does its sums, the Product Manager must forecast sales in units and have them converted in an agreed way into sterling Net Sales Value.

Fixed and Variable Costs

Costs, as is well known, come in two basic shades, 'fixed' being those that will be incurred irrespective of sales volume, and 'variable' (or 'marginal') being those that do vary with volume. Fixed costs for a launch product are very high as a proportion of total costs at the beginning until sales pick up, since origination charges must be accounted for; then they settle down to a fixed amount, and variable costs take over as the major part of total costs. This applies particularly to consumer products and services. With capital goods, fixed costs probably represent a much larger proportion of total costs, since fewer products are made.

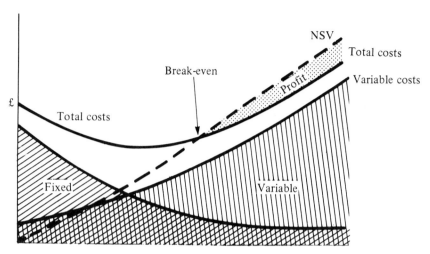

Figure 6.1

Variable costs

Variable costs are those which vary with quantity produced, stocked and sold, and which would not exist at all if the product was never made. They will include production costs such as raw materials and packaging materials, and direct labour and some warehouse and distribution costs. Although of course the more product sold the higher will be the total variable cost, curiously enough, it is usually the case that the variable cost per unit of sale remains about the same. So we have made it so in our example.

Let us assume a healthy doubling of sales in three years and from these deduct variable costs which we will assume to be half total sales cost.

Year	1	2	3
NSV	100	150	200
Variable costs	50	75	100
Contribution (before marketing)	50	75	100

We arrive at figures which can be said to be the contribution that our product makes to the overheads of the company, to the fixed expenses of the business as a whole. However, this is fairly academic because without some marketing action we would never achieve the sales anyway.

Marketing costs

The method of arriving at a marketing budget is discussed later in this chapter. Together with our marketing budget we must, for the purpose of our costing process, include sales costs, those directly related to the job to be done with our new product.

For our launch, we shall need relatively heavy expenditure, let us say 20% of turnover in Year 1, reducing to 15% in Year 2 and to 10% in Year 3. For service and industrial product launches, these percentages will be smaller, perhaps nearer 5% on a going basis.

Year	1	2	3
NSV	100	150	200
Variable costs	50	75	100
Marketing	20	23	20
Contribution (after marketing)	30	52	80

Fixed costs – product related (identifiable)

Fixed costs are those that remain constant within a given time period and a given range of output. Some companies now deduct those costs which are fixed, such as the salary of an extra production man, warehouseman or salesman, but solely related to the new product. As volume increases significantly, so might these costs, even though they are called 'fixed'. When this is deducted from NSV one is left with the important 'product contribution'.

Year	1	2	3
NSV	100	150	200
Variable	50	75	100
Marketing	20	23	20
Fixed (product related)	2	2	3
Product contribution	28	50	77

Product Contribution

Now it is reasonable to say that our new product contribution figure, does tangibly contribute to the other costs of the company. Indeed, some companies go no further than this as far as Product Managers are concerned. As has been explained earlier, they say that it is not possible to apportion most fixed costs fairly to individual products, so that as long as all contribution targets are met, the company will prosper.

It is suggested that there are so many 'ifs' and 'buts' about every financial breakdown that there ought to be no more of a problem with fixed costs than with other costs. Further, that without the all important ability to arrive at profit, the proper role of the Product Manager becomes castrated, sublimated to a consideration of turnover. Digressing for a moment into what is euphemistically called 'product rationalisation', which is just another way of saying eliminate something from the range, it is well nigh impossible to justify such action when contribution is the rule, since one can never, with hand on heart, say that the loss in contribution will be made up by extra sales elsewhere, even though the product for the 'chop' is non-profitable.

Other Fixed Costs and Depreciation

To get to profit, we must now deduct the last element, all those costs which are fixed and which can reasonably be apportioned to our product, the payment of factory rent, the cost of machinery amortized over so many years, plant maintenance, part of the telephonist, the post room, the security organisation, perhaps of top management, and so on.

'Absorption costing' is the name given by accountants to the practice of spreading fixed costs over all products. Fixed costs *can* change with volume of business; they are not necessarily fixed for all time. For example if sales continue to increase, a new forklift truck will be required, or a new warehouse, or a new production line. Company fixed costs can also change over time because of the cumulative effect of new product introductions requiring more staff, bigger factories, an extra canteen, offset by the extent to which a new product replaces or partially canabalises existing products.

There is one compensating factor to fixed costs which must be allowed for, and that is depreciation. A lorry or a typewriter or any other piece of machinery or fixture cannot last for ever. If a car is amortized over six years then one-sixth of its value can be written off each year, so that fixed costs can be reduced.

Thus the profit picture looks like this:

Year	1	2	3
NSV	100	150	200
Variable costs	50	75	100
Marketing	20	23	20
Fixed costs (product related)	2	2	3
Product contribution	28	50	77
Other fixed costs (less depreciation)	50	20	10
Profit before tax (PBT)	(22)	30	67
Tax @ 52%	–	4	35
Profit after tax	(22)	26	32
Cumulative profit after tax	–	4	36 = 8% of NSV

An alternative breakdown used by many companies might be this :

NSV	100	
Factory fixed costs	45	
Factory variable costs	45	
Factory administration	2	
Production costs	92	
Gross profit	8	
Distribution	8	
Marketing	15	These are part
Sales	5	fixed and part
Administration	2	variable costs
Net profit (before tax)	(22)	

Cash Flow

Let us, however, stay with the first breakdown and see if the cash flow picture presents such an acceptable situation as the profit picture.

Up until 'Product Contribution' the figures remain the same.

Cash inflow

The Product Contribution is the extra income for the company. Assuming that no other fixed costs are involved because they are already allocated to other products, and in any case because they do not appear as part of the Revenue Account, then corporation tax at 52%, or the rate ruling at the time, will be paid on Product Contribution. However, this will actually be paid in the following year, not in the year in which the contribution is made. So:

Year	1	2	3
Product contribution	28	50	77
Tax	–	15	26
Cash inflow	28	35	51

Cash outflow

The money we actually have to spend will include expenditure on *fixed assets*, such as new plant and machinery, modification to production lines, premises and so on, together with expenditure on *working assets*. These latter comprise three basic factors,
  – cash tied up in stocks;
  – work in progress;
  – credit given to customers, offset by credit we take in paying our bills. In a word, liquidity.
So these equate to stocks + debtors – creditors. In year 1 these will be high, to pay for the build-up of stocks and for delivering more and more product before being paid for it. Years 2 and 3 will be lower, but if sales really catch alight, then perhaps they will not be all that much lower. In other words, one must fund success. This is why it is as much of a problem if one is over target as if one is under target, although for different reasons.

Let us assume that expenditure on fixed assets halve after the first year, and that expenditure on working assets are 20% of NSV in Year 1 and thereafter 20% of *additional* sales.

Product Management Choice

So after three years, if we were working on a contribution target, we would have a healthy looking 155. But the actual cash we received would only be 54. Our profit figure would be even lower at 36 which represents only 8% on a turnover (at NSV) of 450, about the same as we might get if we had put our money in the Post Office! Of course, we can always say that subsequent

Year	1	2	3
Cash inflow	28	35	51
Expenditure on :			
Fixed assets	10	5	5
Working assets	20	10	10
Cash outflow	30	15	15
Net cash flow	(2)	20	36
Cumulative cash flow	(2)	18	54
In comparison :			
Cumulative Product			
Contribution	28	78	155
Cumulative Profit			
After Tax	–	–	36

years will be much more profitable. They will if everything else stays the same. Unfortunately, very many things can happen in as long a time as three years.

As Product Manager, which is to be our choice of financial control, contribution or profit? Almost certainly, we shall have to conform to company procedure. One thing is sure: positive cash flow is a very important factor which could make or break us. In 1971 Rolls Royce were wound up a year after they had made the greatest paper profit in their long history. There were many reasons, but lack of cash flow was one of them. In the long term, one cannot have cash flow without a profitable operation. In the short term, one priority must be positive cash flow.

Examples

There are many advantages for Product Managers working on both profit and cash flow forecasts. The cynic might say that the easiest way for a Product Manager to increase the profitability of his products is to persuade his cost accountant to reduce the overheads that he has apportioned to those products. Any paper reduction in the one will almost directly result in an increase in the other, as can be seen from the first example. But the most obvious and important advantage is to check the implication of marketing decisions.

Example 1   Suppose that sales did *not* double in three years, but increased more slowly with, say, a 50% increase. The picture then might be:

Profit

Year	1	2	3	3 years total
NSV	100	125	150	375
Variable costs	50	63	75	
Marketing costs	20	19	15	
Product related fixed costs	2	2	2	
Product contribution	28	41	58	127
Other fixed costs	50	20	10	
Profit before tax	(22)	21	48	
Corporation tax	–	–	25	
Profit after tax	–	21	23	44

Cash Flow

Product contribution	28	41	58	127
Tax	–	15	21	
Cash inflow	28	26	37	
Expenditure : Fixed assets	10	5	5	
Expenditure : Working assets	20	5	5	
Cash outflow	30	10	10	
Net cash flow	(2)	16	27	41

Now, how do we stand after three years? Contribution has come down, from 155 to 127. Profit has actually gone up, from 36 to 44. Net cash flow has reduced from 54 to 41. The result, if all our figures are right, is that *lower* sales has resulted in *higher* profits. If we were only watching contribution instead of profits, lower sales resulted in lower contribution.

Example 2 Suppose that our sales did double in the three years, as before, but both raw material and packaging material costs were 20% higher than first estimated and that we have not been able to increase our prices. The two major costing changes will be variable costs and expenditure on working assets, since cash tied up in working stock will increase. What is the picture now?

Profit

Year	1	2	3	3 years total
NSV	100	150	200	450
Variable costs	55	83	110	
Marketing costs	20	23	20	
Product related fixed costs	2	2	3	
Product contribution	23	42	67	132
Other fixed costs	50	20	10	
Profit before tax	(27)	22	57	
Tax	–	–	27	
Profit after tax	(27)	22	30	25

Cash Flow

Product contribution	23	42	67	132
Tax	–	12	22	
Cash inflow	23	30	45	
Expenditure : Fixed assets	10	5	5	
Expenditure : Working assets	24	12	12	
Cash outflow	34	17	17	
Net cash flow	(11)	13	28	30

After three years, our contribution has come down, from 155 to 132. Profit has also come down from 36 to 25; and net cash flow is down also, from 54 to 30. So higher material costs have adversely affected all three key indicators. The implication clearly is that prices must rise.

Example 3   In practice, with such an initial error in costs, we should have been forced to put our prices up. This would probably have resulted in less sales volume, unless, perhaps, an increase in marketing funds compensated for any tendency to lose sales. Doubtful but possible.

Let us see what might happen if, with a 20% increase in material costs (which are 55% of NSV), we increased prices by 10% but kept volume of product sales stable by spending an increased 25% of turnover at NSV in Year 1, 20% in Year 2 and 15% in Year 3.

Profit

Year	1	2	3	3 years' total
NSV	110	165	220	495
Variable costs	55	83	110	
Marketing costs	28	33	33	
Product related fixed costs	2	2	3	
Product contribution	25	47	74	146
Other fixed costs	50	20	10	
Profit before tax	(25)	27	64	
Tax	–	1	33	
Profit after tax	(25)	26	31	32

Cash Flow

Product contribution	25	47	74	146
Tax	-	13	24	
Cash inflow	25	34	50	
Expenditure : Fixed assets	10	5	5	
Expenditure : Working assets	24	12	12	
Cash outflow	34	17	17	
Net cash flow	(9)	17	33	41

Now after three years, contribution, instead of dropping from 155 to 132, is not so bad at 146. Profit, instead of dropping from 36 to 25, is not so bad at 32. Cash flow, instead of dropping from 54 to 30, is up a little at 41. So acknowledging the material cost increases, putting prices up but taking avoiding action by increasing marketing funds, is considerably more to our advantage than simply trying to absorb the extra costs, *if* sales were to react as suggested.

Conclusions   What conclusions can we draw from these three examples which consider both profit and cash flow analyses?
  (i) Product Managers must consider the consequences of marketing action in financial terms, difficult though it may be at times to arrive at particularly accurate figures.
 (ii) It is necessary to consider both analyses since marketing action may cause the three indicators of contribution, profit, and cash flow to move in different directions.

(iii) A knowledge of contribution by itself can be misleading. Far better, if at all possible, to go as far as profit after tax.

(iv) Cash flow analyses can show how quickly it is sensible to create sales expansion, which is very much a marketing decision.

(v) Finally and very importantly, to eliminate the need for laborious 'number crunching' by busy and often not very accurate executives, every product launch should have computer models prepared for just this purpose. The consequences of marketing action then become almost instantly available, with ease and accuracy.

Break Even Analysis and Payout

As has been said earlier, the launch of a new or improved product requires a plan by the Product Manager based on a finite pay-out period. This is the period of time over which all origination and launch costs are paid for. Money is usually borrowed, at least in theory if not in fact, for the heavy launch operation and this must be paid back from the profits of continuing sales.

The point at which, on current expenditure, NSV and costs match – the break even point – is an important milestone along this road. Initial borrowings still have to be paid back but now, every sale is earning a profit.

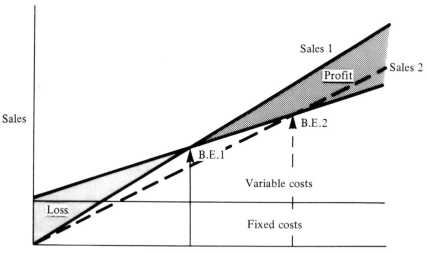

Figure 6.2   Time scale

As can be seen from Figure 6.2, which is similar to Figure 6.1, if sales are not up to the expectations shown by 'Sales 1' then the break even point and the payout period will be delayed. Thus cumulative costs are necessary for this analysis, to compare with cumulative sales as time goes on.

Service Costing

Many service organisations are also involved in manufacturing processes of various kinds, such as 'Oyez' with their very considerable legal expertise who sell stationery with legal connotations. However, there are services which come directly under the concept of a 'pure intangible', such as consultants. For these the major element of costing is manpower at varying levels of experience and competence. Some of this manpower may be considered a fixed cost such as the telephonist or post room supervisor, but at the more senior level a costing based on man hours per assignment is necessary.

Employee cost

As a rough rule of thumb, the cost of an employee is two and a half times his salary. Obviously this needs to be checked out for every organisation, but adding to the salary such items as bonuses, share of profits, NHI contributions, pension contributions, cost of car usage, part of a secretary, and so on, will almost certainly double the salary cost. So, for example, an executive on £10,000 will cost the company £25,000 or thereabouts.

Working hours

Over how many hours can this cost be apportioned? How many possible fee earning hours can an employee work? First of all there are not 365 working days in the year, even though many hard pressed executives would maintain that there are. From this number one must deduct:

Saturdays and Sundays	104	days
Bank holidays (not counting carry overs)	7	
4 weeks' holiday	20	
Average sickness	5	
Others (dentist, funeral, seminars, etc.)	5	
	141	

Thus there are 224 possible working days on which to base costs. This must now be converted to working hours. From 0900 to 1700 with an hour for lunch is 7 hours, but what percentage can we call 'efficient' since part of that time will be spent on work for assignments which never materialise, on attending the inevitable meetings, in filling out time sheets? From experience, few executives could honestly claim more than 80% efficiency. As an example, our executive earning a salary of £10,000 must have his cost to the company of £25,000 broken down by the total number of fee earning hours open to him or her. There are 1254 such hours (80% of 7 hours a day for 224 days). This amounts to £20 per hour with no allowance for profit.

Time sheets

For any possible application of these costs to a particular client, the number of hours worked on that client's problems must be recorded. However inaccurate they may be, the maintaining of time sheets is the only practicable method. Perhaps these time sheets should require hourly records, or even half hourly, depending on the number of different assignments that one might be involved in each day. They will not of course be filled in every half hour by the executive. His remembrance of the day is likely to be recalled at the end of the day, faulty though memories might be. To leave their completion for longer than a day is asking for too much guesswork.

These time sheets will represent the basis of costing and of pricing to the client. It is obvious that the 'product mix', the utilisation of the right level of employee for the particular job in hand, is crucial; perhaps more so than for actual tangible products and certainly much more difficult to forecast.

This then replaces for service operators many of the 'manufacturing' elements of the costs in the previous examples; otherwise most of the preceeding comments on costing and profitability apply in just the same manner to service organisations.

Pricing Influences

The most sensible and advantageous price for any product in the market place is the most difficult marketing decision that any Product Manager will have to make. In an earlier chapter, the point was made strongly that price should not be based on 'cost plus'; that is, to ascertain costs, add on a normally anticipated company profit margin, and sell the product at the resultant price. In spite of the fact that many companies do just that, it is wrong. The price charged should be *that which the market will bear*, providing always that it returns an acceptable profit. This is very easy to state but very much more difficult to work out in practice.

Influencing factors

Here are twelve influencing factors; some or all of them will apply to the vast majority of products and services.

(i) *Use value* Is there a real degree of need in the market place or must one work hard to create even a spark of enthusiasm?

(ii) *Competition* In any competitive market there will be a spread of prices. The product positioning will decide whether one wants to be the same as competition in the middle or upper or lower price range, or above or below him or them. If we are entering a new market then we must assume a future spread and price ourselves accordingly.

(iii) *Demand extent* Is the demand widespread both geographically and by market sector? Does it represent deep penetration of the market or a skimming of the surface? In what part of the product life cycle does the product category lie?

(iv) *Demand intensity* Those markets where need is great for short periods of time, such as anti-freeze, or cold drinks in hot weather; or where need is great in specific areas, such as sound proofing for houses under the flight path at Heathrow.

(v) *Demand elasticity* In some markets price is a key issue, such as for washing powders. Movements of a few pence can make significant differences to sales. Such prices tend to be elastic. In other markets, such as the top end of the cosmetic business, differences of many pence perhaps make little difference to sales. The 'added value' of image is much more important.

(vi) *Derived demand* There are some product prices which are affected by other product prices when there is really no direct relationship. For example, most people will accept that if we must pay more for our petrol at a petrol filling station then we can expect to pay more for our car wash. In fact, of course, there is absolutely no relationship directly between the cost of petrol and the cost of water. Another example is the cost of insuring our house. Most will accept a relationship between the cost of our house on the open market and our insurance premium. In fact, a nearer direct relationship is between our premium and the replacement cost of our house. Building industries being what they are, there are often considerable differences by area of the country.

(vii) *Supply and demand* At any point in time there is an equilibrium between these two factors but the point of equilibrium can vary over time; which is why a greengrocer can charge more on a Friday and a Saturday when demand is greater, than on other days of the week.
To price one's product too high can lead to eventual sales at lower prices to clear stock. To price oneself too low can lead to quick sale, shortage, allocation.

(viii) *Capacity* Over– or under-capacity can obviously react on prices. Bricks are in an over-capacity situation because the building programme has been so very low. The ice cream manufacturer cannot build up his productive capacity for the one hot summer in five, or he would not be economically efficient in the other four years.

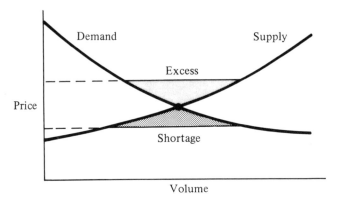

Figure 6.3

(ix) *Distribution* An exclusive distribution policy such as for Estée Lauder with only five hundred department store outlets, or Unipart with only 200 distributors, will affect price; as will selling through agents such as double glazing installers; or direct, such as Scotcade and other direct response advertisers.

(x) *Psychology* The expected price for the product can be almost wholly in the mind. Snobbery plays its part as with After Eight Mints or Rolls Royce cars. The story of the advertising campaign in the States for RR which said 'the only thing you can hear is the ticking of the clock', and the Chief Engineer back in England saying 'I must stop that b . . . y clock', is apt.

(xi) *Government* Since the government, national and local, with all its ramifications, is responsible for spending over one third of total GDP on products ranging from Fairy soap to a nuclear reactor, they strongly influence most of our markets, not only as buyers, but as tax impositors, legislators, creators of codes of practice, heavy leaners on recalcitrant industries, and in many other ways.

(xii) *Marketing policy* Finally, our own marketing policy will to an extent dictate pricing policy. As was said in Chapter 4 on strategic planning, there are essentially four different policies:
  – Passive: follow the leader;
  – Active: set the pace oneself;
  – Exploitive: based on a uniqueness with scarcity value;
  – Penetrative: requiring large volume movement.

All these factors play a part in our appreciation of the market's reaction to price differentials. And if the prospective buyer does not like the price, he or she may well find fault with the product. Even El Greco fell foul of this trap when he tried to gain a higher price for a picture than the priests of the church concerned thought should have been charged. Their rejection of the picture on other grounds held up El Greco's career for some time.

Special factors affecting service pricing

Whilst generally being confined to services, some of the following factors also affect industrial products:

(i) *Some prices are fixed* by other organisations; dentists fees, for example, chemists' national health prescribing charges, opticians charges. They may be fixed by government agencies in collaboration with the profession, or imposed on them, and they may be fixed by the profession's own association such as for solicitors.

(ii) *Imposed by buyer* In a curious way some prices are not set as prices but as services delivered. Whilst building societies are in a highly competitive market, the customer decides what he will invest in relation to what he thinks he can get for his money. The latter, of course, is dependent on market forces prevailing at any one time.

(iii) *Commodity prices* In what the economists call a 'purely competitive' market, such as grain or metal, where any farmer with, say, wheat to sell can enter the market at any time, he will sell at the market price on that day. This price is primarily a factor of supply and demand but other factors can influence it. For example, share prices on the stock exchange can be affected by a well-directed public relations exercise.

(iv) *Tender prices* Tendering is one of the most inefficient ways by which any two people can do business. They result in the lowest quality for the highest price since those in markets where tendering is a way of life will tender down to the lowest price possible if they really want the contract, which means cutting as many corners as possible. At the same time, those tendering get perhaps one in ten tenders. Whatever the ratio, they *all* have to be paid for, together with the time consuming procedures used to arrive at the successful tenderer. Eventually the tender prices must reflect these extra costs. Time lags, trying to forecast inflation, specifiers who cannot possibly know the latest abilities of every tenderer, people who tender but who do not want the particular contract but only to stay on the specifier's tender list, and very many other factors, make tendering a poor way of doing business.

(v)

Proposals The alternative to tenders is for the specifier to specify his problem and ask for proposals for solving that problem. Whether this be for a very complicated computer modelling operation or for supplying baked beans to the armed services, the specifier will get better value for money. 'Negotiated tenders' increasingly used in the building industry become a halfway house between tenders and proposals.

(vi) *Basic plus extras* Many services provide a foundation service such as wiring a house, for which the fee can be highly competitive, in other words low, and endeavour to obtain extra business such as installing kitchen equipment, on a much higher fee basis. Great care must be taken to avoid any accusation of 'switch selling' which is both immoral and illegal, and the end result will depend on the extent to which extra business is likely to result.

(vii) *Guarantee pricing* Some services can be sold on the basis that either a guaranteed result will occur or the total fee need not be paid. Some commando sales forces or merchandising teams are sold on the basis that certain sales results will occur. For this to be not too much of a gamble, it is usually sensible to include in the original proposal a test operation, on the results of which the final 'guarantee' will be based. This sells quality, and quality must be delivered.

(viii) *Time cost* Services such as consultancy, are almost impossible to set a price tag on, often because the problem to be solved is not clear. Very seldom does a consultant finish up solving the problem posed in the first place. A large carpet manufacturer in commercial woven carpets set a consultant the problem of halting declining sales. He finished up reorganising their design department. In such cases one can only give an average man hour rate and an approximation of the number of man hours it is guessed will be required. The contract must be won on experience and expertise, with price as very much a secondary factor.

(ix) *Status* Some service companies, such as A.C. Nielsen, the world wide retail audit company, have never charged low prices and never succumbed to the temptation of extra business from good customers by lowering their prices. They sell quality and therefore reliability of the data they provide. That is not to say that they do not allow discounts for quantity or for existing clients using other of their audit facilities. All pricing is based on the quality of the company concerned, in keeping with the status image they wish to present.

(x) *Decision maker* Often in both service and industrial marketing, there is a 'Decision making unit' (DMU) which may comprise some nine different people at different levels, all with an influence on the final purchase decision. It may be sensible in this situation to aim the price at one particular level of decision maker, dependent upon his or her ability to authorise the expenditure. To obtain the business at a price which, say, the Office Manager can authorise, may be preferable to having to go as far as the Financial Director.

Marginal Cost Pricing

It should be recognised that 'marginal' has just the same meaning as 'variable' when used by accountants.

Total profit is a result of the number of unit sales of a certain product at a certain price, rather than simply the profit margin per unit. To sell one unit with a 100% profit margin is not as beneficial as selling ten units at half that margin. So profit, price, and volume are positively related.

Initial sales of a new product are relatively small and if costs had to be apportioned over a small sales volume, the resulting price would probably be too high for the market. Or, conversely, if the price were in line with the market, a very large red figure at the bottom of the profit and loss account, would highlight the loss. Purely as an internal bookkeeping transaction, therefore, some companies load the new product only with those additional costs which it incurs. The assumption is made that, for example, a factory already exists and that the existing product sales have already paid the rent and the heating bills, etc. To produce a new product from the same factory requires only a little extra electricity, a few more man hours, a little extra time for the progress chaser. The *extra* cost of these is the only figure that need be shown against the new product. Add to this the normally expected profit margin, and the end selling price is very reasonable.

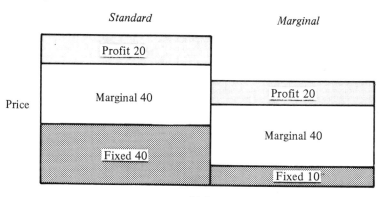

Figure 6.4

Strictly speaking, marginal costing does not include any fixed costs. Essentially, only marginal costs, plus perhaps a few product related identifiable fixed costs, are apportioned to the new product. The Product Manager who happily accepts this method for launching purposes could find himself in a fool's paradise: it is basically a false situation. Sooner or later the product must stand its fair share of costs. One cannot expect it to be subsidised by other products for ever. One year is probably as long as is sensible for marginal cost pricing to enable the product to get off the ground.

The eventual conversion to standard costing can cause substantial problems. Suddenly a product shown as profitable can become unprofitable, simply through bookkeeping.

There may be some justification for marginal cost pricing where there are exceptional conditions; for one particular order from a favoured customer, perhaps; when tendering for an important contract; where factory capacity is not fully utilised; where dumping from overseas occurs. But that justification must be set against the possible harm that might result: customers expecting the lower price to be maintained for ever, forcing competitors down in price and so lowering the general market level; too many company products being marginally costed with the subsequent burden on standard costed products, causing them to be uncompetitive or far less profitable. And finally, perhaps the use of this method as an excuse for poor marketing.

Contribution Pricing

Another way of considering price is to base it on the greatest 'yield', a term used in some companies to encompass marketing funds and profit. The method begs a tremendous problem, to be able to estimate sales volume at varying price levels. Assuming that this can be done reasonably, then there is a spread of prices, as in the example below which, related to volume gives total gross revenue (not NSV it will be noted).

Price	Volume	Revenue	Var. cost per unit	Total var. cost	Contr-bution	Fixed costs	Yield
11	600	6 600	4	2 400	4 200	1 000	3 200
10	740	7 400	4	2 960	4 440	1 000	3 440
9	910	8 190	4	3 640	4 550	1 000	3 550
8	1 120	8 960	4	4 480	4 480	1 000	3 480
7	1 410	9 870	4	5 640	4 230	1 200	3 030
6	1 800	10 800	4	7 200	3 600	1 200	2 400
5	2 500	12 500	4	10 000	2 500	1 200	1 300

By deducting variable costs which, per unit of sale, is usually a static figure up to a certain point, we arrive at total variable costs, and taking this from revenue gives us contribution. However, fixed costs still have to be deducted. Over a certain volume these might increase if one needs a new warehouse or trunker. The resultant figure is 'Yield' which must cover the marketing funds necessary to achieve the volume of business and our profit. Where this yield is the greatest is, in theory, the price level most advantageous for us.

One can sensibly use this method as a start point for a product launch where there are no directly competing products. It must then be considered in the light of all the other market factors which will pertain. In other words, contribution pricing sets an 'ideal' price from the company point of view. It can also be used to see whether it might be better to go for increased volume and deep penetration, or for exclusivity. In other words, it can be an aid to marketing planning but seldom an end in itself.

Discounting

Both standard trade discounts and promotional discounts are a form of price cutting and, as such, are powerful marketing tools, but they can be very expensive indeed. It is easy to give money away, far more difficult to make it.

Effect on volume

Here are two ways of looking at the problem. In the first, assume we have a product to sell at £1 each on which we wish to make 25% profit. We believe that we can sell 100 of these 'widgets' with normal trading and put £25 in our pocket. Assume that any discount to the trade comes straight out of our profit.

So normally we sell at 100p per unit and have 25p for ourselves. If we sell at 90p (10% discount) we only get 15p for ourselves. We therefore need to sell 167 units at 15p to get £25 for ourselves (actually £25.05) and 167 sold at 90p is £150.30.

Discount As % of full selling price and as pence per unit	Profit	Volume (units)	Selling price per unit (£)	Turnover (£)
–	25	100	1.00	100
5	20	125	0.95	119
10	15	167	0.90	150
15	10	250	0.85	211
20	5	500	0.80	400
Increase				
+5	30	83	1.05	87
+10	35	71	1.10	78

N.B. Sterling figures are to the nearest £.

If we cut the price by only 5% we must sell 25% more volume and get 19%

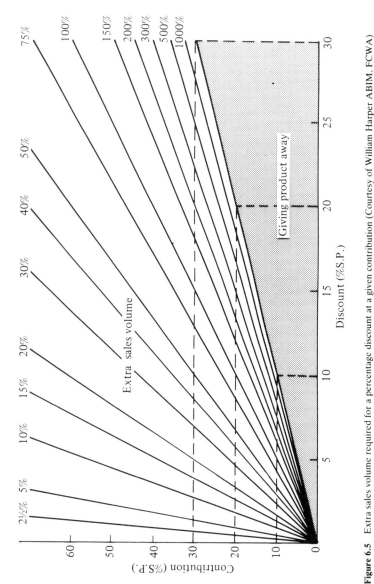

Figure 6.5 Extra sales volume required for a percentage discount at a given contribution (Courtesy of William Harper ABIM. FCWA)

more income, simply to keep £25 in our pocket. If we cut the price by 20%, by no means unknown in this day and age, we must sell *five times* more volume and get *four times* more money, just to keep £25 in our pocket. Now unless one is a miracle worker, or our original forecast was wild, that is patently impossible. Suppose that with a 20% cut we *only* doubled our revenue, which would in itself be an impressive result, we would be £200 short and, with only £25 to make up the difference, we would be £175 in the red. Of course, this is theorising, but it could happen in practice too. One might consider the much smaller volume and turnover requirements from *increasing* the price, rather than reducing it.

Effect on contribution

In the second illustration, the 'sun rays' in Figure 6.5 are concerned with contribution as a percentage of the selling price. If our present contribution is 33%, as in the earlier costing examples, and we gave a discount of 20% we would have to increase sales volume by an extra 150%, in other words multiply sales two and a half times, to maintain the same contribution. As can be seen, if one gives a 20% discount and contribution is less than 20% of the selling price, then one is actually giving product away.

Lessons

Two immediate lessons arise from these examples.
   (i) Never make a deeper cut than absolutely necessary. This requires the Product Manager to test different discounts first, before committing himself. It might well be that a 10% cut, as an example, could be more advantageous in terms of contribution and profit, than a 20% cut.
  (ii) Never make a cut open ended. Always make it for a finite quantity of product if at all possible. That way the cost becomes a known factor. A cut for a specified time period mortgaging future sales for the present, might be justifiable in terms of pre-empting competition, but it might also run away with so much profit as to be completely self defeating.

Financial Ratios

The only true measure of profitability is in relation to capital employed. So say the pundits. But that is an accountant's ratio and not of great help to Product Managers.

Product Managers need two or three comparisons between indicators of marketing activity to measure their progress along the marketing plan's action path. There are a number that may be sensible depending on the market and type of company. One ratio applicable to almost everyone is

PROFIT: TURNOVER

Turnover is best at NSV. In companies where contribution is more widely used then the ratio is

CONTRIBUTION: TURNOVER.

In those markets where marketing costs are relatively high, such as most fast moving consumer goods, then a necessary ratio is

MARKETING EXPENDITURE: TURNOVER

In some service companies one may need

FEE INCOME: NUMBER OF CLIENTS

or

FEE INCOME: NUMBER OF CONSULTANTS

With very many unit items in a range it may be sensible to watch

SALES: STOCKS

There are numerous ratios that can be used. Two ratios involve four indicators. Keeping records of these and comparing them with forecasts will be an invaluable aid to financial control.

The Marketing Budget

As a cost centre as well as a profit centre, the Product Manager must be accountable for the money he spends. These costs, comprising the marketing budget, need to be well founded, properly agreed and properly controlled. They must be related to the job to be done; in other words, the requirements of the marketing plan. However, there are a number of different methods of arriving at this requirement converted into financial terms. First, however, let us consider the budget make up.

Above and below the line

Some company budgets are split between what is 'above' and what is 'below' a line. In fact, this line was and is a very tangible black line, originated by Procter & Gamble for its requirements of its advertising agencies. All advertising on which the agency received 15% commission should be above this actual line printed on their budget forms, and everything else, broadly concerned with promotional activity which was based on fees, should be below the line. Such a line seems to have become a fact of life for many companies, although primarily for those in the consumer goods markets.

In such markets where advertising is often not only necessary but vital, it may be sensible to spend some 60% of the budget above the line and 40% below. This ratio, or a ratio most pertinent to a particular product category learnt by experience, should be adhered to. There is an example of changing that ratio radically which is often quoted, that of fruit squash in the soft drinks market. Manufacturers are supposed to have given in totally to the demands of powerful multiple grocers and placed all their money with the trade, that is below the line. As a consequence two major marketing factors have resulted:

  (i) Firstly there is *little or no consumer franchise* for individual brands. No one minds now whether they get Suncrush or Kia Ora or Sunfresh or any of the other branded names which used to be well known because none of their manufacturers has given the consumer a reason to prefer one brand over another. They have spent virtually nothing above the line for years. There is one exception – Robinsons – which has never stopped advertising to the consumer and for which people have a definite preference.

(ii) The second factor is that of *private label* or 'own brand'. Over 40% of all squashes sold are retail house names, a higher proportion than for virtually any other product category sold through the grocery trade.

Budget make up

Above the line, then, comprises all media advertising expenditure *plus* all media production costs, artwork, blocks, films, etc. Below the line comprises everything else. In detail:

(i) All forms of sales promotion: special promotional discounts, competitions, premiums, coupons, and so on;

(ii) Public relations and product publicity – two separate types of activity;

(iii) Exhibitions, trade fairs, conventions, conferences, seminars;

(iv) Printed literature: from display material to erudite brochures.

(v) Direct mail;

(vi) Packaging design, but not product development, usually a separate budget;

(vii) Market research – regular and ad hoc. Note (a) that in companies with large research budgets this may well be a separate budget; and (b) that this heading does not relate to product research in the laboratory or technical sense;

(viii) A final element, if one is wise, is to add a 'reserve' of 5% of the total below the line part of the budget. It will be spent before one receives it.

Method of calculation

The marketing budget must be based on some reasonable and logical method of calculation. It should not be a figure pulled out of the air, as so often seems to be the case. There are at least eight different methods which can be applied in differing circumstances. Indeed, several different methods might quite sensibly be employed in any one company, although not for a single product.

The historical method   In relatively stable markets, whilst there may well be changes in expenditure by individual brands, the amount spent by the total market sector is probably fairly stable too. In such circumstances the same amount of money that has been allocated to a brand annually over the last three or four years has been perfectly adequate and performed well. It is therefore quite reasonable to suppose that it will serve well for next year, plus inflation of course. This method assumes that last year's budget will be replicated next year. Research suggests that almost half of all companies use this method.

Turnover proportion   Another frequently used method is to say that a fixed percentage of turnover is available for marketing funds. On average in consumer markets this is 5%, but averages are only averages. Budgets based on ½% up to 13% have been known and for some cosmetics as much as 40%. Buzby from British Telecom was said to represent 0.08% of turnover. After one has been in the market for some time a judgement figure is not hard to come by. To assess it of course requires a forecast of next year's turnover which, hopefully, is a reasonable forecast.

Percentage increase   One theory, which is perhaps not always tenable, is that if one is expected to achieve a 10% increase in turnover next year, one must have a 10% greater budget. Percentage increases, however, depend very much on the start point. 10% on 100 is not very much but 10% on a million is rather more.

Case rate   In many markets which have significant volumes and which are relatively stable, it is possible to say that for every case sold one can afford to spend so much. If the forecast for the first quarter of the year is exceeded we have more to spend in quarter two, but if they are below expectations we have less to spend. It could be argued that if we are below forecast in quarter one, we should spend more next quarter, not less. However, in big markets that thinking just is not affordable.

The case rate method is the nearest one can get to spending in relation to business as it occurs. It does assume that during the last quarter of the company's fiscal year, one has a chance to catch up any deficit. It also assumes that one can adjust one's spending within three months. In practice that can often be difficult and even incur penalty payments. It also assumes that changes in costs will not radically affect the affordable case rate.

Task   The pundits say that we should decide what must be done next year to achieve our marketing plan of action, cost out this action at next year's prices, add it up, and the total represents a sensible, defensible budget. This makes obvious sense and indeed is the only method open to a new product launch. The problem is in forecasting next year's prices. However, this is not an insurmountable problem within the general uncertainties of forecasting and budgeting.

Brand share   A less definite method, although one where some statistical work is supportive, is to hypothesise that if you wish to achieve a brand share of 10% next year, then the budget must be 10% of what the total market is estimated to spend annually over a period of years.

Competitive   In some markets, mainly oligopolies where perhaps two brands dominate, an expenditure at least as great as those individually is necessary to enable one to be heard adequately. Certainly in many markets where competitive product differences are minimal, it is sensible to relate expenditure in some way to major brands.

Advertising and profit   Finally, as a method this suggests that during the year there is a flexibility to spend more at some times and accept less profit, providing one achieves one's profit target at the end of the year. Whilst this does give the Product Manager total control, it can play havoc with cash flow and expenditure budgets and it can only really relate to products which do fluctuate significantly through short term manipulation of promotional activity. These are the exception rather than the rule.

Obtaining agreement

After all the tortuous reasoning, whatever method is chosen, the resultant budget must be justified to and agreed with top marketing and financial management. It may well be that the Product Manager is forced to accept a different budget for perfectly sound reasons, perhaps to do with the cash requirements of the company, or priority given to a different group of products. But the possibility or even probability of this occuring should in no way result in budgeting in a haphazard fashion. It must be based on a rational method which is capable of justification based on cogent reasoning. Certainly no Product Manager should accept an imposed budget with which he profoundly disagrees. Nothing can be one hundred per cent watertight but the Product Manager should know better than anyone else what is required to be done next year and the likely cost of that action. For that he should be prepared to fight – but perhaps not to the death !

7   Market Research

Facts, not fancy – Range of choice –
Defining a need – Desk research – Audits –
Field surveys – Procedure – Questionnaire
design – Sampling – Industrial research –
Reporting – Obtaining value for money –
Margin-of-error table

Facts, Not Fancy

'To manage a business well is to manage its future. To manage its future is to manage information.' To know what is happening in the market place is the basis of good decision making. It ensures that risk taking is minimised. The alternative of guessing is fraught with peril. To have a 'feel' of the market, 'flair', 'hunch' is all very necessary, but is never a substitute for real knowledge.

Past history

It must never be forgotten, however, that all factual data is past history. Whilst computer data banks can bring us nearer to the present than ever before the information available is still about yesterday. Trends are therefore generally very much more important than absolute figures; and for any trend to be evident there must be comparative figures. If an attitude study today said that 30% of people hate your product, is that good or bad?

you do not know unless it can be compared with the same data from some earlier time. If then only 25% of people hated you, then the new 30% is bad; but if before, 35% of people hated you, then the new 30% is good.

Not all research data requires such a bench mark for comparison: reaction to a product change as part of a product development programme, for instance. But even then, the knowledge that, say, ten percentage points clear preference over competition results in a 'winner' is valuable knowledge to have. So generally it is wise to build up a bank of research data and use it for comparative purposes whenever relevant; and, in commissioning new research, to have a thought to that which went before.

Researching the future

There *are* attempts made to find out what people might do in the future – many electoral polls do just that. But they will always be suspect for the simple reason that all of us, as individuals, find it difficult to think of ourselves in a different situation. We really cannot decide how we might act in a given set of circumstances. When those circumstances actually do happen, many other influencing factors, both personal and external, might be different too.

Figure 7.1

One relatively frequent endeavour of Product Managers seems to be to find out what price potential or existing customers might pay for a given product. All that can be said for certain about the answers to such research, is that the 'Don't knows' don't know. Those who say they will or will not pay a given price might well change their minds when they see what is actually available within a set of alternatives when the time comes.

Accuracy and precision

No research data is 100% precise although it may be statistically accurate and there is certainly no point in treating a computer print-out of research data as gospel from which figures can be quoted with absolute certainty. Virtually all market research is based on a small sample of the total available. The degree of statistical accuracy which one can apply to a given sample can be worked out. Examples are given later in this chapter. Product Managers should ensure that they obtain this for every piece of research data that they might use, before committing themselves to decisions as a result of it. For most research projects, accuracy to within ±5% is sufficient, bearing in mind that the tools of marketing are blunt weapons. The marketing action that can be taken cannot be so finely tuned that the high cost of exactitude in research data can be cost effective. It should be noted that fierce arguments have raged over the years between the value and usefulness of qualitative as against quantitative research without any clear guidelines emerging. Both have their devotees and their uses.

Range of Choice

As can be seen from the 'Research Menu' below, there are many methods of gathering information, ranging from desk research to major 'Usage and Atittude' studies:

Desk
    Own files: records, company data home and overseas;
    Government;
    Trade associations;
    Reference libraries;
    Published and subscription services;
    The media;
    Trade fairs, conferences, seminars;
    Field intelligence from sales force, suppliers, customers, colleagues.
Exploratory
    Brain storming, unstructured interviews with trade, consumers;

Store checks;
Group discussions;
Observational studies;
Pilot surveys.
Syndicated services
Consumer panels;
Retail audits;
Omnibus surveys;
Media surveys.
'Ad hoc' surveys
Methods – personal, mail, telephone, in home, in hall, outdoor, etc.
Product testing;
Name, pack, position testing;
Pre-and post-advertisement testing;
Usage, purchase habits, opinion and attitude surveys;
Market segmentation;
Distribution: dealer attitudes;
Corporate images;
Model building.

It is not the purpose of this book to examine each of these as a research technique but to concentrate on the Product Manager's usage of research as an aid to decision making. There lies the key. What are the gaps in our knowledge? Are they important or just nice to know?

The London office of a famous international advertising agency, became so constipated with paper at one stage that one man was employed for one whole year to cut down the amount of figure work that was jamming not only the computer but also executives' minds.

Two years ago, a major discount warehouse chain opened new premises in Ruislip with laser controlled cash tills. The quantity of paper pushed out by the computer was so great that executives spent most of their time studying print-outs and little at their proper job functions. It was not, of course, the computer's fault. A human being had programmed it in the first place. The program had to be drastically curtailed to produce only essential data.

Defining a Need

Research must never be used as an excuse for inaction. 'The matter is under consideration' really means 'Never heard of it!' 'It is under active consideration' means 'We are looking in the files for it'. 'We are seeking clarification' really means 'We are filling in the background with so many details that the foreground goes underground!' And far too often 'We're conducting a survey' really means 'We need more time to think of an answer!'

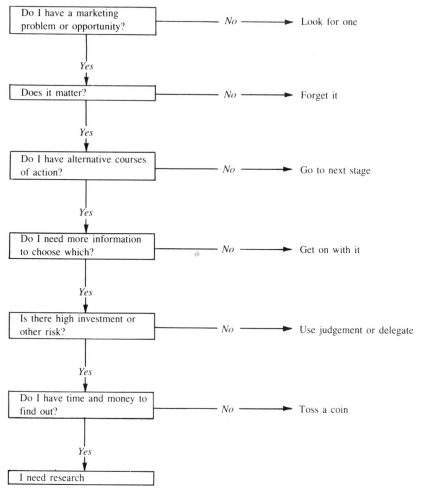

Figure 7.2

The essence of defining a need for regular or specific research is to be quite clear what is the problem to be solved and then to see if the information can be obtained from existing sources. If not, then the research requirement is clear. So let us examine in more detail desk research, regular data, and field surveys.

Desk Research

The amount of information that can be obtained simply for the asking is legion. No specialist research should be carried out before checking that the information required is not already available. Among a vast number of potential sources, can be listed:

(i) Own company – branch offices; overseas branches; other divisions; associated companies; distributors; agents;

(ii) Own sales force – on the spot reports can be invaluable, either personally observed or obtained from customers. Beware however, that they are factual. Both salesmen and customers can be highly subjective in their relationships with each other;

(iii) Government – Ministries; Customs & Excise; HMSO; Census Office; Companies Register; publications such as *Monthly Digest of Statistics* and *Annual Abstract of Statistics*; There are government indexes to their publications;

(iv) Trade associations – industry boards; trade unions; employers' organisations;

(v) Specialist press – editorial departments; journalists; press cuttings services;

(vi) Information offices – Chambers of Commerce; Overseas Export House; commercial libraries;

(vii) Specialist bodies – doctors; nurses; British Tourist Authority; road safety laboratories;

(viii) Educational authorities – universities; colleges; research institutes;

(ix) Overseas – trade attachés of UK embassies abroad; exchange organisations; financial institutes; other sources as for UK;

(x) Competition – considerable help may be forthcoming from one's competitors who are often interested in the same things. Sometimes the cost of research projects can be shared.

We are singularly blessed in the UK with a wide range of available 'good' data and the means by which that data can be up-dated and extended, which is better than that available in most other countries of the world. And not only information concerning the UK. Information providers have long recognised that wise Product Managers must keep abreast of overseas developments which may affect their own markets or provide opportunities for them to benefit in their own countries.

Audit Research

Retail

For virtually every consumer product category, from automotive to DIY, from petfoods to beer, there is a regular monitoring of retail markets by companies such as Nielsen and Stats MR, which give valuable data and trends, enabling Product Managers to steer their activities with greater accuracy by pinpointing problem areas and opportunities and watching the effects of competitive activity at retail point of sale. They are not confidential. Anyone who pays his money can buy the data. Like all research they are not, and cannot be, one hundred per cent accurate since they are all based on samples. Nor is there much point in trying to correlate ex-factory sales with retail audit data except in so far as trends are concerned. There are many reasons for this but three predominate. First, any comparison on a time basis is suspect. If, for example, one compares ex-factory sales at, say, 28 February, the retail auditors will have started their work halfway through the month and go on into the first week in March. Their auditing will cover a three week time span. Secondly, product may have been delivered to a central warehouse in London and finish up as retail sales in Coventry some weeks later. Thirdly, retail audits are of defined retail categories. But a bar of chocolate is sold not only through confectioners: it is sold in garden centres, petrol filling stations, cafes, and kiosks throughout the land. Indeed it is doubtful if any retail audit actually accounts for more than some 75% of ex-factory sales, and for some product categories considerably less.

Consumer

This third problem is often a good reason for opting for a consumer audit rather than a retail audit. Audit companies such as Attwood and AGB carry out diary panel research asking housewives, sometimes husbands and teenagers, to fill in a diary when they purchase certain defined products with details of source, price, brand, promotion, and so on. Or they are asked to keep products, packets or labels in a special dustbin for regular auditing. Again, in an imperfect world, nothing is one hundred per cent accurate. To keep the panel 'fresh' a proportion of it is often renewed at regular intervals, just as the housewives are getting used to it, which is of course the reason for freshening it. Whilst her purchase is recorded whatever the source, does she know for example, what a 'multiple' is? Do you know what a multiple is? (Officially it is a group with ten branches or more.) Further, if the purchase is not recorded until next day, or two days later, might she not forget the exact price paid or other details?

Industrial and 'Other'

Syndicated retail and consumer audits are not available for every market, sometimes because companies within those markets are comparatively small and cannot afford, or are not prepared to afford, the considerable cost of setting up such an audit and the subsequent reports on a regular basis, usually bi-monthly. And too, because from the audit companies' points of view, the potential revenue from the few companies to whom they could syndicate their reports, would not be a profitable operation.

For those companies and for those in industrial markets, a possible alternative monitoring process can be obtained by using Department of Trade *Business Monitors*. There is a *Monitor* for most industries which records home production to which is added imports and from which is deducted exports, both obtainable from Customs and Excise at Southend. The data is based on manufacturers' returns and Bills of Lading, with all the problems of time and accuracy engendered by them. Further, they are based on Standard Industrial Classification numbers (S.I.C's) and Standard International Classification Numbers. These categories and sub-categories may not exactly coincide with Product Manager's requirements. However, they can be extremely helpful.

Field Surveys

> 'Measurement is the foundation of science
> and
> Classification is the basis of measurement.

Be quite sure what needs to be measured. Choose a research company with experience in the type of problem-solving required – from your own experience, or that of your colleagues, or of your agency, or with assistance from the Market Research Society or the Industrial Marketing Research Association. Discuss your problem with them. Not 'I want to do motivational research into the owners of radio sets' but 'It would help me to know if the ability to receive many different transmitting stations is important to men, women, teenagers, etc.' Unless the Product Manager has a research background, leave the professionals to recommend techniques; simply pose the problem. There are so many different types of research and, as in any branch of business, some techniques are in fashion at a given point in time and others are not.

If the Product Manager is quite sure that the information he or she needs is not available through other published sources and that it is essential information to have, then he must commission research especially for that purpose. Note 'especially for that purpose'. Once a decision to originate research is taken, there is a great temptation for Product Managers and others in the organisation to say 'Since we are doing research, wouldn't it be nice to know if. . . .' In succumbing to such attractive blandishments, the research gets bigger and bigger, the questionnaire longer and longer, the sample size required grows, no longer can an interviewer stand in a street to ask her questions, she must knock on doors and be invited in, with as many as three call-backs when required respondents are out, and so on almost ad infinitum. The consequence – costs rocket. Every time the Product Manager says 'Yes' it costs him! Be clear and firm in defining the research objectives and do not waver.

Procedure

Whilst some ad hoc research can be carried out swiftly, it pays to plan it properly, step by step. Provided there is time, for markets where there are a large number of possible respondents, the procedure to go through will be something like the following. The procedure in markets where there are relatively few people to interview, mainly very specialist, or industrial, or service markets, is discussed afterwards.

ACTION	COMMENT
Define objectives	– Ensure information essential and not available elsewhere.
Choose research company and discuss	– From previous usage, personal recommend, personal vetting, MRS or IMRA.
Choose broad method of research	– From full scale survey to in-home placement test. From telephone, to postal, to street or home interviews.
Obtain initial costs	– Ensure budget availability.
Validate hypothesis	– Group discussions, questions on omnibus surveys, etc. to assist in deciding what questions to ask.
Originate and validate questionnaire, and code	– Vital to establish that answers will provide information required and that length is commensurate with type of interview. Pilot questionnaire on small sample
Decide sample size, type and location	– Probably done at the same time as previous step.
Decide analyses required, and computer program package	– Presentation of data in meaningful, manageable and and understandable tables and charts.
Re-cost	– Ensure budget availability.

Carry out fieldwork	– Check that questionnaires are coming in smoothly and that fulfilment of quotas is satisfactory. Ensure crosschecks on proportion of interviews.
Convert questionnaires to computer usage	– To punched card or tape. Crosscheck accuracy. Ensure editing reasonable.
Analyse data	– Check for statistical significance.
Prepare technical report	– Methodology. Relationships between data. Done by research company.
Prepare marketing report	– Can *only* be done by Product Manager.

Questionnaire Design – What do we ask?

> 'Never underestimate the intelligence
> of the consumer. Never overestimate
> his knowledge.' (Dr Gallup)

A properly constructed questionnaire requires an expert to compile it. There are four prime guidelines:

(i) Each question must be capable of an answer which means the same to everyone.

(ii) The answer to one question must not lead the respondent to answer another question in a preconceived way.

(iii) Checks are necessary to ensure that, as far as possible, respondents do understand the question and are answering honestly.

(iv) The questionnaire length should not lead to tiredness in answering the later questions on the form. The location of interview is relevant in this respect. Too many questions asked at a railway station or in an airport lounge or in a shop or busy street, can easily lead to irritation or snap answers. In the calmer situation of home or office, a longer series of questions can be asked.

Questions must be unequivocal. For example, it might be thought that a simple question such as 'Did you visit your bank last week?' is perfectly understandable and unequivocal but, of the seven words in that question, five of them are capable of different interpretations:

'Visit'	– Did you go with a friend or for your own purpose? Did you go inside or to the night safe or cash machine?
'Your bank'	– Was it the Post Office, the Trustee Savings Bank, one of the joint stock banks, a merchant bank? Was it to the

branch that holds your account or to another?

'Last week'   – Does this mean in the last seven days from today, or the
                   last calendar week and does the calendar week start on
                   Sunday or Monday?

All these words are capable of differing interpretations and since every answer will finish up as a dot on a piece of magnetic tape to be added to all the other similar answers, the end print out could be misleading and *no one would ever know.*

In order to ask that question, one might require as many as eight questions, one of which would probably be a check to ensure that the respondent was answering correctly, such as:

   (i) Have you a bank account? (If 'No' close interview.)

  (ii) Who with? (Write in.)

 (iii) Is there a branch of your bank in this town? (If 'Yes' proceed. If 'No' go to Q8.)

 (iv) Do you visit it weekly? (Once in 7 days.)
                     monthly?
                     less often?

  (v) Did you visit it within the last seven days?

 (vi) Do you have a current account?
                     a deposit account? (Check question.)

(vii) On your last visit what did you do? Cash cheque, etc?

(viii) Did you visit a branch of your bank in any other town in the last seven days?

Then there is the question of honesty. If 100 people were asked 'Did you clean your teeth last night?' probably most would say that they did, rather than run the risk of public social stigma. But in fact, probably less than 50% would have done so. Perhaps a better way of putting it might be to ask first whether they have toothpaste in their bathroom now, the brand name, then the same about a toothbrush and then their total teeth cleaning actions throughout the day.

Even the inflection of a voice can change the meaning of a sentence sometimes.

    'General Amin says he has uncovered a plot. 12 arrested.'

    'General Amin *says* he has uncovered a plot. 12 arrested.'

The emphasis on the word 'says' changes a factual statement to a doubting comment. Which is why field workers should maintain a consistent, objective and unflappable mien, disregarding all facetious remarks and all extraneous comments. Since resting actors and actresses tend to act, they are not always suitable material as substitutes for experienced interviewers. All these considerations require a questionnaire to be validated on a microcosm of the eventual sample so that snags and problems can be ironed out, before committing oneself to a major survey. Whilst this is a function of the research company, the Product Manager must be sympathetic to the need and also ensure that it occurs.

Sampling – Who do we ask?

Since for all research where there are many possible respondents, it would be quite unaffordable and, indeed, quite unnecessary to ask everyone possible their views on a particular subject, a small representation of the total, a sample, is chosen. It follows that the chosen few must really represent the total. There are several methods by which the sample is chosen, based on statistical probabilities. Whilst they are the technical province of the professional researcher, Product Managers are involved in a number of ways.

Margins of error

How accurate does the information need to be? If 20% of people say that they hate you and that is accurate to ± 5%, does it matter that the 20% could really be anywhere between 15% and 25%?

(i) For random samples (which are 'random' only in the statistical sense, they are very specifically defined in the research sense) margins of error can be ascertained by using statistical 'standard deviations'. (It should be noted that 'quota' samples tend to have greater margins of error than the examples below.)

A range of + or −3 Standard Deviations means that 99.7% of all deviations from the standard, will be within this range. This is very comprehensive indeed. Usually for marketing purposes 2 standard deviations are sufficient which encompasses 95% of deviations from the 'norm'. 1 standard deviation is not usually sufficiently accurate since it encompasses only 68% of deviations.

(ii) For research questionnaires, the principle to remember is that the formula for measuring degrees of accuracy is based on the percentage of different *answers* to a particular question and that 50/50 is the worst possible case.

For example,

Do you drive a car?

Yes 50%
No 50%

In percentage terms, any other answering proportion will be more accurate because more people will be giving one answer.

Do you drive a car?

Yes 60%   Yes 40%
No   40%   or   No   60%

(iii) The formula for working out the error based on an accuracy of two standard deviations is twice the square root of the two percentage answers to the question, divided by the sample size.

$$e = 2 \sqrt{\frac{p \quad q}{N}}$$

$$\text{margin of error} = \text{Twice} \sqrt{\frac{\text{Answering one way} \times \text{Answering other way}}{\text{Number of respondents}}}$$

So for a sample of 100, taking 50/50 answers, the margin of error is likely to be ±10%

$$e = 2 \sqrt{\frac{50 \times 50}{100}} = 10$$

Thus 95% of all answers on a sample of 100 will lie between 40% and 60%.

(iv) How far would we have to go to double the accuracy, that is to reduce the margin of error from ±10% to ±5%?

Taking our formula,

$$5 \text{ (the error)} = 2 \sqrt{\frac{50 \times 50}{N}} = \frac{2 \times 50}{\sqrt{N}}$$

$$\sqrt{N} = 20$$

$$N = 400$$

Therefore, to double the accuracy we must *quadruple* the sample and thus quadruple the cost of the research.

(v) If there are several possible answers, each must be worked out separately.

Do you drive a car often (once a week)?	45%
seldom (Once a month)?	35%
never?	20%

The margin of error must be worked out for:
45/55
35/65
20/80

A Table of margins of error will be found at the end of this chapter.

Number of breakdowns

The total size of the sample will depend, among other things, on the number of breakdowns for which answers are required. If one started with a sample of 5000 adults, a very large sample and ample to represent the total adults in the country, and then broke it down by:

50% in our market
males and females
4 age groups
4 socio-economic groups
with and without children
13 television areas

which requires 1664 different breakdowns, one is reduced to a sample 'cell' of 3 people – which is a sample of no-one! One cannot have so many breakdowns, even from so large a sample as 5000. If one really did need them all, then one must start from the bottom line and work up. Using the formula above a total sample requirement of some 38,750 adults would be necessary at a cost of perhaps £775,000. Obviously unaffordable.

Cost

So along with realism as far as the number of breakdowns required is concerned, must go budget constraints. What is sensibly affordable? What can I get for that money? What can I do with the information? Is it worth it?

In conjunction with the research agency, the Product Manager should consider the sample breakdowns in detail. Does the research need to be national, for instance? Perhaps six carefully chosen geographical areas can give almost as good data and be perfectly adequate for our purposes. Might it be sufficient to have age groups by area and, separately, socio-economic groups by area, rather than area by age group and by socio-economic group. And so on.

Methodology

A rather clumsy word to describe the method by which the data is obtained. Must it be a long questionnaire asked of the total sample? Might it be acceptable to ask fewer but more basic questions of the total sample, and then obtain more in-depth data from a microcosm of the total sample?

Might it be acceptable to telephone respondents rather than interview them eyeball to eyeball, recognising that many homes do not have a telephone and that it is easier for the respondent to prevaricate or give hasty answers?

Might it be sensible to post questionnaires, knowing that one will be lucky to receive more than 10% back and that the respondent will read the whole questionnaire before answering any question, so that replies might be biased?

Could the same information be obtained by inviting specialist groups to a series of central locations and carrying out 'in hall' interviewing? For some research, 'in hall' use by correspondents of computer keyboards with video screens can cut down interviewing time drastically and yes, even the most unsophisticated can very quickly and very happily press a limited number of keys, depending on the screen's instructions. All these, and many other methods, cut costs and may be suitable for the task to be done.

Cumulative significance

There are some types of research, sometimes called 'dipstick' research, where individual field samples need not be statistically representative of the total but which, carried out at regular intervals, eventually cumulate to a statistically representative sample.

In launching a new product in the consumer world, for example, where one is eagerly waiting for results almost from day one, to take 100 housewives in, say, the London area is by no means statistically significant. But to do this every week for the first four weeks and then, perhaps, at four weekly intervals, soon starts to build up trend lines which can be relied on reasonably well for the area concerned, whatever the purists say.

Industrial Research

In many industrial and specialist markets and in many service markets allied to industry types, the number of customers or decision makers is relatively few. In consequence, to obtain a statistical sample as used in consumer research is impracticable. Since information gained by means of independent and objective research is every bit as necessary in such markets as in consumer or larger markets, how can it be obtained?

Unlike consumer markets, where specific knowledge of particular markets is not specially necessary, industrial research can only be carried out by researchers who understand industrial markets and who may specialise in particular types of market. In general terms, the researcher will select particular companies within an industry, decide on the type of person to be interviewed, from Works Director to Foreman, from Contracts Manager to Shipping Manager, and make an appointment to see them. When he goes along, he perhaps has a sheet of paper with a list of pertinent headings which he keeps in his pocket as an aide memoire, but seldom a formal questionnaire. His interviewing is done by getting the respondent to talk, rather than by conducting a question and answer session.

His report will be an amalgam of his expert interpretation of all his interviews added together; which is why he must understand the particular industry, although not necessarily be part of it. With such professional researchers, the research report will be just as actionable as for a very much larger field study, originated on statistical bases.

In terms of cost, there is probably little difference between industrial and consumer research. Fewer interviews and less statistical analyses are probably counterbalanced by the higher cost of experts who perhaps can only carry out two interviews a day by appointment.

Reporting

Essentially the research company should render a technical report and the Product Manager should interpret the meaning of the data from the marketing standpoint. There is often great temptation to endeavour to obtain 'top line' data before the full information is available. The research has been carried out and the data collated ready for statistical analysis and interpretation. It has been a long time in the field and now the Product Manager feels that he wants to be the first with some really original information. Beware of temptation. If too much pressure is put on the research organisation, mistakes are liable to be made in order to satisfy 'the client'. In any case, data concerning one or two aspects of a market study can be very misleading without a knowledge of the remainder. And it may well be that to obtain this special information first, puts the analytical process out of order and the end result may be to delay the real 'meat' of the research. So leave the research company to produce the report in its own way.

The technical report should not only itemise the methodology but be very clear as to the statistical significance of various tables and figures. What can be added to what? Which way do columns total? What are percentages and what absolute numbers? What comparisons can legitimately be made? Can one percentage a percentage? What is the time scale? What unusual factors bear close study? What require further investigation? And so on.

The Product Manager's marketing report should go back to the original objective for carrying out the research. What was the gap in knowledge? Has it been filled, and if so, how? How can it be used for decision making? How does it compare with previous research? Can it be of help to other product groups in his company? To whom should it be presented and who should have copies?

Value for Money

Buying reserach is no different from buying a radio. You get what you pay for. It will play you a tune without any trouble but the discerning ear can detect poor quality reproduction. The Product Manager must be able to discern poor quality data. There are many ways of cutting research costs. Use unqualified interviewers and engage resting actresses. Keep magnetic tape or punch card operators tapping away for hours on end so that they soon become quite oblivious to what they are punching. Some questionnaires are optically scanned, which avoids this problem. Cut down on supervision. Use old sample names and addresses. These methods and many more will cut costs, but reliability will become more and more suspect.

Use a company you know or that someone you can trust knows, or stay with the professional lists from the MRS or IMRA. Ask for references and check with those references. Brief them properly with your marketing problem and let them recommend the technique for solving it. Respect them and they will respect you and give you good service.

Do not 'forget' them once you have commissioned the research. Keep in touch and check, check and double check. Problems are bound to arise. If you are in touch they can be solved to *your* satisfaction. Ask to accompany an interviewer in the field. See some of the questionnaires as they come in. Ensure that the tabulations are as you agreed them. Allow sufficient time but do not let the research company use that as an excuse for lethargy. Set and agree deadlines at varying stages along the way.

> Research should be rather like a 'passé'
> strip tease artiste —
> past history but with a great deal of interest.

Margin of Error Table

Sample Size	Percentages giving particular answer									
	5 95	10 90	15 85	20 80	25 75	30 70	35 65	40 60	45 55	50 50
100	4.4	6.0	7.1	8.0	8.7	9.2	9.5	9.8	9.9	10.0
200	3.1	4.2	5.0	5.7	6.1	6.5	6.7	6.9	7.0	7.1
300	2.5	3.5	4.1	4.6	5.0	5.3	5.5	5.7	5.7	5.8
400	2.2	3.0	3.6	4.0	4.3	4.6	4.8	4.9	5.0	5.0
500	1.9	2.7	3.2	3.6	3.9	4.1	4.3	4.4	4.4	4.5
700	1.6	2.3	2.7	3.0	3.3	3.5	3.6	3.7	3.8	3.8
1000	1.4	1.9	2.3	2.5	2.7	2.9	3.0	3.1	3.1	3.2
2000	1.0	1.3	1.6	1.8	1.9	2.0	2.1	2.2	2.2	2.2
3000	0.8	1.1	1.3	1.5	1.6	1.7	1.7	1.8	1.8	1.8
4000	0.7	0.9	1.1	1.3	1.4	1.4	1.5	1.5	1.6	1.6
5000	0.6	0.8	1.0	1.1	1.2	1.3	1.3	1.4	1.4	1.4

Percentage plus or minus at 95% confidence level (i.e. two standard deviations)

8   Forecasting

*Purpose – Use of Statistics – Structure –
Time span – Source of data – Choice of
method – The sales forecast – Recording –
Extrapolation – Moving averages – Exponential smoothing – Least squares –
Curves – Correlation – Delphi – Behaviour
models – Regression – Standard deviation*

Purpose

In essence the Product Manager's job is to manage events; events created by
his own actions or thrust upon him by changes in the market place. Such
events are constantly happening. As a result, the Product Manager is
frequently having to make decisions, often of a minor nature, but some quite
major. And for each one he must say to himself 'I wonder what will happen if
I do this or that?' He is constantly throwing himself into the future –
forecasting.

   If he has some past history to go on, then arriving at the best decision is
made easier. Some of the risk of future action as a result of his decision is
reduced – some of it, not all of it. The less back history that is available, the
more guesswork is inevitably involved. Some people might substitute the
word 'prediction' for 'guesswork'.

   Forecasting is the projection of past events, altered to allow for future
events. It is what is most likely to happen, given certain assumptions. The
essential nature of a forecast is a range of probabilities, hopefully not too

wide a range, based on past experience and with explicit assumptions about the future. The purpose of forecasting is to minimise risks and maximise opportunities. The probable results of proposed action options must be forecast before the event.

MANAGEMENT

■

To manage constantly changing events for profit requires frequent

DECISIONS

*Based on wise
choice of 'good'
available data
for controlled
action to*

PROJECT INTO THE FUTURE

Figure 8.1

Use of Statistics

All this seems perfectly logical and reasonable. Yet it is extraordinary the number of people, even in marketing positions, who believe that the logic of statistics is not worth applying because the forecast is seldom exactly right. Lies, damned lies and statistics! They appear to believe that holding a wet finger in the air or turning over their seaweed will be just as good.

Some research that was carried out at the beginning of 1980 among consumer goods companies who, one would have thought, would have been even more aware of the benefits of scientific forecasting than industrial or service companies, showed that over one third of them thought that scientific forecasting was 'not important'. (ADP Network Services Ltd. *Marketing Techniques of Consumer Companies in the UK.*) Which only goes to show that a great deal of serious forecasting must have been poorly executed, or that no attempt has been made to use scientific methods through ignorance or inability, to evince such a low confidence factor.

Since marketing decisions affect virtually every facet of the organisation, it is imperative to assess their effect as accurately as possible. The fact that no forecast can be completely accurate except by good fortune, implies a necessary discipline to ensure the maximum degree of accuracy possible within the constraints of expenditure and time to ensure the minimum possible risk.

The Structure of Forecasting

In talking of 'forecasting' we are generally considering three elements, two of which are not strictly forecasting:
  (i) The collection and assessment of past data;
  (ii) Its projection forward – extrapolation;
  (iii) Deciding future events and their effect on the forward projection.
The first two of these are, as near as makes no difference, mathematical certainties. In many markets which are quite stable – going up regularly, static, or going down regularly – with little internal movement going on, one really need go no further. It is quite surprising how little dynamism there is in some markets. But of course all Product Managers must consider what may happen 'next year' and how those events may change individual product results. Call it crystal ball gazing, guesstimating, or what you will, the Product Manager's feel of his market and a sound knowledge of the effect of past events on results, forms a good basis for melding the extrapolation of past data into a reasonable forecast.

The further into the future or the greater the proposed change, the more problematical and the less exact become the forecasts. Hence long range planning, perhaps over five, seven or even ten years, must present less certain and less detailed forecasts than short range annual plans.

Time Span

As a general rule, it is sensible to go back three years in order to provide a sufficient base for a projection one year forward. One can use only one year's back data if no more is available, provided the information is available on a fairly frequent basis such as monthly or, better still, thirteen four-weekly periods. With the latter one has no problems with periods of different lengths. However, one year's back data is not really sufficient to provide reliable trends. Extrapolation based on only one year is bound to be suspect. Three years should be considered a minimum.

To extrapolate three years ahead requires at least five years' back information. To probe five years ahead or more probably requires econometric models making all sorts of assumptions such as immigration and emigration with birth rates and mortalities and average family sizes to arrive at population estimates; rates of exchange, gross national products, interest rates, prime commodity rates and so on for the state of the economy and its probable effect on commerce and industry. These are not usually the province of the Product Manager but of the long range planner. Since it is usually only the larger companies that can afford the luxury of such erudite creatures, smaller companies that require long range planning, and this is especially pertinent to industrial companies manufacturing capital equipment, are best advised to go outside for this expert advice.

Sometimes, of course, the availability of back data is minimal. All one can say is that it must be built up, and extrapolation based on more and more data as it becomes available. Until then one is a bit like the daughter of a Spanish father and Jewish mother who did not know whether she was Carmen or Cohen!

Source

Past data is derived from:
   – Published information of all types;
   – Research, regular or specially commissioned;
   – One's own internal records.
To be useable it must be understandable and reliable and relevant.

Use more than one source

No single source can be totally comprehensive nor can it ever be 100% accurate. No retail audit can ever pick up all ex-factory sales and, like all research which is based on samples, will never have total accuracy. *Business Monitors* from the Department of Trade require returns from employers of 50 or more employees, so they do not include all production or sales. Population estimates from the Registrar General are based on censuses which are always out of date, particularly as regards breakdowns of total GB data. Directory lists of industries are partially out of date before they are printed.

It makes sense therefore to extrapolate two different data sources. Inevitably one winds up with two different answers which must be compared as to the discrepancy between them, their reliability, and their accuracy. At the very least, this gives one parameters within which one might reasonably plan. At the most it forces one to decide which is most reliable, and to do all one can to build up the reliability of that source. Too often one is content to leave the source alone and assume that it must be as right as can be when one should be pushing to enhance its reliability. No one is infallible.

Understand the source

There are two important parts to such an understanding. First understand the basis of the data being used. What *is* the data used in the *Business Monitor* for your industry based on? The National Family Expenditure Survey that measures our spending on everything from holidays abroad to building society savings, reports in 'pence per person per week'. This is pretty useless unless one knows how many persons it is based on. What are our company sales based on? Are they ex-factory deliveries, or invoiced sales, or payments received, or fee income? If they are in sterling what adjustments have been made to allow for inflation so that rational comparisons can be made with previous years? If in units, how have various different sizes been added together? Have adjustments been made for returns or mistakes or stock checks?

The other important part to an understanding of past data is to understand the reasons for changes in the data. Are sudden changes due to a factory fire, or a strike, or an industry shortage, or a marvellous summer, or an arctic winter? Are they not real changes at all but simply a result of a change in the basis of collection of the data. In this country, a census of population, of production, and of distribution is generally carried out every ten years. The last census of distribution in 1971 gave 104,000 grocers' shops. The 1981 census was not carried out because the government could not afford it. So the A.C. Nielsen company, for whom this information is vital as a basis for their retail audits, did their own at the end of 1979. This found 62,000 grocers. Obviously they had to change their sample in 1980 which has affected every recorded products' sales data.

Every Product Manager should ensure that there exists a sales record annotated with all non-recurring events to explain any blips up or down in the statistical picture, for *one must not extrapolate figures resulting from non-recurring events*. Memories are very fallible and if the Product Manager has kept no record of influencing factors then the use of untreated past data will result in misleading forecasts.

Allowing for non-recurring events

By far the easiest way, if enough data are available, is to extrapolate backwards, if that is not too 'Irish'. By graphing data before, during, and after the event, it is relatively simple to see where the trend line would have been had the event not occurred. Whether one makes an adjustment based on graphing, out of one's head, or by a computer program, this statistical 'smoothing' must be done so that 'good' data is used for the forward extrapolation.

Choice of Method

A number of methods are explained at some length in this chapter and sometimes more than one method is applicable to a particular set of circumstances. Which is the best method will depend on:

   (i) The *detail* required. For Distribution to decide whether to buy a new trunker may require a forecast of total unit sales only, whereas for conversion to sales targets, much greater detail will be necessary.

  (ii) The *accuracy* required. In a very large market a 5% error may represent a very large sum of money but in a small market, problems of cash flow and other financial measurements may make a 5% error perfectly acceptable.

 (iii) The *frequency* required. An up-dating of a corporate 7 year plan may be required only six-monthly whereas an annual marketing plan may need to be up-dated at least three monthly.

 (iv) The *purpose* for which the forecast is required. If the definitive action of launching a new product, a great deal is at stake. If simply to consider the consequences of two possible courses of action, results are not so crucial. Are the forecasts required to reduce costly stock losses or only as a general guide to warehousing?

  (v) *Availability* of relevant data. Research data only available for one part of the country; test market data only available for certain types of distributive outlet; sales data only available for total market. All these and many more will help decide on the best method.

 (vi) *Product life cycle position* The more 'mature' a product category, the more meaningful will be the relationships between influencing factors.

 (vii) The *cost* of gathering and processing the data. High costs for very sophisticated methods might be quite acceptable for major forecasts on which large sums of money depend, but quite unacceptable for the many minor forecasts required during a year.

(viii) *Simplicity* Recognising the need to 'sell' our forecast to many doubting Thomases, too much 'sophistication' in method might well cause cynical comments about attempting to 'blind them with science'. The simplest method possible is not only preferable in gaining acceptance of our forecast but will be the cheapest and the least difficult to repeat at regular intervals.

The Sales Forecast

Of all forecasts, that for unit sales is most crucial from the point of view of the Product Manager. From a realistic sales forecast stem many other forecasts: production, purchasing, finance; it enables cash flow requirements to be gauged; budgets to be calculated and allocated; capital expenditure requirements to be ascertained; sales targets to be worked out. All these vital management controls are vital to a successful organisation. And this is the Product Manager's responsibility. On his or her forecast rests virtually every other forecast in the company.

In practise, the Product Manager ought to create his annual sales forecast from the marketing point of view. What is happening to the market and to his sector; what is competition doing; what product development is likely; what action is he taking next year? But it is a sales forecast and if he expects his forecast to be accepted then Sales Management must have an input. And in the end, both Sales and Marketing will have to agree since the forecast will be reflected by sales objectives and by each individual salesman's target. If they can and do agree, then it will be easier to obtain the all important acceptance by finance since the conversion to sterling and the relationship to corporate financial objectives are in their hands.

Recording

Before finishing discussion on the 'Collection and Assessment of Past Data' the Product Manager should always remember:
  (i) Clearly state the methods used;
  (ii) State all assumptions made;
  (iii) Give parameters within which any forecast can legitimately be acceptable and outside which re-forecasting must take place;
  (iv) Ensure that data will be supplied in the form and with the frequency required to monitor progress.

Projection of Past Data and Forecasting

Let us now consider various ways of extrapolation.
  First four ways of looking at trends in past data.

Method 1 Moving averages. Best used for data with a regular pattern.
Method 2 Exponential smoothing. A system of moving averages where more weight is given to the more recent data and less to the more remote. Applicable only to de-seasonalised data.
Method 3 Logarithmic graphing. For a steady rate of increase or decrease.
Method 4 Least squares. For analysing the time trend in a fairly regular set of figures.

Since there are some occasions where straight lines are not appropriate, there are some comments on curves.

Method 5 Concave, convex, bell, complex and 'S' curves.

Then two methods are suggested of helping to guide one's future thinking when no useful back data are available:

Method 6 Correlations and regression analysis. Concerned with the relationship of several variables.

Method 7 Delphi. Based on experts' opinions.

Three consumer models follow, as examples only, of this technique.

Method 8 Brand switching.
Method 9 Purchase cycle.
Method 10 Brand share prediction.

And finally the vital necessity of validation based on standard deviation concerned with forecast accuracy.

It must be pointed out that all these techniques are capable of computer analysis. Indeed, the more recent computers can draw the pictures too. Product Managers must realise, however, that the great word GIGO applies – garbage in, garbage out. To leave everything to the computer is a recipe for doubt. There is a human being somewhere who is responsible, and he or she must be briefed and checked. Even though the computer can be a tremendous help, the Product Manager must understand the methods by which data appear on print-outs.

The following methods, whilst in frequent use, are not intended to be exhaustive. They are simply examples of the ways in which forecasting, although more particularly extrapolation, can be done.

Method 1 Moving averages

The 3-year sales at Table 8.1, follow a very normal seasonal pattern. If they are graphed as at Figure 8.2, it is impossible to project them forward, except in the most arbitrary way. By halving the vertical axis, as at Figure 8.3, the picture is much clearer. It is important, in all graphing, to use the most suitable scale for the purpose required. However, there would still be great difficulty in projecting forward with any accuracy.

By totalling sales for the past 12 months, each month (by adding to the first 12 months total the next month's sales and subtracting the sales for that same month a year ago), 'Moving Annual Totals' are obtained. These MATs can then be graphed as they are, or divided by 12 to arrive at 'Moving Annual Averages', and these MAAs graphed as in Figure 8.3. (Sometimes they are called 'Moving Monthly Averages'.) The result is a smoothing of all the past

Table 8.1

Year	Month	Sales	M.A.T.	M.A.A. at Mid Yr. (÷12)	Sales M.A.A. % Diff. +	−	Average Change % +	−
1980	January	114						
	February	131						
	March	163						
	April	138						
	May	102						
	June	65		105		38		
	July	55		106		48		
	August	51		107		52		
	September	121		108	12			
	October	107		109		2		
	November	112		108	4			
	December	101	1260	109		7		
1981	January	125	1271	107	17			
	February	139	1279	106	31			
	March	181	1297	105	72			
	April	152	1311	105	45			
	May	88	1297	105		16		
	June	71	1303	105		32		35
	July	36	1284	104		65		57
	August	38	1271	103		63		58
	September	115	1265	102	13		13	
	October	102	1260	100	2		—	
	November	116	1264	101	15		10	
	December	98	1261	99		1		4
1982	January	116	1252	101	15		16	
	February	121	1234	100	21		26	
	March	174	1227	99	76		74	
	April	119	1194	99	21		33	
	May	101	1207	98	3			7
	June	55	1191	98		44		38
	July	51	1206					
	August	37	1205					
	September	103	1193					
	October	98	1189					
	November	105	1178					
	December	99	1179					

changes and a reasonably straight line which can be projected with confidence. Such a projected line, however, merely represents averages. Seasonal and other factors must be re-imposed, for the forecast to be meaningful on a monthly basis. Since each MAA figure is an average of the preceeding year, it should be plotted at the mid-year position. Thus the MAA for the past calendar year will be *between* June and July, so that in

theory, to compare the MAA with, say, July will require averaging the first
two MAAs. In practice, this is unnecessary unless the trend is significantly
increasing or decreasing. Setting out the percentage difference between the
MAA for the month at its mid point and the 'actual' for that month, enables
one to see the difference caused by seasonal and other factors. On the
assumption that all non-recurring factors have been eliminated from the raw
data, it is safe then to average these percentage differences over the number
of years for which data is available (as at Table 8.1). These differences can
then be applied to the projected straight line to provide forecasts of actual
monthly sales. This system of moving averages can be applied to any
reasonable time length and not only to annual figures – moving quarterly, or
six-monthly figures might be just as useful. The choice depends on the
availability of data in the form required, the differences from normal that
occur, and the time span required for the forecasts.

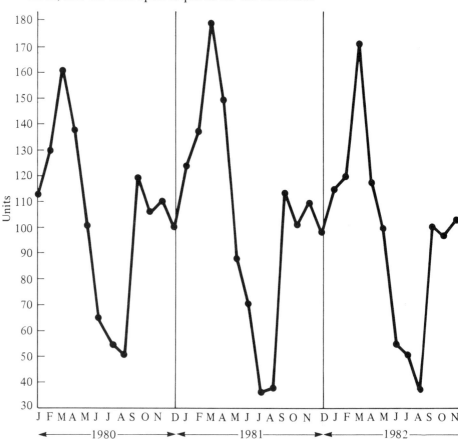

Figure 8.2

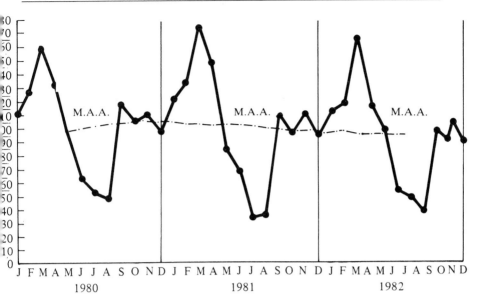

The y-axis labels read (top to bottom): 80, 70, 60, 50, 40, 30, 20, 10, 00, 90, 80, 70, 60, 50, 40, 30, 20, 10, 0

The x-axis labels read: J F M A M J J A S O N D J F M A M J J A S O N D J F M A M J J A S O N D with years 1980, 1981, 1982

Figure 8.3

Method 2 Exponential smoothing

For many reasons, it is sometimes the case that the latest figures available are more important, for future projection, than the earlier ones. In such cases, it is sensible to give more weight in mathematical terms to the more recent figures. This is only applicable to de-seasonalised or annual data.

Method 3 Logarithmic graphing

If figures are increasing or decreasing at a *steady* rate, say 10% per quarter, their plotting on ordinary squared paper would show a curve which is an exponential curve. On log paper, where lines of different values are differently spaced, they would result in a straight line which can be projected forward. Log paper is also useful when it is required to graph different sets of figures with very different values, such as sales for the market and for oneself when one has only a very small share of the market.

Method 4 Least squares

Plotting data of actual achievement on normal graph paper results in points which will never be in a straight line. The statistical method of fitting a line to the points, known as 'Least Squares' can be used to identify the time trend. The addition of all the squared vertical distances between each point and the straight line, must give a significantly low value, for the line to be considered a 'good fit'.

If *Y* represents revenue on the vertical axis and *X* represents years on the horizontal axis, (with *n* the number of years), we need to know *a* the distance up the vertical axis at which the line crosses it and *b* the slope of that line.

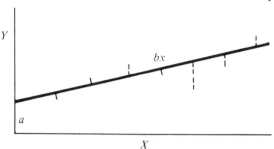

Figure 8.4

There are two formulae to use:

    (i) A straight line is

        '$Y = a + b\,X$' therefore

        $a = \bar{Y} - b\bar{X}$

    (ii)

$$\text{and}\quad b = \frac{\Sigma XY - n\,\bar{X}\bar{Y}}{\Sigma X^2 - n\,\bar{X}^2}$$

(The letters with bars require 'mean' figures to be used – that is, their totals divided by the number of figures involved).

Take the following picture of revenue over the last ten years:

	X (Year)	Y (Revenue)	XY	X²
	1	12.0	12.0	1
	2	13.1	26.2	4
	3	14.3	42.9	9
	4	15.7	62.8	16
	5	17.2	86.0	25
	6	18.6	111.6	36
	7	19.8	138.6	49
	8	21.0	168.0	64
	9	22.3	200.7	81
	10	24.6	246.0	100
Total	55	178.6	1094.8	385
Mean	5.5	17.86	109.48	38.5

To find *b* first, by substituting in the second formula above:

$$b = \frac{1094.8 - (10 \times 5.5 \times 17.86)}{385 \quad - (10 \times 5.5 \times 5.5)}$$

$$= \frac{1094.8 - 982.3}{385 \quad - 302.5}$$

$$= \frac{112.5}{82.5}$$

$$= 1.36$$

Next find *a* by substituting in the first formula:

$$a = \bar{Y} - b\bar{X}$$
$$= 17.86 - (1.36 \times 5.5)$$
$$= 17.86 - 7.48$$
$$= 10.38$$

To draw the straight line of 'best fit' two points are needed, say at 2 years and at 10 years.

If *X* is 2 and 10, therefore, by substituting in the formula for a straight line:

	Y	=	a + bX
For value 2		=	10.38 + (1.36 × 2)
		=	13.10
For value 10		=	10.38 + (1.36 × 10)
		=	23.98

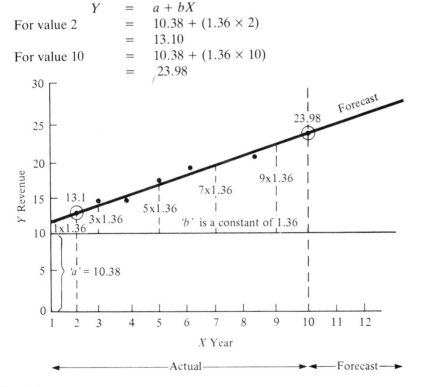

Figure 8.5

Method 5 Curves

Where straight line trends can be assessed and projected, the resultant forecast is usually more reliable than when the trend represents a distinct curve. However, there are many occasions when the pattern is clearly a curve and the continuance of that curve, or a variant of it, is most probable, a product launch or the growth phase of a product life cycle, for example.

Whilst the continuance of an existing curve can be projected fairly accurately, particularly on the computer if properly programmed, changes in the curve shape or direction can only be forecast by experience of and reference to similar market situations. It should be noted that many regular curves can be plotted on logarithmic graph paper, when they will appear as straight lines.

There are four simple types of curve – concave, convex, Bell, and 'S'. Various combinations of these create 'complex' curves.

(a)   (b)

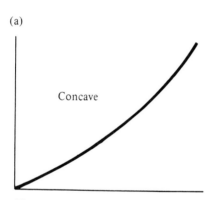

Concave   Convex

Figure 8.6

Examples: (a)   (b)
    1 Launch on a 'roll-out'   1 Growth to maturity in P.L.C.
      expansion area basis.   2 Decline (Curve reversed)
    2 Growth phase of P.L.C.
    3 Supply and demand.

Future Events

There are a number of aids to the effect that future events may have on projected historical data. Some are based on research techniques, some on mathematical applications, most on sheer experience in the market place.

(c)

(d)

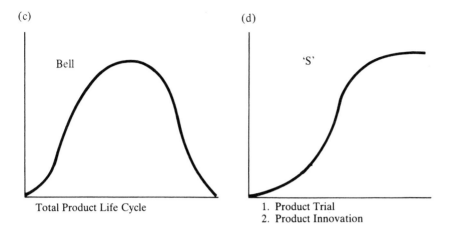

Bell

Total Product Life Cycle

'S'

1. Product Trial
2. Product Innovation

(e)

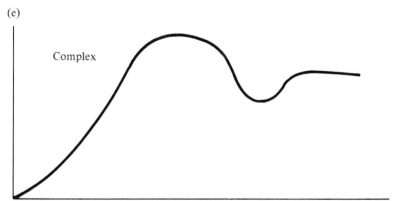

Complex

Typical new product launch in consumer rapid repeat purchase markets
Figure 8.6 (cont.)

Method 6 Correlation and regression analysis

(a) Correlations

In virtually every market, there is an economic or market indicator that reflects, or conditions, that market's behaviour; e.g. total advertising expenditure has a direct correlation with the economy of the country as measured by consumer expenditure; strength of attitude of mind to a particular advertising campaign is directly related to the number and impact of exposures to that campaign; similarly that is correlated with the 'forgetting' curve.

Causal relationships between different factors *can* be of great value in forecasting the future of one of them. It is essential that such relationships be *direct* and *provable*, since some apparent correlations are as a result of a third factor, which may not always be present. Correlation analysis is a statistical method of seeing whether one factor is directly related to another and whether such a relationship is significant. Statistically, there is a 'perfect positive correlation' if the result of the analysis is Plus 1 and a 'perfect negative correlation' if the result is Minus 1. Values between these extremes show the extent to which the factor has an influence. This 'coefficient' figure can show a high degree of correlation at both extremes – either both factors working closely together and influencing each other in the same way (positively) or directly influencing each other in opposite ways (negatively).

As examples, it is to be hoped that advertising expenditure would directly influence sales – that an increase in one would result in an increase in the other – a positive correlation and the nearer the coefficient is to Plus 1, the greater the effect will be. On the other hand it is also hoped that the greater the sale, the lower would be the cost of the production per unit – a negative correlation and the nearer the coefficient is to Minus 1, the greater the cost saving. Therefore, a coefficient at, or close to 'O' indicates that there is little or no correlation between the two factors being considered. This statistical technique can similarly be used to see which of several different factors that might exert an influence, actually does so, and to what extent.

It must always be borne in mind that the data being used is *past* data. The fact that sales reacted positively to advertising in the past, may not hold good for the future if saturation has been reached, or new competitors enter the market, or the product or service being advertised has been redeveloped, and so on. The correlation will only continue to hold good, *all other things being equal.* When market changes occur, experience and reference to similar events in the past may be a guide to the future.

Let us consider the correlation between revenue and advertising expenditure in the circumstance below, with X representing revenue and Y advertising expenditure. The past 8 years' data is available.

	X (Revenue)	Y (Advertg.)	X^2	Y^2	XY
	3.4	175	11.56	30,265	595
	4.3	200	18.49	40,000	860
	3.9	230	15.21	52,900	896
	5.2	245	27.04	60,025	1275
	4.9	275	24.01	75,625	1348
	5.6	285	31.36	81,225	1598
	5.9	325	34.81	105,625	1920
	6.9	330	47.61	108,900	2280
TOTAL	40.1	2065	210.09	554,925	10,772

The formula to use is:

$$r = \frac{\Sigma X Y - \dfrac{(\Sigma X)(\Sigma Y)}{n}}{\sqrt{\left(\Sigma X^2 - \dfrac{(\Sigma X)^2}{n}\right) \times \left(\Sigma Y^2 - \dfrac{(\Sigma Y)^2}{n}\right)}}$$

$$= \frac{10,772 - \dfrac{(40.1)\,(2065)}{8}}{\sqrt{\left(210.1 - \dfrac{1608}{8}\right) \times \left(554,925 - \dfrac{2065 \times 2065}{8}\right)}}$$

$$= \frac{10,772 - 10,350.8}{\sqrt{9.1 \times 21,881}}$$

$$= \frac{421.2}{\sqrt{199,117}}$$

$$= \frac{421.2}{447}$$

$$= 0.94$$

So there is a very high degree of correlation between advertising and revenue and it is positive (+0.94).

(b) Regression analysis

A mathematically based method of defining the extent of one variable relative to others, over time. Results will show which variable has the greatest effect and to what extent. For example, it has been used to forecast demand for canned beer by an equation which correlates sales to income levels, the number of drinking establishments per thousand persons, and age distribution of the population. When more than one variable is used the technique is called 'multiple regression'. For all general use, regression analysis can only be carried out with the aid of a computer and the advice of a statistician.

For each variable, reliable back data is required. It is unlikely that reliable results can be obtained with less than 3 years back data. If sales are to be forecast and it can sensibly be assumed that the predominant influencing factors on sales are distribution, media expenditure, and price, then the equation to use will be:

$$S = B \qquad + Bd\ (D) \qquad + Bm\ (M) \qquad + Bp\ (P) \qquad + Bt\ (T)$$

| Sales Base sales, i.e. starting point. | d = amount of influence on sales of distribution. D = Distribution forecast. | m = media influence M = media forecast | p = price influence P = price forecast | t = time T = year of forecast |

bd, Bm, Bp represent the coefficients of *B*.

Having carried through the equation, the variables must then be checked for reliability. This is done in three ways:

(i) *Coefficient of Determination (R^2).* This shows the effect of the variants in total on the 'Base' or element to be forecast – how much of past variation in sales is explained by the independent variables – in other words, how well the equation fits the basic data. A figure of 1.00 is perfect.

(ii) *'T' values.* This checks the reliability of the relationship between the dependent variables (distribution, media, and price) on the independent variable or base (sales). In other words, it is checking the B Coefficients – the value obtained for each should be at *least* ±2.0.

(iii) *Standard error.* This indicates the likely range of error of forecasts made by the equation. One standard error, of say 2.5, would imply that, for two thirds of the time, forecasts would be within ±2.5 units. Two standard errors of 5.0, implies that for 95% of occasions forecasts would be within ±5.0 units.

There are five possible problems with regression analysis, which must be verified:

a) *Two way causation.* As well as the variables affecting the base (or independent variable), the base may affect the dependent variables. For example, sales may affect price as well as price affecting sales. In such a case, similar equations, using the dependent variable as a base, will show the statistical influence exerted.

b) *Multi-colinearity.* Some of the dependent variables may highly correlate with each other irrespective of the base. The action to take is to omit one of the correlating dependent variables and assess the difference to the results.

c) *Auto-correlation.* Consistent under – or over – prediction might occur. The first step is to see if there is another dependent variable which has not been taken into consideration and which might explain the consistent discrepancy. If this is not the answer, then the results of a prior year might be used as an extra dependent variable.

d) *No real causality*. There may be a high statistical correlation between two or more variables, but it may simply be without any foundation in practicality and both may be dependent on a third variable which has not been taken into account. In such cases, extract one of these variables and proceed without it.

e) *Dormant variables*. A factor, highly relevant to sales, may have changed little in the past and therefore not taken into account as a variable. If such a factor *does* change significantly, it must be identified and included. Practical experience should identify such a factor.

Method 7 Delphi

A recognised method of assessing future events where little or no factual data is available, is the Delphic method, which is based on an intuitive consensus of expert opinion. It can be used, for example, to estimate total market size, or the time at which a known event, such as the introduction of a new technology, might take place.

Some twelve or more people from within the industry concerned, who have a deep experience of the problem area and an ability to think ahead, are asked for their opinions in numerate terms. They must be briefed clearly, so that their estimates of the future event are all based on the same understanding. If twelve people are used, twelve different figures will result. The upper and lower quartiles are ignored. The median of the middle half of the figures submitted is taken and relayed back to the panel of experts with the request that they review their estimates. Some will be changed, others will not. This procedure is carried out three times and the final figure can be accepted with reasonable confidence.

One slight caveat is that the more technical the problem, the more the experts are likely to give optimistic estimates in the short term and pessimistic estimates in the longer term. Extreme estimates should be probed for reasons since they may be privy to technical information not available to others.

Example

Problem: When will the use of lasers for retail cash purposes be widespread in the UK? That is, the year by which 20% of all retail shops will regularly use this method.

Year order	First series	Median	Second series	Median	Third series	Median
1	1985		1985		1987	
2	1987		1990		1990	
3	1989		1992		1993	
4	1990 ⎫		1993 ⎫		1994 ⎫	
5	1990 ⎬		1994 ⎪		1994 ⎪	
6	1993 ⎱	1994	1994 ⎱	1995	1995 ⎱	1995
7	1995 ⎰		1996 ⎰		1995 ⎰	
8	1995 ⎪		1996 ⎪		1996 ⎪	
9	1998 ⎭		1997 ⎭		1996 ⎭	
10	2000		1998		1997	
11	2010		2000		2000	
12	2020		2010		2000	

N.B. Median is the value which splits the distribution into halves. In the table above it is between years 6 and 7.

Consumer Behaviour Models

The word 'model' is simply a blueprint for the method by which an answer is arrived at, using a format suitable to the problem. It is a representation of a physical action in mathematical terms. There are many such models ranging from the very simple to the very complicated. Most, but by no means all, have a basis in statistics and the more complicated, therefore, may require computer assistance. Model building, when carried out by experts, can be so 'tailor-made' to a company's requirements as to be invaluable as an aid to decision making.

Three of very many are considered here solely as examples of what might be possible.

Method 8 Brand switching (based on Markov)

In many consumer markets where there is a reasonably regular 'repeat purchase cycle' and where differences between brands are marginal, there is a substantial element of consumer substitution. Even though there may be loyalty to a particular brand, a promotional incentive on another brand, or a temporary out-of-stock situation, may result in a switch to another brand. The extent of 'brand switching' can readily be found on a regular basis through 'diary panel' type research.

It is obviously sensible to know whether a policy of continually attempting to take business from competition is preferable to a policy of strengthening brand loyalty; the former policy is one of aggression and gaining new customers, the latter of holding existing customers. (The point should be made that this particular model is best suited to an assessment of the market as it exists, rather than as an aid to forecasting.)

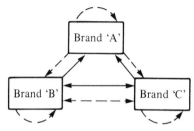

Normal market switching

Figure 8.7

Brands frequently gain or lose customers from each other as well as regaining lapsed customers who have temporarily left the market.

Example

For the sake of simplicity, the following example assumes only two brands in the market. In practice, with a number of brands, mathematical assistance in the form of a computer programme will almost certainly be required.

    Assumption: That 55% of Own Brand users stay loyal.

               That 70% of Brand 'X' users stay loyal, therefore 30% switch to Own Brand.

		Next time purchase			
	Current Share %	Own Brand		Brand 'X'	
		Buyers %	Share %	Buyers %	Share %
Own Brand	40	55	22	45	18
Brand 'X'	60	30	18	70	42
			Total 40		Total 60

Own Brand share remains the same as last time at 40% but with very different make-up of customers, 22% from original buyers but 18% from Brand 'X'.

    Two courses of marketing action are open:

(i) Endeavour to increase take from Brand 'X' by, say, 5% to 35%; or
(ii) Endeavour to reduce loss to Brand 'X' by retaining, say, 60% of customers instead of 55%.

First alternative: (Figures are percentages)

Brand	Share	Next purchase Buyers	Share	New share	2nd purchase Buyers	Share	New share	3rd purchase Buyers	Share	New share	4th purchase Buyers	Share	Stable share
Own	40	55	22	43	55	23.6	43.6	55	24.0	43.7	55	24.05	43.75
'X'	60	35	21	57	35	20.0	56.4	35	19.7	56.3	35	19.70	56.25
Own Total			43			43.6			43.7			43.75	

N.B. A 'stable' state is reached when the new brand share is the same as the previous share – in this case, after the 4th purchase – so that the maximum gain on this policy is of 3.75% from 40% to 43.75%.

This 'long-hand' method of arriving at the answer, can be formalised as follows:

$$Bn = (Po \times Bo) + (Px (100 - Bo))$$

Where Bn = New brand share Px = purchasers from brand 'X'
         Bo = Old brand share Po = purchasers from own brand.

The above circumstances can be arrived at therefore, as follows:

$$Bn = (0.55 \times 40) + (0.30 (100 - 40))$$
$$= 22 + 18 = 40$$

Since a 'stable' state is reached when $Bn = Bo$ and this is the maximum share that can be obtained in the circumstances, by substitution of the two, the new formula is:

$$
\begin{aligned}
Bn &= (Po \times Bn) &&+ (Px (100 - Bn)) \\
&= 0.55\,Bn &&+ 0.35\,(100 - Bn) \\
&= 0.55\,Bn &&+ 35 - 0.35\,Bn \\
&= 0.20\,Bn &&+ 35 \\
0.8Bn &= 35 \\
Bn &= \frac{35 \times 10}{0.8} &&= 43.75
\end{aligned}
$$

Second Alternative

$$
\begin{aligned}
Bn &= 0.60\,Bn &&+ (0.30\,(100 - Bn)) \\
&= 0.60\,Bn &&+ 30 - 0.30Bn = 0.30\,Bn + 30 \\
0.7Bn &= 30 \quad Bn &&= 42.86\%
\end{aligned}
$$

Therefore, the correct strategy is one of aggression to take business from competition (Gain 3.75%) rather than expanding brand loyalty, (Gain 2.86%). Further, the brand share for each gain can be worked out using this model.

Product Launch

The same type of model as for brand switching analysis can also be used for estimating likely share achievement for a new brand launch. The two key requirements are an estimate of the gain that might realistically be expected from competition and the loyalty to the new brand that might occur.

Example

Assume a constant gain of 20% from competition and a maintenance of 90% of the new brand's users.

Again, for simplicity, assume only two brands in the market.

$$
\begin{aligned}
Bn &= 0.90\,Bn + 0.20(100 - Bn) \\
&= 0.90\,Bn + 20 - 0.20\,Bn \\
&= \underline{66.7\%}
\end{aligned}
$$

Thus, the maximum share attainable is 67%. This is an unnatural situation, of course, since both the above factors will change in time. Nevertheless, its use can reflect the various shares that might be achieved for different levels of brand switching and thus give sensible guide lines for setting targets. Further, after the experience of the growth pattern in a test market, further expansion of distribution and sales can be forecast quite realistically.

Method 9: Purchase cycle (based on Markov)

Certain products have a 'fad and fatigue' cycle – people are in the market for some weeks and then leave it, usually for a longer period of time, but both their periods in the market and out of the market are fairly regular. Products such as salad cream, custard, particular brands of chocolate bar can be in these markets. The question is, will a policy of trying to prolong the time in the market be preferable to a policy of trying to bring consumers back in earlier. The former is a policy of finding new uses and new ideas for the product concerned and the latter one essentially of reminder.

IN	OUT	IN	OUT	IN	OUT

The formula which can be used in such cases is:

$$
S = \frac{P}{(1 - P)^2}
$$

Where S = the SUM of purchases *after the first* and P = the Probability of purchase.

Example

From diary panel research, it has been ascertained that 50% of purchasers who purchase in any one week are likely to buy in the following week as well, also that of those who did *not* buy in any one week, 28% of them will buy the following week. The two alternatives available are:

(i) Increase length of time *in* the market from 50% to say 55%;
(ii) Bring people back earlier by increasing the 28% to say 33%, or conversely reducing the 72% who stay out to 67%

First alternative:

For current position:
$$S = \frac{0.50}{(1 - 0.50)^2}$$

$$= \frac{0.50}{0.50^2}$$

$$= \frac{0.50}{0.25}$$

$$= 2$$

For new position:
$$S = \frac{0.55}{(1 - 0.55)^2}$$

$$= 2.72$$

Therefore, it is only possible, in these circumstances, to increase the length of time *in* the market, from 3 weeks to 3.72 weeks. (Above formula gives time *after* the first purchase occasion.)

Second alternative:

For current position:
$$S = \frac{0.72}{(1 - 0.72)^2}$$

$$= 9$$

For new position:
$$S = \frac{0.67}{(1 - 0.67)^2}$$

$$= 6$$

Therefore, it is possible to reduce time that people are *out* of the market from 10 to 7 weeks, which is a saving of 3 weeks, compared with the first alternative which only gives an extra three-quarters of a week. The strategy should therefore be one of reminder and the effectiveness of this can be forecast.

Method 10: Brand share prediction (Parfitt & Collins)

For both new product launch prediction and also for existing brands, a more sophisticated and probably more widely used model is that based on the work of J. H. Parfitt and B. J. K. Collins. Full details of the statistics of the model are not appropriate here since they are many and complicated.

Essentially this model is used in relatively stable and existing consumer repeat purchase markets. It requires consumer panel data of two basic types:

1 Cumulative growth in new buyers; in other words penetration. Within this one must take account of the seasonality of the product group concerned, since obviously there are likely to be more new buyers at the time of normal seasonal upsurge in demand.

   Further the time of entry of each new buyer into the market is important since the sooner a buyer enters, the higher will be that buyer's repeat purchasing rate.

2 The average rate of repeat purchase. The ultimate success of any brand in these markets depends on the willingness of consumers, once having tried the product, to continue to purchase it.

   Whilst advertising and sales promotion with good product distribution can affect the rate of entry of new buyers, product satisfaction must be experienced for repeat purchase. A knowledge of the rate of repeat purchase for each buyer is necessary also, since an avid user will make more impact than a desultory user. In fact, users are usually grouped into 'heavy, medium and light' users. For predictive purposes the average repurchase rate is necessary.

Such a model can predict, not only success or failure in the market place, but whether marketing action needs taking on the fronts of advertising, sales promotion, selling, distribution or the product itself.

Validation: Standard deviation

Forecast accuracy. No forecasting system will ever give completely accurate results. It is therefore necessary to have some means of evaluating the extent to which a forecast is likely to be wrong. A convenient way to do this is to calculate the 'standard deviation' of the past errors over a convenient period. The necessary steps are:

(i) Find the deviation between forecast and actual figures over the period;
(ii) Square these deviations and add them all up;
(iii) Divide by the number of deviations *minus 1*;
(iv) Take the square root.

Example

Month	Actual revenue	Original forecast	Deviation	Deviation^2 (All positive)
1	90	92	+2	4
2	105	108	+3	9
3	98	100	+2	4
4	93	90	−3	9
5	101	100	−1	1
6	104	105	+1	1
7	100	98	−2	4
8	96	98	+2	4
9	92	90	−2	4
10	103	100	−3	9
11	98	102	+4	16
12	105	103	−2	4
			TOTAL	69

There are 12 deviations, therefore divide the sum of the squares by 11 = 6.27.

The 'Standard Deviation' is the square root = 2.5.

Having found the Standard Deviation, it can reasonably be assumed that forecast figures will be within *2 Standard Deviations* either side of the forecast. Thus, in the example, if the forecast for next month is 95, it is reasonably certain that the actual figure will be between 90 and 100.

This assumes that the inherent accuracy of the forecasting method remains unchanged. In practice, it is wise to check for accuracy occasionally so that any deterioration can be quickly allowed for. As a general rule:

68% of deviations will lie within ± 1 Standard Deviations
95% of deviations will lie within ± 2 Standard Deviations

In the example, it is 95% probable that if the forecast is 95 units, then the actual will be between 90 and 100. However, 1 in 20 (5%) of forecasts will still be outside these limits. If one needs to define the limits with even less risk, then 3 Standard Deviations can be taken, which will result in ±7.5, so that the actual will lie between 87.5 and 102.5.

9 Product Range Management

General range policy – Basic principles –
Range analysis – Range action – Product
life cycles – Range development

General Range Policy

'The product range is the foundation of company profits.' Whatever other criteria there may be for judging a company, the reaction of individual actual and potential customers is primarily based upon the products or services offered for sale. Their attitudes may be influenced by other factors such as advertising in all its many varied forms suggesting 'added values', but for that to be successful it must be related to the product. It cannot make the product appear to be something that it patently is not. A glossy packaged holiday brochure may arouse false expectations of a 5-star hotel in Paradise for an hotel worthy of no stars even in Hell and, unfortunately, a sale may be made. But it is not likely that the package will be profitable, once word gets around and the inevitable court case occurs, as it surely will do.

Planned basis

To make for sale, rather than to sell what is made, is at the very heart of marketing – a philosophy which many companies, especially in industrial markets, have yet to practice. The commercial and industrial scene is littered with the skeletons of companies who failed to grasp this nettle, of keeping their product range related to customer need – British Leyland, Hesketh, Lesney, even De Lorean.

Far too often a product range has evolved over many years like Topsy, haphazardly and with no really comprehensive plan. Products have been added, hardly ever taken off, because of a short lived market opportunity, because production has required something extra to keep manufacturing lines busy, because of a change in raw material availability, because of the need to use by-products of the manufacturing process, because of the whim of a chairman, or as the result of ill conceived mergers.

As a past Industrial Director of NEDO and Head of Unilever Marketing Division is reported as saying in 1979, 'In some industries, the product range is obsolescent or oriented to slowly growing markets. Too many companies play about with too wide a range of products, instead of concentrating on the ones that really count.'

Customer benefits

'Products are pathways to customer benefits.' If there is no discernible benefit to sufficient customers to represent a profitable operation, then the product has no future. The sooner that is realised by every Product Manager the better it will be for the business health of this country. Products are not sold, they are bought. For a sale to be satisfactory it must be of benefit to *both* sides of the transaction. And since customer requirements are not rigid and since the speed of increase of technology offers continuously different ways of satisfying customer requirements, a product range must be kept continuously up to date in the light of ever new customer attitudes and expectations.

Remember that 'new' products hardly ever exist. The first ball point pen, the first use of lasers, the first credit card happens very infrequently. The vast majority of 'new' products on the market are developments of existing products.

So the first step of every newly appointed Product Manager is an appraisal of his or her existing product range in relation to current and future customer needs.

Basic Principles

In general, a company's range of goods or services for sale should be such as to:

Attract prime customers

Those people, be they business decision makers or domestic consumers, who have been designated in the marketing strategy as of the greatest importance to the future well-being of the company. It may be tempting to set out to attract many other 'minority' groups and perhaps, if they can provide enough business, it may be sensible to do so. But we must always put our bread and butter first. The jam is nice to have but useless with no bread to go on. Best to do what we know best. The hazards of diversifying into unknown fields may seem Elysian but may turn out to be Dantean. One cannot help wondering if British Rail's excursion into the photographic reproduction and processing market as a means of attracting more customers to travel by train is not ill conceived.

Sell the year round

Whilst virtually every individual product has particular seasonal appeal, products within a range should, if humanly possible, so complement each other that there is never an 'off' season. Lawn mowers and hedge clippers; fertilisers and insecticides; anti-freeze and car polish. The benefits of such a complementary range is enormous, in cash flow, in maintaining a presence in a trade or to customers, in evenly utilised production and distribution systems, in communication.

Have few slow movers

These are anathema. They create a positive disinterest among own staff and customer alike. Just another number on the computer print-out. They lead to production and distribution problems, out of stock situations and their attendant headaches of split orders, split deliveries, leading to a host of customer and sales force problems.

But this dictum has to be married to having a sufficiently large range to attract those designated 'prime' customers. These VIPs must have no excuse to go elsewhere for their total business because of their inability to obtain one or two products from you. The product range should be sufficiently comprehensive to satisfy any reasonable customer requirement.

Services Can this apply to services? In most cases, yes. Insurance companies, for example, increasingly offer a wider range of coverage to both business and domestic customers. Insure your home, its contents, personal valuables, your car, yourself, and so on. Building societies are increasingly offering traditional banking services covering many facets of personal finance. Whilst the addition of more and more services offered to the same customer may bring in substantial extra revenue, some of those services may create more problems than they are worth, particularly when they stray into realms that the company really does not understand.

Capital items Can this apply to capital items of equipment which are inevitably slow to move anyway? Possibly. Everything is relative, some are slower than others. The computer hardware sold by Honeywell takes a long time to sell but, once sold, can create a much more frequent demand for software and systems and other services. The 'core' product in such cases, is obviously the centre of the product range; without it one has no range. On the other hand the software on its own has provided much lucrative business for many computer bureaux and suppliers.

Be saleable

This sounds such a truism that it ought not to be worthy of mention, but is it? For a product to be saleable a salesman must *sell* it, not just mention it but really sell it. Not just take an order for it, salesmen are too costly to be order takers. When face-to-face with the buyer he or she must explain the market context, customer trends and attitudes, competitive products, the virtues of his own product, the benefits derived by the potential customer in buying or stocking it. At the very least, a twenty minute job, much more for some specialist products and services, and perhaps involving visual presentations involving a number of decision makers. How many products can a salesman sell like this in the course of a year? In many consumer goods companies salesmen are on a six or eight week journey cycle. This means that they will call on one buyer on average only six or eight times in one year. Of course they may call on bigger customers more often and smaller customers less often. Their call rate may be twelve to fifteen calls a day.

In industrial and service selling, where calls are usually by appointment, the rate is more likely to be two a day or less, and often six or seven calls must be made over time on different people before a sale is made. If a salesman is really selling, he can probably do this for only one product, or one product range of similar products, at one selling occasion. To try to switch to another product group and do the same again to a busy buyer is often hopeless. For anything but the 'lead' line for that one selling occasion the salesman is an order taker only.

And the salesman is not only selling existing products. He must sell new products, sales promotions, act as consultant, trouble shooter, intelligence gatherer, sometimes collect money, move or transfer stock, and a hundred and one other jobs. This all adds up to a probability that the salesman can only *sell* a limited number of products in any one year; in consumer goods companies perhaps no more than eight. In industrial markets for repeat business certainly no more than that to the same buyer. In specialist companies, more or less depending on the speciality, probably less.

So which products in a range are sold? Those which the individual salesman finds easiest to sell, those which have the biggest demand, that have the best back up in terms of promotional effort, that offer the salesman the biggest bonus. Are these few products out of the total range the best products for the company in terms of profit and the future well being of the company base? The Product Manager should do everything possible to ensure that this is so. And in the larger companies, with several Product Managers, he must accept that he will not get his pound of flesh on every selling occasion and that some products in the range will *never be sold*. Thus Product Managers should do their utmost to ensure that the product range, and particularly new product introductions, are really saleable.

Range Analysis

Within these overall company considerations, Product Managers should analyse those products for which they are responsible in light of the following twelve considerations which will lead to rational action:

CONSIDER	*ACTION*
The customer	
Competition	
Coverage	
Raw materials	Leave alone
Production	Alter
Distribution	Find companion
Sales force	Exclude
Export	
R & D	
Profitability	
Corporate needs	
Product life cycle	

The Customer

Is the product still 'right' for today's customer needs? It is a true saying that yesterday's luxuries are today's necessities. The television set is the last item which a bankrupt disposes of. A fourteen year old boy asked his parents one night, 'Before television was invented, when you used to listen to the radio, what did you look at?' Social attitudes and actions are constantly changing. Water fluoridation is fairly generally accepted now as a dental attribute. Pollution is not accepted, filtration methods are in great demand, even in countries bordering the highly polluted Mediterranean. Increase in noise levels engenders demands for sound proofing and double glazing. As consumers, we tend to upgrade our purchase size of products like washing powder believing that this represents a better buy and yet the average family size tends to decline with many more one parent families and single OAPs. The growth of car ownership has made the definition of a pedestrian as a 'motorist who has found a parking space'.

Competition

Is the range still competitive or can others offer attributes that our range does not possess? The smaller pocket calculator or the calculator with a greater number of uses; the 'hands on' computer with comprehensive print-out facilities; the insurance policy with car 'no claims' bonus protection. The major stimulation of a capitalist society is the constant urge to beat competition so as to safeguard and expand profits.

Coverage

Does the range cover all reasonable customer requirements for the product category within the market sector concerned? As individuals, we tend to grow bigger, upwards as well as outwards. Arguably, garment sizes seem to take no heed of this fact. The casual shirt is very much a unisex garment these days. Does sizing take this into account? Containerisation of goods for both home trade and export continues to expand, particularly as business moves from rail to road. Metal and plastic strapping for goods to be sent by container is continually required for new types of product. Tensions, widths, lengths, fastenings may often be non-standard initially but lead to an additional standard requirement in the range.

Raw materials

Are the sources of supply the same as before and are they reasonably stable? The supply of most common fish types such as herring has been disrupted by over-fishing and the need for conservation. Fish fingers are perhaps less based on the traditional cod than in the past. Many processes use potash, the main source of which in the Western Sahara is the subject of territorial dispute. Many food processes include protein, some of which can now be derived from grass, perhaps leading to cheaper raw materials. Other food ingredients, such as colourings, are the subject of controversy with the possibility of legislative change.

Production

Have production processes changed through new technology or other reasons and has this led to changes in costs and therefore profitability? Does this require changes in specifications or in sales emphasis? For certain rarely used types of lead pencil such as 10H or 10B, new production can make five years' stock available almost before one can stop the machine. 'Synthetic' sausage casing enable a great deal more automation to take place in factories processing these staple elements of our diet, even to the extent of enabling production of a straight sausage, not that anyone wants such an animal.

Distribution

Are there new problems of delivery requiring specialised transport or warehousing or stock control for certain products in the range? Regulations for many types of bulk chemicals are much more stringent now, rightly so, than even a few years ago. The reprehensible glue sniffing by some youngsters for 'kicks' must require a greater degree of security at depots and warehouses for all types of adhesive and indeed, perhaps for many aerosols.

Sales force

With possible changes in sales force structures and the continual reduction in the size of sales forces, are products in the range still 'saleable' as discussed earlier in this chapter? With specialist services, such as accountancy for example, it is often the case that selling is carried out by a combination of direct mail and direct selling by professionals of the service specialization, rather than professional salesmen. Thus for a service to be sold effectively it follows that there must be sufficient professionals with a bent for making a professional sale, which is by no means everyone's forte.

Export

Are the inevitable special problems caused by different cultures, attitudes, market requirements, compensated by the business gained? It is an intriguing fact that the nationality of the wearer of a bra can be deduced from the position, shape and size of cup, as Playtex know well. Exporting is a specialist subject. Each overseas country is a separate market to be studied and satisfied in its own special way. To try to sell a product range designed for the UK in overseas countries with no changes, is seldom sensible. Perhaps petrol is the same wherever in the world it is sold, except that many countries call it 'gas'. Perhaps Scotch whisky is the same throughout the world, but in parts of southeast Asia, one reason for purchase can be to generate 'heat', in the sense of virility.

Research and Development

Has the company's expertise in, and control of, each product in the range remained the same? If expert advice is a bought-in commodity, or production is carried out by an associate company, or overseas main plant, or other supplier, then one has little control. This implies that the ability to keep up to date is limited for some items in the range. If so, perhaps concentration on those lines over which one does have knowledge and control, might be more profitable. A very large PR company had no real abilities in the financial PR world so it bought a small City PR firm and merged it within itself. A year later it had to be hived off as a separate entity since financial PR was such a different market sector that the general run of PRO simply could not understand it.

Profitability

Is each product in the range sufficiently profitable? They will certainly not be equally profitable. The 80/20 rule tends to apply with 80% of profits derived from 20% of the range. Can one do anything about the other 80% of the range? Is sales effort concentrated on the right lines? The profitability of the range is the sum of the profits from individual lines obviously, with the profitability of the major sellers of prime importance. How can a company such as Carron, the baths and sinks group, with a history going back to 1759 and a reported one-third share of all the stainless steel sinks sold in Britain, become so unprofitable that they have to call in the receivers? Perhaps one can allow small profit margins from small sellers but certainly not from major planks in the range.

Corporate needs

Does the emphasis resulting from all the above factors marry in with the company's overall requirements? If a company is promoting a new market, the Abbey National building society opening High Street money shops, or Wedgwood opening shops within shops, then the company may be more concerned with brand share or market penetration than with short term profits.

Product life cycles

Finally, where is the product category in its life cycle? Has it many years of growth ahead of it, is it settling down in maturity, or is it in decline? This is such an important marketing concept, on which a great deal of action can be based, that it is dealt with separately in this chapter.

Range Action

Having examined each product line and each variant against all these twelve criteria, the action required will be virtually self evident. Broadly the action will be one of four. The product line will:

- *Be suitable* as it is. No change is desirable or required.
- *Require alteration* for which a development programme must be initiated.
- *Benefit from a companion product.* A variation in size or shape or colour or package or usage, etc.
- *Be excluded* from the range as no longer necessary, perhaps a positive hindrance taking up time, effort, money, giving a bad image.

Thus a clearly defined product development programme emerges from a close study of the existing range. And, to repeat, most 'new' products are in fact variations from existing products. Further, the criteria necessary for an effective 'screen' to sieve new product ideas will, to a large extent, also derive from the study.

Product Life Cycles

Overall view

A very great deal of work has been carried out on this British concept of the life of a product group through the years, both here in the UK and in the USA. Many academic papers have been written about its practical application in various types of market. As yet, its actual usage in companies does not, from personal observation, seem to be widespread. Perhaps this is because the concept of PLCs may have been presented as positive in too dogmatic a way and perhaps because there are so many 'ifs' and 'buts' as far as individual products or brands are concerned.

It is strongly recommended that all Product Managers use it as one marketing tool among many; primarily for use in considering the future shape of product categories, of market sectors; only secondarily for assessment of the future of individual products. As will be seen, it does have applications for both but, in the main, as pointers to marketing action within a product category. Indeed, it is not stretching credulity too far to say that the application of the PLC concept can be fundamental in the broad sweep of marketing action required. But within that broad sweep there is much scope for individual product development.

The concept

Introduction   Essentially the view, strongly supported by factual evidence, is that a product introduced into the market place in a fresh new form or way, positioned to satisfy a customer need differently or a new customer need, forms the nucleus of a new product category since other suppliers, seeing the opportunity, will start to jump on the bandwagon. It presupposes that a degree of customer need is evidenced.

After a period, during which the introduction to the end customer is spreading, and this may take a long time for a product such as say, teledata, or a short time for a product such as ready mixed Campari soda, the market will start to grow significantly. To repeat, this assumes that a degree of need is established. It should be pointed out that in some types of consumer market, as many as two-thirds of product launches fail to remain in the market.

Growth   The dividing line between introduction and growth is by no means exact, it is a whole grey area. But that essential 'feel' of a market which all Product Managers should strive to cultivate will soon tell whether there is real growth, rather than simply gaining distribution and customer awareness.

The growth phase is the most lucrative part of the whole product's life cycle. It is dynamic, things are happening, opportunities abound, new people are coming into the market all the time, these create scope for new features, new distributive outlets, line extensions. It should be the most profitable phase although a difficult one for cash flow because one is having to fund expansion.

As is the case with each phase, the growth phase may be short lived for say, a new drug which, after all its clinical trials, has immediate obvious advantages, or long lived like instant coffee which, as a product category, has been expanding for many years.

Maturity   Sooner or later the steam starts to go out of the market, the rate of expansion slows, there are no new customers to be found. They have all decided for or against the new category and, apart from a few new entrants and a few old ones dying away, there is no more 'give' in the market. Now one is fighting competitors for any business expansion, for the only way to gain extra sales is to take them from someone else. Many markets, such as tea, survive for years and years in the mature phase. Sometimes one is surprised at the longevity of some markets and brands. For how many years have products like Tarmacadam, Perkins marine engines, Radio Luxembourg, Elastoplast, Hoover, Persil, Typhoo tea, Mars bars, been with us? But many mature phases are very short lived. Skateboards caught many napping. Product categories that rely heavily on fashion appeal tend not to last for long, although miniskirts and stiletto heels lasted longer than their particular trades expected. It is debatable, for example, how much longer digital watches will remain before we revert to analogue faces, albeit with a different liquid quartz movement.

Decline Eventually the market category starts to die; almost inevitably, because something else is in the growth phase and is becoming an acceptable substitute. It will be a bold company that maintains a presence in the decline phase, once the rot has set in. There are occasions when this can be profitable, indeed, sometimes an individual product's sales can actually increase in the decline phase, because everyone else is leaving the market. This happened with Mansion Guardshine in the solid wax polish market and still there is a sufficiently hard core of users for Reckitt & Colman to have quite a profitable business. On the other hand, three British toy manu- facturers all had their products in the decline phase when Mattel came across from the States to supplant them and all three went bankrupt. Result, famous names like Triang and Pedigree are defunct.

If one remains in the market when it is in decline, the important principle is to 'milk' the product for every penny possible. Large marketing budgets are quite superfluous.

Some examples

Introduction	Growth	Maturity	Decline
Video discs	Video tapes	Audio tapes	Records
Direct debit	Credit cards	Cheques	Cash
Erasable pens	Felt tips	Ball point	Fountain pens
Health nibbles	Pizzas	Hamburgers	Steak & Kidney pud
Disposable suture guns	Disposable sutures	Suture needles and nylon	Needles & catgut
Viewphone	Notelets	Headed letters	Writing pads
Teledata	C.B. radio	Television	Newspapers
Personal computers	Hands-on computers	Main frame	Time sharing
Personal holidays via computer	Time sharing apartments	Package tours	Personal booking

Practical application

So these then are the four phases of the Product Life Cycle. In America some organisations use a fifth 'Pre-introduction' or 'Pre-commercialisation' phase which takes account of all the development problems. However, in this country the four represent the standard.

Wherever the product category lies on the PLC curve (which statistically

PRODUCT LIFE CYCLES

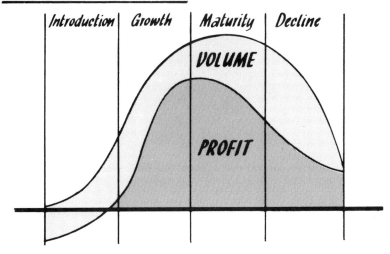

Consumers	Experimenters	Trendsetters	Followers	Traditionalists
Approach	Educate	Inform	Compete	Remind
Sell	Concept	Brand	Brand	Uses
Promotion	Selective	Broaden	Total Market	—
Vehicle	Salesmen	Salesmen and advertising	Salesmen: advertising and sales promotion	Sales Promotion
Tactics	Penetrate	Market Development	Product Development	No change
Profit	Nil	High	Falling	Doubtful
Investment	High	Small	Develop	Nil

Figure 9.1

is a bell-shaped curve) will decide the broad lines of marketing action. The chart in Figure 9.1 shows eight marketing factors which change as the PLC changes, but there are many more. De Paul University of Chicago lists 23.

Here we shall first take five key factors and see how a transition from one phase to another affects their implementation in order to illustrate the practical sense of Product Management involvement with PLCs:

– Customer type;
– Sales appeal;
– Sales method;
– Price;
– Profit.

Introductory phase In every developing market there exist people who, in PR terms would be called 'opinion formers'. They love experimenting with new things and they often have the cachet and authority which makes them leaders. They will not be sufficiently numerous to represent an attractive customer profile in the long run but, if one can get them to initiate movement in the market, one is much more likely to succeed than without them. However, they are scattered over the face of the earth, are difficult to winkle out and, when found, must be persuaded to try the new product or service and stop using the 'old' way. They will argue and question, so that personal eyeball to eyeball confrontation is necessary.

Marketing action: All this implies a particular customer type who must be educated by personal selling into the concept of the product usage. All this is very costly and not likely to lead to immediately profitable sales. The product concept is the important factor, not the brand name or price although neither is ever unimportant. Salesmen should be the communication vehicle if at all possible, particularly for industrial and service products. For consumer products, almost inevitably some form of media advertising is necessary but PR activity to opinion formers is often sensible.

Growth phase Once the market has begun to expand, the type of customer subtly changes, to the Jones's and those who keep up with the Jones's; to those who are not prepared to be too adventurous but who, once the new product seems to be heading for acceptance, wish to be seen to be in the van of the trend. Now too, many other suppliers have joined in, so that there is growing up a recognisable product category with a spread of prices and brand names. New customers still need to be persuaded into the market through education but this is gradually taking on the shape of information about particular brands and brand names rather than concepts become paramount.

A major communication vehicle is still the sales force but one's net must now be spread wider to more people so that salesmen must have a back up, usually of advertising. Whilst price is still subsidiary to being in the trend, it becomes increasingly important as more suppliers offer greater choice, especially when the rate of growth starts to weaken. Because more and more suppliers may be found in the market, all helping to push it into continuing growth, the cost of exploiting it for each supplier, per unit of sale, becomes relatively less so that, with expanding volume, profitability is high. In fact, the profit to sales ratio is probably higher in this phase than at any other moment in the product's life.

Marketing action: This implies a subtle change of customer profile and of positioning. One is developing the market, widening the appeal, informing and carrying out a branding job, through salesmen and advertising. Price becomes more of a marketing weapon and profits are good.

Maturity phase   Now the number of new customers has dropped to a trickle. Those that are left are the followers. There is nothing new to say. Everyone knows the product category and the brands. Salesmen are just order takers. What can one give them to talk about? A promotion, a line extension, a new package, relaunch advertising? Now every marketing tool in the book must be used to gain any competitive edge.

Price is a vital ingredient of the marketing mix within the promotional scene. Indeed, if price was too low at launch resulting in lower than necessary profit margins, now is the time when the mistake will really hurt, for one may not have sufficient funds available to compete adequately against strong competition. Profitability may, indeed should be still attractive, even though less per unit of sale than before. In fact profit may start to slip whilst the market is still growing, indicating the onset of maturity.

Marketing action: Strong branding operation with heavy advertising and sales promotional expenditure. Highly competitive. Profits less.

Decline phase   Once the market really is in decline, one should only stay in it if it is still profitable and providing one has other company products in growth phases, otherwise one is thought of as a company which is old and bereft of ideas, wholly traditional and not likely to succeed in the future. Not an ideal image! To stay in the market is to recognise that one is faced with customers who themselves are very traditional, dyed in the wool, subject to little persuasion. Perhaps they need an occasional reminder that the product still exists but it is a sheer waste of money to do more. One should take the maximum profit possible. It may be possible to price up a little for people who are determined to stay with such a product come what may, as some compensation for declining sales.

Marketing action: Take the money!

Other Practical Applications

Two other points are of particular importance for Product Managers: cash flow and product development.

Cash flow   As the diagram illustrates, cash flow is generally negative in the introduction and growth phases, the former because of the high cost of getting first time sales and the latter because one is sending out increasing quantities of product before one gets the money for it; the penalty of funding expansion. When the growth starts to ease up and turn to maturity, cash catches up and one has simply the normal debtor situation. Cash flow is positive. In decline, of course, it is often better still since it is the reverse of the growth phase.

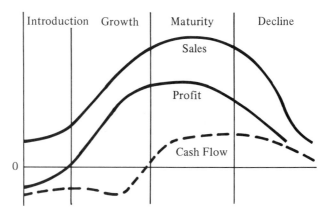

Figure 9.2

Product development   Throughout the whole of this section on PLCs we have been concerned with a market sector, a product category as a whole. The marketing applications, however, apply to the Product Manager's individual products within that market sector. If he has pioneered the market and led the way into the growth phase, he will inevitably help his competitors, since it is up to him to push that market to the greatest heights possible. And because it is now highly profitable, he will want to stay in that growth phase for as long as possible. This means that he should plan for product development or market development to avoid any possibility of losing momentum.

As soon as he senses the rate of expansion beginning to flag, a major new product improvement must be ready to slot in to regenerate the market and particularly his own brand, so as to push himself back into growth. As the impetus of the 'booster rocket' dies away, he should plan for the same thing again and perhaps a third time. There is a limit, of course, to renewal and the third effort may result in a 'pimple' rather than a peak since how new is new is new is debatable. Credibility will only go so far.

In consequence, the PLC for an individual product may look more like this.

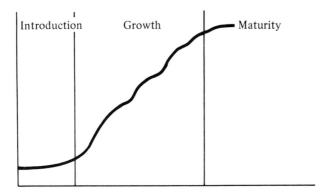

Figure 9.3

In the USA the three major car manufacturers expect a new model to reach the end of the growth phase after about five years, at which time a new model must be ready to take its place. After seven years the old model is taken off the market, unless it really still shows considerable buoyancy. Such planned obsolescence often makes good sense. If BL are right and they never did make any money out of the Mini, perhaps they should have done the same.

If one is not the pioneer but intends to enter the market later, then by far the best time is when the market is dynamic, when change occurs, when there are some weak brands to take business from first, in other words in the

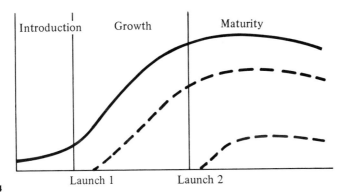

Figure 9.4

growth phase. If one enters the market in its growth phase then one is likely to grow at the same rate at least. But if one enters the market in its mature phase, then one may grow against the market trend for a short while but very soon conform to the static nature of the market.

Position on Curve

It has already been said that virtually all marketing actions will vary depending on one's position on the PLC curve. This begs the question 'Do you know where you are on the curve?' According to some not very recent research 87% of companies using the concept do know, which implies that 13% do not. There really should be little problem if one has total market data as well as one's own, and studies profit to sales ratios, communication methods in use, size of marketing expenditures, and all the other factors that change as the cycle changes.

Caveats

Customer viewpoint   One must always consider the market and its position on the curve from the customer's point of view. To illustrate this, it may be remembered that several years ago the price of instant coffee went through the roof, to £1.60 for the most popular size. This was caused by frosts in South America which decimated the crop for that year. At that price customers refused to buy and sales dropped radically until a year later when prices eventually came down to 99p and the market reverted to normality. Instant coffee has been in the growth phase for years. Tea, on the other hand, has been in decline for years, ameliorated to a certain extent by the expansion of teabags. *Both* trends were halted and reversed during the high priced coffee time. False conclusions could have been drawn for both product categories because they were not a true reflection of consumer change.

Market segmentation   One must be extremely careful to apply the PLC to a market segment as defined by usage. Lasers are in use in many different markets ranging from geological surveys to retail cash tills and video discs:
- For demonstration and display they are still in the introductory phase.
- For retail cash tills they are very much in the growth phase. Perhaps for video discs too.
- For surgical operations they are probably beginning to change from growth to maturity.
- For detecting flaws in a metal they are very much in the decline phase.

Hence it is so necessary to clearly define the product category in terms of a market sector or segment.

Product managers

Finally, even the type of Product Manager may be different depending on the cycle phase. The sort of person required to oversee a new product introduction is likely to be an entrepreneur, ready to take risks, able to grasp opportunities quickly and sense danger signs, willing to stick his neck out. Such a person may be totally bored if forced to look after a product in the mature phase where battling for an extra one per cent share is the order of the day and sales promotion probably takes up a great deal of time. Fortunately marketing takes all sorts!

Table 9.1

PRODUCT LIFE CYCLE EXAMPLE

(All figures in £'000)

Year	Sales £	Sales %	Variable cost £	Variable cost %	Fixed cost £	Fixed cost %	Marketing cost £	Marketing cost %	Profit £	Profit %	Funding* £	Funding* %	Net cash flow £
1	500	—	250	50	250	50	100	20	−100	−20	30	6	−130
2	600	+20	360	60	150	25	100	17	−10	−2	60	10	−70
3	800	+33	560	70	150	19	100	13	−10	−1	100	12	−110
4	1400	+75	980	70	160	11	140	10	+120	+9	200	14	−80
5	2100	+50	1470	70	160	8	210	10	+260	+12	340	16	−80
6	2700	+29	1890	70	160	6	270	10	+380	+14	490	18	−110
7	3200	+12	2240	70	180	6	320	10	+460	+14	640	20	−180
8	3600	+11	2520	70	180	5	360	10	+540	+15	610	17	−70
9	3800	+6	2660	70	180	5	380	10	+580	+15	400	15	+180
10	4000	+5	2800	70	180	5	400	10	+620	+16	400	10	+220
11	4000	—	2800	70	180	5	400	10	+620	+16	200	5	+420
12	4000	—	2800	70	180	5	400	10	+620	+16	200	5	+420
13	4000	—	2800	70	180	5	400	10	+620	+16	200	5	+420
14	3900	−2	2730	70	180	5	390	10	+600	+15	200	5	+400
15	3800	−3	2660	70	180	5	380	8	+580	+15	190	5	+390
16	3500	−8	2450	70	180	5	350	5	+520	+15	180	5	+340
17	3000	−9	2100	70	180	6	300	5	+480	+15	150	5	+330
18	2200	−27	1540	70	160	7	220	5	+280	+13	110	5	+170
19	1700	−23	1190	70	160	9	170	2	+200	+12	90	5	+110
20	1500	−9	1050	70	150	10	150	2	+150	+10	80	5	+70
Total	54,300		37,840	70	3,480	6	5,540	10	7,550	14	4,870	9	—

*Mainly Debtors.

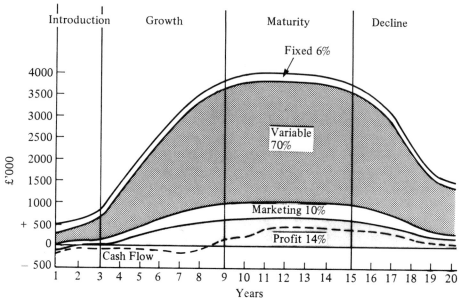

Figure 9.5 Product life cycle example (Percentages are averages over 20 years)

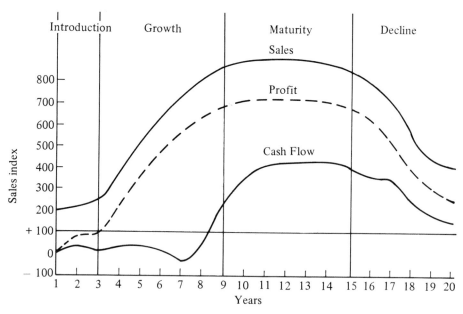

Figure 9.6 Product life cycle example (Figures based on index of 100)

10   New Product Development

*Control – Method – Source of ideas –
Cluster and Gap analysis – Ideas pro-
cedure – Criteria – Successful ideas –
Screening – Naming – Research and testing
– Network analysis*

Control

It is essential that there be only one executive, with clear cut responsibility for product development for a particular market sector or product group and with clear authority to obtain work from the various departments of the company such as production, quality control, purchasing, accounts, sales. To exercise that authority within a controlled operation, he must have a budget since the alternative of having to go cap in hand to others for money to progress an idea implies complete lack of authority. Money gives power.

New product development cannot be carried out by committee. It must be accepted as of vital importance by top management or it will fail through lack of commitment. It must be carried out on a long term, continuous basis and cannot successfully be picked up and then set down again. It must involve at various stages all the skills and talents available in the organis-ation, from production to research and development, from finance to selling and distribution.

Method

The logical process of arriving at successful product development is:
- Collect or originate new ideas;
- Screen all ideas to find the likely winners and give reasons for rejections based on objective, rather than subjective, grounds;
- Carry out a business analysis of those ideas which pass through the screen;
- Check the technical and manufacturing feasibility of ideas still valid;
- Test market.

Source of Ideas

Development ideas can come from many different sources:

A new product manager taking over an existing range who feels that most items in it are as worn out as an old woodpecker in a petrified forest:

A new product development manager someone specifically appointed to the role of finding and developing new products with no other responsibilities. There has been controversy over the years concerning the merits of such a person being wholly restricted to this task. The 'pros' tend to concentrate on the experience gained at gathering, evaluating, developing, and testing ideas, and the 'cons' on the fact that, with no other on-going responsibilities, the very important 'feel' of a particular market place is missing. Existing Product Managers obviously have this, although their prime responsibility is to their existing products.

Perhaps the answer lies in the size of the company. A large company can probably afford a specialist New Product Development Manager, unencumbered by other responsibilities whereas a small company probably cannot.

Research and Development In highly technical markets, such as electronics or drugs, where years of research, clinical trials, technical and scientific analysis, and original research may be necessary, it is seldom that Product Managers, even if professionals of the technique concerned, can contribute directly to the research. In general terms however, a 'steer' by them to R & D appears to become increasingly required since they do know their market trends better than anyone else. With no imput from the practical market place, scientists might beaver away for ten years before reaching a break through. But their 'Eureka' can soon turn to gall if it turns out that a competitor had the same answer a year ago. Companies can no longer afford

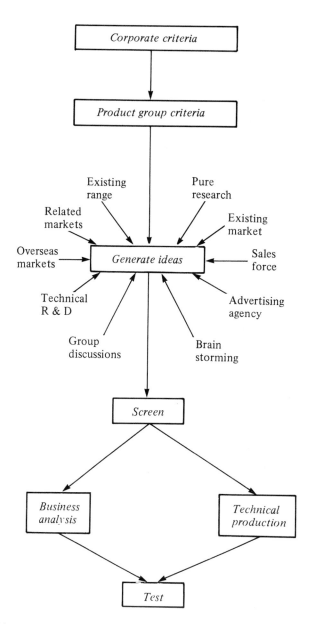

Figure 10.1

the luxury of such pure research freedom, hence the need for a Product Management input.

Nevertheless, many good, marketable ideas can and do originate from R & D. In fact one source, Booz Allen & Hamilton, operating on 150 US companies, considered that 60% of new ideas came from a combination of Marketing and R & D.

Overseas markets   It is sensible for every Product Manager to keep watch on comparable overseas markets through his own company if it be international, or specialist publications, or special research companies set up for just this purpose, or from sales agents, or from attending overseas exhibitions and fairs. Not infrequently, products successful in overseas markets can be successful in the UK, albeit perhaps with some modification. The USA is especially prolific in this sense of course, through their very advanced economy.

Sales force   A prolific source. Every salesman has a customer who says 'If you had brought it out in a red colour, I could have sold twice as much', or 'Put two handles on instead of one', or 'Make it small enough to go in the boot of a car', and so on and so on. Salesmen *are* in the firing line, and so often are their customers. Some of their ideas can be good. A few can be very good. Every effort must be exerted to encourage salemen to suggest new ideas on their weekly report forms or in some other way.

Advertising agencies   The metier of an advertising agency is to think in conceptual terms. All day long, creative types are striving to find effectual selling ideas. Whilst many of these may not have directly practical application, the origination of an idea *from the potential customers' viewpoint*, is all important. That is the agency's starting point, their experience.

From among many concepts which are capable of arousing interest from a specific market sector, some are bound to be capable of manufacture or, in the service sense, of implementation. If therefore, the person responsible for new product development has such an agency, it is sensible to involve them in the search for marketable ideas.

Friends, colleagues and others   Most people of one's aquaintance have ideas from time to time, certainly one's secretary, sometimes the Chairman's wife. The problem is to harness them.

Brainstorming is one method to which some companies give considerable credence as generating original ideas. It involves a number of people with no recognisable research base getting together and simply letting ideas flow. There must be no attempt to relate ideas to rationality; no criticism of any idea, no matter how zany it may be. That ideas flow cannot be denied, but unless they are then put through an effective screen to sieve out those that are obviously non-starters, a great deal of time and money can be wasted. Indeed, because of the sheer weight of ideas that can result from a brainstorming session, a great deal of time is often spent on the screening process, and it might be sensible for the New Product Development Manager, or whoever is responsible, to appraise such ideas critically even before screening.

Group discussions Among customers or potential customers discussions which are properly controlled in the research sense can be extremely useful. It is seldom that individuals can foresee a future need or desire and therefore articulate a new product. What they can do, however, is to discuss their present preoccupations and highlight problem areas which, in turn, might lead to marketable propositions. A housewife saying 'I hate dusting, it always makes me sneeze' might lead to a duster with an inbuilt battery suction action! A trainer of racehorses complaining of the time lost through a horse recovering from a strained tendon, might suggest the usefulness of a Slendertone type of muscle exerciser which can be used whilst the horse is idle.

Related markets executives Discussion of the future of related markets with executives of those markets, including the usually very knowledgeable specialist press editors, can often lead to valuable new thinking about one's own market future. Sometimes, too, they can see the future of one's own market more clearly than oneself, being rather remote from it. Take furniture, for example; if the domestic dwelling of the future has, among other things, a combined dining/sitting room with picture windows and self-coloured plastic walls, within which are situated the television set, video recorder and player, the personal viewer remote control telephone, the home movie screen and the computer controls for putting the cat out, the effect on the shape and type of furniture might be dramatic: lounging chairs with automatic turning device depending on the part ofthe wall brought into play, for instance.

Existing markets examination using perhaps Gap analysis sometimes also called Cluster analysis. There are a number of ways of carrying this out which can be applied to service and industrial markets as well as to consumer products. One starts from the premise that there are usually only two really important reasons for customer discrimination between suppliers of the same or similar products. Numerate research on this basis to ascertain the reasons why decision makers decide on a particular company or brand name in preference to many others, may well throw up ten or a dozen relevant reasons. Simple or multi-regression analysis will put an order of importance on each reason and it is generally the case that two will stand out as being of major importance.

For example, the most generally proffered reasons for conference organisers' choice of a suitable venue are:

– Separate and total accommodation – no noise from children or kitchens, no-one sleeping out;
– Good car parking;
– Easy accessibility;
– A smart image;
– A reasonable price;
– Professional audio-visual equipment;
– An interested hotel manager;
– Knowledgeable conference staff.

Of these, probably the two most important for many conference organisers relate to accommodation and price. If an hotel with conference facilities analysed say 32 competitive venues in its region, including itself of course, very objectively on these two criteria, either through specially commissioned research or, more likely, through the proprietor's own knowledge and scored each venue out of ten for each criterion, the sort of clusters shown below might materialise.

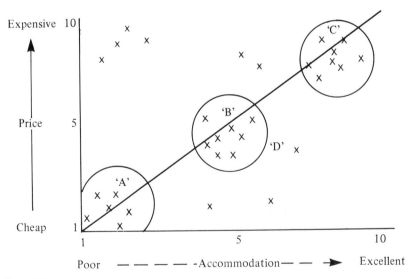

Figure 10.2

Three clusters along the diagonal might logically be expected –
    'A' Poor and cheap;

'B' Average and medium priced;

'C' Good and expensive.

Supposing the hotel concerned placed itself at 'D' believing that, for the fairly good accommodation offered its prices were below average, how might this help it? If nothing else, at least it knows where it stands relative to competition and therefore its strengths and weaknesses in the market place. However, in its vicinity there is no one with 'Excellent' accommodation at an 'Average' price. Should the hotel decide that that was a gap worth filling, it might, with government grants, enhance its conference accommodation, perhaps by building a special wing; increase its charges a little, but not radically; and tackle a sector of the market which is relatively untapped. Or, it might argue, if no grant were available or no rebuilding possible or desirable, that if it could find some other attraction such as first class car parking facilities, better than most others in the region, it could increase prices with the same accommodation. Or, if no-one else in the region had an expert on audio-visual aids, it could hire such a person and offer a service specialising in the use of such aids. Separate Gap analyses would be done for each of the important criteria.

Type of Idea

As an aid to the generation of new ideas by some or all of these methods, it might be helpful to think of the sort of developments which are possible, illustrated by some common examples with which we are all familiar.

From the product viewpoint

(i) *Physical* Bisto gravy granules; Angle sliced giant green beans; Chunky dogmeat; Instant custard; Freedent chewing gum.
(ii) *Companion* Flush non-bleach lavatory cleaner; Windmill brown bread; Cracotte extruded crispbread; Krona margarine; Turkey rolls; French bread pizza.
(iii) *Convenience* Polaroid glasses; Kodak handled cameras; bottled water; Snack pots.
(iv) *Packaging* Pentel disposable fountain pens; 110 camera film; cling film; wide necked bottles; one-piece cans; bubble packs; Tetrapaks.
(v) *Price* Brute 33; Fairy Soap; Kellog's Special K; Estée Lauder; Rimmel.
(vi) *New concepts* Disc camera film; Time switches for recording radio and TV programmes; noise sensitive light switches; solar heating; domestic computors;

From the market viewpoint

Market

Existing   New

	Market	
Existing	Market Penetration (i)	Market Development (ii)
New	Product Development (iii)	Diversification (iv)

P
r
o
d
u
c
t

(H. Igor Ansoff 'Corporate Strategy')

Figure 10.3

(i) *Market penetration* If the market is still dynamic and not yet saturated, the possibility of widening sales appeal by slight product changes exists – a new size, a new colour, a new flavour – the *News of the World* colour supplement. This is usually the easiest development to achieve since one is taking known products in known markets.

(ii) *Market development* Here, one is taking a product one knows all about but putting it into a new market or sector – agricultural hedgecutters into a domestic world; guttering from the construction world to retail DIY; car accessories from original equipment into the replacement market; merchandising teams from the grocery world into the book selling fraternity.

(iii) *Product development* The reverse of 'Market Development', taking a new idea into a known market. A photographic laboratory specialising in school photographs, setting up a training programme for photographers so that its developing process is not detracted from by poor film; 'hands on' computer manufacturers becoming involved in paper recording; Sterling Health's Baby Wipes.

(iv) *Diversification* – which some might call 'the blind leading the blind'. Putting products one knows nothing about into markets one knows nothing about. There have been so many failures through the acquiring company having no understanding of the market structure, make up, problems of the company taken over, that one wonders whether the only considerations taken into account by companies in the take-over field are financial ones. Noah may have made a success of floating a company when everyone else went into liquidation, but he was exceptional. Even the great Imperial Tobacco has had to shed its poultry meat and eggs businesses after disastrous results and their American hotel and restaurant chain does not exactly hang happily around the giant's neck. Fortunately, diversification decisions are seldom the lot of Product Managers or NPD Managers. Someone at a higher level, probably a board director and eventually the full board, is the decision maker on a corporate basis.

Number of Ideas

How many marketable ideas can one company successfully handle in the course of one year? And how many marketable ideas emerge from the totality of ideas progressed by the Product Manager or NPD Manager? There is no one single answer of course.

Strike rate

According to one source, Booz, Allen & Hamilton from the United States, a strike rate of only 2% can reasonably be expected in consumer markets.

New ideas	58
After screening	12
After business analysis	7
After technical development	4
Tested	3
Successful	1

From these figures, it is evident that even two thirds of product ideas which get as far as test market, eventually fail. Whatever the success rate, there is no doubt that a very great deal of time, money, effort, trust, and prestige is wasted through a poor development programme, sometimes with very adverse and long lasting effects.

Saleability

The ability to handle products that have been developed to the stage of test marketing, depends primarily on the capability of the sales force and the amount of selling time that is taken up with existing products, sales promotions and all the other extra-curricular duties loaded on to them. It is also related, in part, to the dynamism or sluggishness of that particular market. Some markets, such as video, probably expect constant innovation, and salesmen require something new to talk about fairly frequently. In others, such as washing powders, a really new product is a rarity.

To generalise, always a dangerous occupation, perhaps six new product ideas to sell into a test market is the maximum that one sales force can handle in one year. If the figures above are anything to go by, and in the UK the number of patents converted to marketable propositions tend to bear them out, then only two of the six will be successful; and for one sales force to have to sell nationally two new products in the course of the year is probably as much as they can handle, with all their other work.

This means that one only needs about 100 ideas to achieve the two 'winners'. In consumer markets they will not be too hard to come by. In large equipment industrial markets and in service markets such figures will almost certainly be out of the question. But then it would probably be unrealistic to think in terms of launching six new ideas into test markets too. So perhaps everything should be scaled down commensurately. In the agricultural machinery market, for instance, where innovation is not infrequent, perhaps one or two new ideas a year put into the market place from one company should be the goal. And a goal there should be, for if none is set little will happen, and there is considerable danger of being up-staged by competition.

Criteria

To bring some discipline into the search for marketable ideas, definite criteria need to be laid down, based on the company's policies, existing skills, and finance available, so that broad guidelines are established within which the search for new products can be concentrated. This avoids costly and time consuming involvement in areas which are not likely to be of benefit to the company. Criteria such as the following might be laid down:

   (i) Company policy is based on remaining in its existing markets; or allied markets; or it is completely open to any market opportunity.

  (ii) It wishes to make use of existing sales and distribution organisations; or it wishes to expand these; or diversify them.

 (iii) Existing production capabilities and knowledge must be utilised; or the company is prepared to consider acquisition; or expansion; or origination of other production facilities; or joint operations.

 (iv) The company is in an industrial market and wishes to remain so; or it is prepared to go into consumer or service markets; or other market sectors.

  (v) It is not interested in any development which is not capable of a turnover of £1 million within three years; or the minimum volume of sale must be 70 tons per week.

(vi) The company intends to develop its own products; or is prepared to factor other companies' products; or to buy other products, inventions, names.

(vii) It intends to find products which require only a limited promotional budget and which can be introduced into the particular trade slowly and carefully; or it is prepared to spend £1 million a year to gain quick market advantage.

(viii) Any new product must retain the existing company image of prestige products at premium prices; or highly competitive products suitable for mass markets; or cheap products sold on price.

(ix) The company does not wish to enter a crowded market where all brands have small shares; or it does not wish to enter an oligopolistic market where two or three companies have the market sewn up; or where private label is strong; or where buyers are restricted to a few nationalised industries.

(x) It wishes any new product to be capable of commanding a high profit margin; or it is prepared to accept small margins with high volumes.

Successful Ideas

These criteria should have some bearing on the considered success factors for new products within an industry. Product Managers should be able to articulate these after experience in the market place. There is some evidence now that at least part of the reasons for the success of new products can be attributed to:

The company

(i) Top management commitment and involvement in the future of the company, rather than undue attention to day to day management.

(ii) A track record of skill and experience in both developing products suitable for the market place and in test marketing, in being able to read the signs.
'Success was rarely associated with doing one thing brilliantly but with performing well over a whole range of operations' concludes Rothwell of Sussex University concerning engineering machinery.

(iii) Total control over the development; not having to rely on others, such as overseas laboratory or manufacturing plant.

(iv) Financial capability and the will to do the job properly.

The Product

(v) A distinct and recognisable difference from competing products. A 'me too' product gives a potential customer no reason for changing supplier. A 1982 survey by KAE Surveys taken among grocery multiples showed that one of the main reasons for refusing a new product by as many as 74% of buyers was 'No product advantage'.

(vi) Factual evidence that it will satisfy a customer need or desire. Conversely, 'Lack of attention to market needs is the common denominator in new product failure' is the conclusion from wide ranging surveys into agricultural machinery by Sussex University, reported in 1981.

(vii) Sufficient volume of business in the long term to be of continuing interest to both company and customer.

The market

(viii) A dynamic, expanding market with sufficient activity to be constantly in the forefront of customers' minds.

(ix) The presence of weak brands and products from companies who are slow to react. Easier to obtain a toe-hold by the ability to take business from weak brands first before attacking the big boys.

(x) A stable market. One of interest for a considerable part of the year and which is not likely to be a seven day wonder.

Screening

The sifting process by which new product ideas are actively progressed, put to one side, or swiftly rejected, requires a formalised screen or sieve which although allowing some flexibility, imposes a discipline on choice in order to avoid personal, subjective likes and dislikes. There is some evidence that a major reason for failure can be that the Product Manager responsible for development becomes so enamoured with and beholden to his idea that nothing will move him off it.

This screen must be based on the criteria which have been set in the first place and, since it is highly probable that a number of new product possibilities appear at first sight to be of equal merit, it is often advisable to formulate a system of scoring points for each element in the screen. For example, if one criterion is that a new product must be capable of gaining wide distribution quickly and a second is that it must be capable of a turnover of £1 million within three years, then the turnover potential might be considered as of greater importance and weighted more heavily than the distribution criterion.

It is impossible to carry out research into the potential market for every idea and is totally unaffordable. For initial simple screens, therefore, scoring must be done on personal judgement and kept simple. Those ideas that clear the initial screen may be put through a more complicated one later, for which some research, probably only of a desk nature, will need to be carried out. At least, if the idea is a variant of an existing product then some data will be available. If however, it is completely innovative, some customer research may be necessary.

At the conclusion of the screening process, one has a league table of ideas with an order of merit and, almost certainly, comparatively few ideas which stand out from the mass. These become the priority and will require researching in greater depth to establish the nature of the market opportunity.

The following three possible screens have varying degrees of simplicity or complexity.

Screen 'A' is very simple. One either scores points out of 100 against each criterion or, even more simply, ticks each idea as 'Above average', 'Average', or 'Below Average'. At the conclusion of scoring twenty or so ideas, there will be very few indeed with ticks 'Above Average' for every

Criterion	Score	Above Average	Average	Below Average
MARKET Degree of need Volume Growth potential Stability Competitiveness				
MARKETING Range fit Sales and distribution Total promotion Pricing Profitability				
PRODUCTION Ability Facilities Raw material supply Packaging				

Figure 10.4 Screen 'A', a simple screening system.

SCREEN 'B'

		Very Good	Good	Fair	Poor	Bad
New Product	Unique characteristics Difficulty of imitation Expected life (for marketing) Absence of seasonal effect Few variations in design, types, sizes Complementary to present products Compliance with legal requirements Price advance over competitiors' products Technical advance over competitors' products Expected profitability					
Marketing	Size of market Growth prospects of market Stability of market Excess of demand over supply Company familiar with market Strength of competition Impact on present products Impact on relation with customers Suitability of present selling facilities Suitability of present distribution facilities Time between launch and saturation Speed of launch and developing sales Export potential Comparative promotion cost					
Technical	Suitability of existing know-how Utilisation of spare tech capacity Availability of new tech staff Relationship to projected R & D work					
Production	Suitability of buildings and services Suitability of present equipment Suitability of staff know-how Availability of suitable staff Availability of suitable materials Absence of labour relation problems Value added by manufacturing Fuller utilisation of spare capacity Maintenance of balanced work load Ability to meet delivery requirements Ability to hold requisite stocks Minimum re-layout, re-equipment required Suitable packaging/despatch facilities					
Financial	Availability of finance Effect on overall Company profitability Effect on overall Company volume Effect on break-even point Effect on overall working capital Rate of return on investment Fits present terms of trading					
Summary	Compatibility with New Product Policy Overall business prospects of product Low risk of failure					

Figure 10.5 Screen 'B'

criterion. These are obviously the one or two to progress. Almost as important, one can give reasonably objective reasons to the various originators of the ideas as to why it is not intended to proceed with their idea. This should placate them so that they will continue to send new ideas. For this screen, no research is attempted. The Product Manager or NPD Manager will simply use his own judgement.

Screen 'B' has many more criteria and a five point semantic scale instead of the three point scale in Screen 'A'. Again, little or no preliminary research will have been carried out before applying this screen.

Screen 'C' is more complex since it combines a weighting factor with the scoring and expands the criteria even further. Peter Krausher, the originator, has spent a great deal of his commercial life involved with product development and can be considered an expert. All the scores are collated in the matrix at the end of the screen. Only three ideas in the example given, A, E and H, score at all respectably but, compared with the maximum possible score of 138, none is worth pursuing.

SCREEN 'C'

A COMPREHENSIVE SCREENING SYSTEM

(From Peter M KRAUSHAR's *New Products and Diversification*

Once the need is seen to find markets suitable to the company's current profile or to its future characteristics if important changes are planned, it follows that the company's strengths and weaknesses must be examined particularly closely in this context. Such an analysis combined with the development policy criteria should result in the definition of what factors are important in the search for new markets and in the relative importance of each individual factor.

Screening systems have been found useful for this purpose. They incorporate all the relevant factors and it is possible to weight the factors' according to their importance

An example of a screening system which has been used very successfully for some years is shown below :

1.   *Growth*   *Weighting Factor*

    (a)   Sterling Sales Trend   3

        Declining market   −2
        Static market   −1
        Growth in line with population   0
        Growth faster than population   +1
        Growth much faster than
            population growth   +2

    (b)   Volume Trend   4

        Declining unit sales   −2
        Static unit sales   −1
        Growth in line with population   0
        Growth faster than
            population growth   +1
        Growth much faster than
            population growth   +2

    (c)   Long-Term Prospects   6

        Almost certain decline   −2
        Probable decline   −1
        Likely static market   0
        Probable growth   +1
        Almost certain growth   +2

2.   *The Market*

    (a)   Current Market Size (R.S.P.)   3

        Under £2m.   −2
        £2m. − 10m.   −1
        £11m. − 20m.   0
        £20m. − 40m.   +1
        £40m. +   +2

    (b)   1

        Strong C2DE bias   −2
        Some C2DE bias   −1
        Strong ABC1 bias   0
        General appeal   +1
        General appeal with some
            ABC1 bias   +2

Weighting Factor

(c) Age Group Characteristics   2

Concentration among old persons   −2
Strong bias among older age
    groups   −1
Little difference by age   0
Some bias among young age groups   +1
Strong bias among young age
    groups   +2

(d) Area Profile   1

Concentration in one or two
    areas   −2
Strong regional differences   −1
National appeal with Northern
    bias   0
Uniform appeal nationally   +1
National appeal with Southern
    bias   +2

3. *Stability*

(a) Economic Factors   5

Very sensitive to economic
    conditions   −2
Fairly sensitive   −1
Some sensitivity   0
Should be reasonably stable   +1
Strong continuous demand   +2

(b) Seasonality   3

Sales concentrated in one
    month of the year   −2
Strong seasonality in one
    part of the year   −1
Two peaks during the year   0
Some seasonality   +1
No seasonality   +2

4. *Marketing Skills*

(a) Penetration of Branding   3

Dominated by two or three
    major brands   −2
One dominating brand with
    own brand element   −1
Fragmentation among many brands   0

Two or three brands with strong own brand element	+1	
Commodity market moving towards branding	+2	

(b) Companies in the Market   5

Three or more major marketing companies in Market	−2
Market divided among two major marketing companies	−1
One major company in market	0
Market divided among two or three unsophisticated companies	+1
Market fragmented among a number of unsophisticated companies	+2

(c) Marketing/Sales Ratio   3

Very high expenditure	−2
High expenditure	−1
Average for consumer goods	0
Low expenditure	+1
Very low expenditure	+2

(d) Product Differentiation   5

Little prospect of product advantage	−2
Uncertain prospect of product advantage	−1
Some prospects for slight advantages	0
Some prospects for important products advantages	+1
Good prospects for important product advantages	+2

5. *Image*

(a) Company Image   2

Weakens company image	−2
Inconsistent with image	−1
Makes no difference to image	0
Strengthens image	+1
Strengthens image very considerably	+2

Weighting Factor

(b)   Brand Images   4

    Cannot use company brand names   −2
    Unlikely to use brand names   −1
    Can possibly use brand names   0
    Company brand names would be sensible   +1
    Brand names would be positive
      helpful   +2

6.   *Production*

(a)   Technology   5

    Very different technology unfamiliar
      to company required   −2
    Fairly different technology
      unfamiliar to company   −1
    Different technology but familiar to
      company   0
    Similar technology   +1
    Similar technology some capacity
      available   +2

(b)   Buying Resources   3

    Severe buying disadvantage compared
      with competition   −2
    Some disadvantages   −1
    No difference from competition   0
    Competitive advantages   +1
    Strong buying advantages   +2

7.   *Selling and Distribution*

(a)   Sales Force   6

    Present sales force completely
      unsuitable   −2
    Sales force compares badly with
      competition   −1
    Equal to competition   0
    Some competitive advantages   +1
    Sales force capacity and strong
      competitive advantage   +2

(b)   Distribution   5

    Completely different outlets from
      those covered now   −2
    Large extension needed to current
      distribution   −1

Some extension needed	0	
Small extension needed	+1	
Present distribution completely suitable	+2	

Such a system, however crude, helps to ensure that all possible factors are taken into consideration and that every market is considered on a comparative basis. Each company should establish its own system and the scores and weighting factors will depend greatly on its characteristics.

If the above screen is applied to say eight markets, the following pattern could result.

Maximum   Market Idea

Factor	Score	A	B	C	D	E	F	G	H
Sterling sales trend	6	6	0	−6	3	3	0	−3	0
Volume trend	8	4	−4	−8	0	4	0	−4	−4
Long-term prospects	12	0	0	−6	0	12	0	−6	0
Current market size	6	0	6	3	0	0	6	3	−3
Buying by class	2	1	1	1	−1	2	1	1	0
Age group characteristics	4	0	0	0	2	2	0	−2	0
Area profile	2	1	1	1	0	2	−1	0	1
Economic factors	10	5	5	0	−5	10	−5	5	0
Seasonality	6	−3	0	0	3	3	6	0	3
Penetration of branding	6	6	0	3	−6	3	0	3	0
Companies in the market	10	10	5	5	−10	5	5	5	5
Marketing/sales ration	6	3	0	0	−6	3	0	0	3
Product differentiation	10	5	0	5	0	5	0	−5	0
Company image	4	0	2	0	2	−2	2	0	4
Brand images	8	0	0	4	4	0	0	0	8
Technology	10	5	0	−5	−5	−5	0	0	5
Buying resources	6	0	3	0	−3	0	0	3	3
Sales force	12	6	0	6	−6	6	0	0	0
Distribution	10	5	0	5	0	−5	0	0	10
TOTAL	138	54	19	8	−28	48	14	0	35

Naming

For a comparatively small variation to an existing product this represents no problem but for a substantially different product, or for a completely new one, the question of naming can be very important. Does it really matter over much what it is called? After all, if H.J. Heinz II will forgive the use of his name, who, in their right minds would have thought of using the name 'Heinz' for anything, at least in this country? Or 'Mars', which might be fine for today's intergallactic mania, but one could hardly have foreseen that forty years ago at its birth. Or 'Otis' for elevators; although a sign hung beside an out-of-action lift in a music publisher's which read 'Miss Otis regrets' reflects a useful relationship with a one-time popular tune. Or 'Europe' for the land mass to the west of the River Don named by the Greeks after their goddess of that name.

Many marketing people will say that the name is all-important. That it is important there can be no gainsaying. A name that trips off the tongue, that seems 'right' for the product, that stands out from its competitors, that does not mean nasty things in a foreign language – as Rolls Royce discovered when they wanted to call a model 'Silver Mist', not realising the 'mist' in German means manure – that can be given some degree of protection legally in most countries, is undoubtedly a substantial marketing asset. A particularly appropriate name was coined by a group of protestors about high rates in the Borough of Kensington, they called themselves the 'I-Rates'.

Product Managers should never forget that any name requires effort and expenditure to establish; must be worked at continuously so that it becomes associated with a particular set of values in peoples' minds, so that it will eventually conjure up an immediate image. It is the *image* which is all important. For certain products, there is the possibility of associating the new product with an existing, well known name. Should this be done? As usual, there are pros and cons.

(i) The cost of creating awareness of the new product will be much less by using a known name than the cost of originating a new name.

(ii) But to use an existing brand or company name will hug to the new product all the problems as well as the good points of that name.

(iii) Further, to ride on the back of an existing name could adversely affect that name, if the relationship between them is not close.

(iv) If the new product is never likely to be able to command a sufficient marketing budget in its own right, then one has no alternative to adopting the known name, or not putting the new product on the market at all.

(v) One of the dangers of launching a companion product is that it might cannibalise the existing product rather than add an extra selling unit. This danger is increased if the same name is used. A separate name can sometimes act as a spur to competition, to the benefit of both.

Research and Testing

The importance cannot be overstressed of continually probing and checking as an idea becomes a reality and is developed and refined, in as objective a

Price versus sportiness

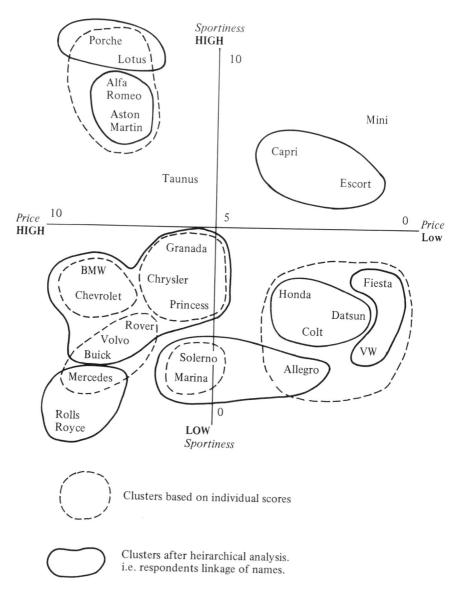

Figure 10.6 UK car market – cluster analysis. Attitude to brand names (not based on fact)

way as possible. So many mistakes are made through believing that one's
own reactions are similar to those of one's target audience. All the
techniques of research should be employed within the confines of realistic

budgets. So frequently, development work in the consumer world is carried out by males when the consumer is very likely to be female. It should never be forgotten that there are three types of male who do not understand women – the young, the old and the middle aged. Further, be warned against using one's own colleagues and employees of the company for research purposes. If the company has its own home economists, or specialists in the laboratory sense, well and good. But ordinary folk within the same organisation are not unbiassed. They all have some preconceived notions which might impinge on a rational judgement, even if they are only the result of internal politics.

A cardinal rule is to test comprehensively. Whilst separate tests and checks should be carried out for such elements as attitude to the new idea, methods of use, side usages, eye appeal, packaging, name, price, storage and a host of others, each will affect the other. For example, price cannot be divorced from name, eye appeal, packaging and selling position; so that, as one progresses with the development, one should constantly bring in other marketing factors. At the end, the only true method of research is to endeavour to sell the product in its normal market environment and closely monitor results: to test market, in other words.

This chapter, and indeed this book, is not the place to enumerate all the many ways of gathering information from the market place for consumer goods, industrial goods or services. Each Product Manager should know those that are relevant to his or her own market. The next chapter deals, in some measure, with test marketing.

Network Analysis

Purpose

Network planning, sometimes called 'Critical Path Analysis', is a management tool which is designed to ensure that every project, requiring complex action from many different individuals and departments, can be executed according to plan. It can be applied to product development programmes involving the manifold detail of check and counter-check, right up to test launch, to the taking of an exhibition stand. Networking can be a valuable tool for Product Managers in:
   – Clearly showing responsibilities;
   – Ensuring proper thought is given to the effect of one department on another; what cannot happen before something else occurs;
   – Highlighting where bottlenecks and problems might occur;
   – Giving parameters of time for certain activities and showing where time restraint will affect the end result;

- Enabling proper control of the overall operation;
- Giving flexibility where rigidity might have been self-defeating;
- Ensuring the reasonable attainment of the objective without mis-understandings and disruptive panics.

In short, 'it is a management tool of great impact which makes possible the more effective discharge of a project'. (L.J. Rawle, Unilever) Beginning with the development of Polaris, where the US Navy created a technique called 'Programme Evaluation and Review Technique', PERT for short, and parallel work by Dupont on 'Critical Path Method' we now have a highly useful method of gathering together the threads of a complex marketing operation to ensure successful implementation.

Method

   (i) List each department or outside agency that will be affected;
  (ii) Discuss with each Department Head the contribution to the project required from him;
 (iii) List every facet under the relevant department;
  (iv) Notate every item which cannot be done without an input from another department; e.g. production tools cannot be ordered until the pack has been designed;
   (v) With Heads of Departments' assistance, put each item in order of action;
  (vi) Then, again by discussion, put a time period against each, which shows how long it will reasonably take, providing everyone else performs their part on time;
 (vii) Create the network as explained below;
(viii) Give each department that part of the network that applies only to them, but with the inputs required from other departments;
  (ix) Monitor progress constantly; an out of date network is a menace;
   (x) Meet regularly to consider progress and amend the network as necessary. Note that if an amendment is required to an action which is on the 'critical path', the end date will have to be amended.

Creation of network

This is a simple operation but it requires great attention to detail. An examination of the 'Launch Network' for a mythical launch of a range of domestic scissors, will be found helpful. For the purposes of space, very few 'activities' are listed. In practice there would certainly be more. However, the Product Manager does not have to go into great detail for individual departments. As long as the important steps are included, unnecessary detail will only confuse.

Figure 10.7

LAUNCH NETWORK EXERCISE

PRODUCTION

Task	Weeks
Product specification	
Detail plant requirements	2
Schedule production	
Set up quality control	
Check warehousing capability	2
Install new production and packaging plant	
Test	
Train staff	
Produce test batch	
Provide costs	3
Produce sell-in quantities	
Despatch to depots	2

BUYING

Task	Weeks
Order plant requirements	13
Get raw material quotes	4
Order raw material Check deliveries	6
Get packaging material quotes	
Obtain dummies for product packaging	4
Order outers and product packaging	6
Order display and promotional material and special forms (order: computer)	4

DESIGN

Task	Weeks
Produce packaging specification	
Design pack sizes and shapes, inners and outers	4
Create surface design	
Check dummies	2
Carry out: Travel test Shelf test	
In home placement test	6
GO/NO-GO	

AGENCY

Task	Weeks
Create advertising strategy & agree	2
Create theme	2
Prepare roughs of advertisements and storyboards for TV commercials	4
Concept test and get IBA cc clearance	
Obtain finished artwork Shoot TV films	8
Get NPA cc and IBA cc clearance	2
Send to media	
Plan media budget and agree	4
Book space and time	2
	4
Plan sales promotion	
Create material Budget and agree	6

FINANCE

Task	Weeks
Financial forecast	
Pay-out plan	2
Cashflow chart cost	
Budget	2
Computer codes and analyses Order forms	4
Get legal clearance for brand name and sales promotion	14
Re cost	2
Provide funds	4
GO/NO-GO	

SALES

Task	Weeks
Prepare sales plan	
Key A/C sales conference	4
Pre-sell multiples and get listings	4
Sales conference and sell in	6

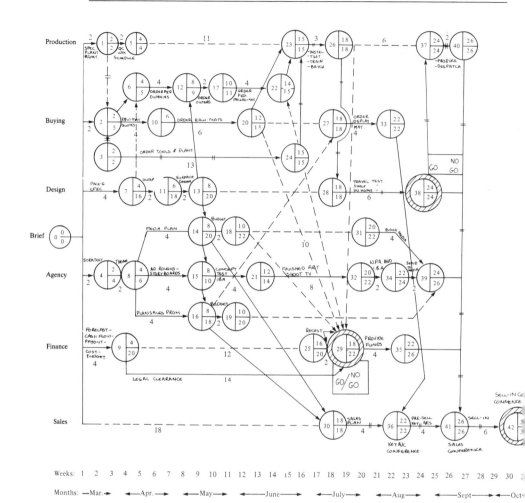

Figure 10.8

There are excellent books and articles on Networking and much academic discussion has taken place on its merits, demerits, and practices. What follows is a very much truncated explanation but sufficient for the operation to be grasped by Product Managers who may not be familiar with it.

There are ACTIVITIES designated by a solid line with arrow, showing the activities of each department.

6 →

There are DUMMY ACTIVITIES designated by a hatched line showing where one activity cannot occur until someone else has undertaken their bit.

Each 'Activity' or 'Dummy Activity' starts and finishes with an EVENT designated by a circle, to show the end of an activity.

Within each 'Event' circle (or roundel) there is a number which is simply a reference number starting from the beginning, usually working from top to bottom, left to right. There is another figure showing the earliest time by which that event can occur, the 'EARLIEST EVENT TIME' and, below it, another which shows the latest time by which the event can happen, the 'LATEST EVENT TIME'.

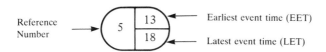

Finally there is also a figure under each 'activity' to show how long that activity will take. Everything is laid out against a time scale. That is all!

Finding EET and LET

To find the Earliest Event Time (EET) one adds each activity

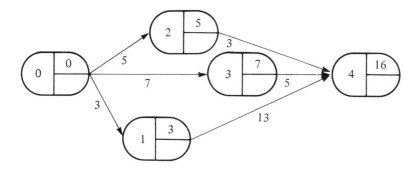

time to the previous one. However, where several activities join together, as for a sales conference for example, that event, the sales conference, can only happen after the longest activity time.

One carries on, adding activities together, until the end. Having arrived at the end, the number of weeks that all activities will take to reach the desired objective is now known.

Now we turn round and come backwards, doing exactly the same thing, except now subtracting each activity time, rather than adding them. These show the Latest Event Time (LET) at each event.

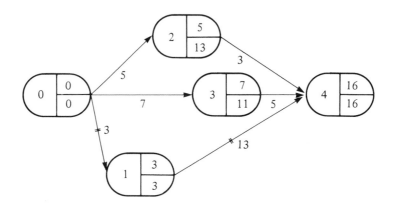

For most events, there will be a difference between EET and LET which is called the EVENT SLACK. But for some, perhaps between 10–15% of them, there will be no Event Slack. One can do the same thing for activities. Where there is a difference in the times, there is an ACTIVITY FLOAT. And for events which have no Event Slack, and activities which have no Activity Float, they are critical. The pathways along which these lie is the CRITICAL PATH. Such pathways, for there may be more than one, are usually marked with crossed lines.

Any event that lies along that path that can no longer take place for whatever reason, *will* put back the end date of the project. It will not happen on the due date if there is any hitch along any critical path.

Use of computer

It can readily be seen how useful and important a network is for an operation involving several or many different departments with many different events. It *must* be kept up to date.

There are computer programmes for network analysis which can help to take some of the chore out of the origination and maintenance of the project. Indeed, for engineering and high technology projects, where networks are frequently used, computers are almost a necessity. It is thought that it is feasible for manual control of up to 600 activities to be acceptable, although after some 200 it is perhaps wiser, and certainly easier, to involve the computer. But 200 activities is quite a large number. There is little need, for marketing use, to have so many. In consequence, the manual preparation and control of a marketing project by network analysis is not only perfectly feasible, but probably preferable. By checking each event personally one can bring into play all one's experience and knowledge of the people involved, as well as the activity.

Cancellation or delay

For many operations originated and controlled by Product Managers, finite data cannot be available until that operation has been physically attempted. The real cost of producing a batch of product in a factory for example. So that there should usually be built into the network of a marketing project a 'GO/NO-GO' position, perhaps more than one. These should be strategically placed so that a round table discussion followed by an individual decision to proceed or do further work before going any further, can be made. This must mean that the project will not be completed by the original timetable, so everyone is aware of the problem, the reason, and the solution. The network can be reorganised after the problem has been cleared.

11 Testing And Test Marketing

To test or not to test – Purpose – Limitations – What to Test – Methods – Concept testing – In Home, In Hall tests – Store tests – Area and Regional tests – Timing – Seasonality – Purchase cycles – Evaluation – Modelling

To Test or Not To Test

Adventurous marketing calls for admirable qualities of entrepreneurial flair, sound judgement, and willingness to take a risk. The degree of risk will decide whether it is sensible to mitigate as much as possible against financial loss, by testing various elements of product and marketing mix before finally committing the company to an irreversible course of action. And since it is possible that two thirds of products which are put into test market fail to create worthwhile sustainable business, the watchword should be to test rather than not to test.

Occasionally, however, it might be sensible to take the risk of nationally marketing the product at one fell swoop. If the ease of replicating the product by competition means that one's lead time is extremely short for instance; or if the product has already been tested by competition and differences are slight; or if clinical trials of an ethical pharmaceutical, for example, after five years are approved by the appropriate authority; and for very high capital cost products where sales in an area in a comparatively short time span would be too few, both to warrant a test and to recoup sufficient finance to start paying the bills.

Purpose

A test market is a controlled experiment. It represents the first time that *all* facets of the marketing mix have been brought together in a near normal market situation. The accent must be on *control*, which means *measurement*. Failure to ensure either leads to an abortive test.

There are many reasons for testing. Among them may be:
- To evaluate the performance of the product, its concept and the marketing mix;
- To be able to assess the national picture that might pertain;
- To assess the speed of gaining distribution and trial;
- To see how competition reacts;
- To provide persuasive evidence to the trade and others on a wider basis;
- To act as a pilot for a future range of innovative products;
- To suggest the next step in a development programme;
- To train production, sales force, distributors, in a new market opportunity;
- To provide reasonable proof of financial viability so as to attract investment;
- To reduce risk.

As with all facets of marketing, the prime objective should be clearly defined right from the beginning. Control and measuring methods will largely depend on the nature of the objective.

Limitations

(i) Any test market chosen cannot be the same as the eventual market, whether that be a geographical region, national or international, if for no other reason than that of time. In fact within the UK no single region can perfectly replicate the national scene, whether one considers a town, a television area, Registrar General's area, retail audit area, or any other.

It follows, therefore, that differences must be anticipated and allowed for in any marketing model used for measurement. Obviously one wants to obtain some idea of potential national sales from a test market. Many considerations may hang on the answer, from the availability of cash to the problem of buying expensive machinery. Allowances can only be made by examination and comparison of as much finite data as possible, such data as demographic profiles, number and type of distribution outlets, competitive products available, seasonality, psychological attitudes, and so on. Above all, a good track record of successful test marketing, and the knowledge gained from this, will be the best arbiter of market differences and what allowances should be made as a result.

(ii) With a small area, it may be difficult to obtain a large enough research base for research results to be meaningful.

(iii) This equally applies to distribution. Insufficient distribution of a reasonably specialist product may result in insufficient opportunity for trial. But perhaps more of a problem with regard to distribution, lies in the concentration of buying power in many industries. Where retailers are concerned, for example, there may be reluctance on the part of the multiple head office to restrict distribution of the test product to the test area branches only. Indeed, they may be physically unable to do so because of central warehousing and despatch problems related to their own regions.

(iv) The presence in a test area of a new product immediately tells competitors almost everything they may want to know. If they are wise and they watch the test closely, they can obtain invaluable information which may enable them to pre-empt one by going national first. Most applicable to a highly competitive market where lead times are short, of course.

(v) The test can divert sales force time from the money spinners of the company, out of proportion to the new product's ultimate value to the company.

(vi) Small quantities of product may have to be produced or imported from parent companies or other plants, which in themselves, cannot be profitable.

(vii) There is always a tendency to 'hothouse' a test area. Everyone, from Managing Director down, may wish to 'sample the air', partly no doubt from genuine interest, but all too often from a desire to show keenness and advance knowledge. Until the test area has been left alone to the normal salesman on the ground, one cannot place a great deal of reliance on measurement.

(viii) In the UK, with all the many media choices available, it is extremely difficult to match media to geographical areas. National press editions, where regional, cover large areas. Television stations all have some overlap areas. Magazines are often national or, even where regional editions are available, may not take advertising in only one area, although many do.

(ix) There is a danger of a new product carrying an existing name, adversely affecting that known name, either through cannabalisation or by being thought of as not so good.

(x) There is also a danger to company image and sales force morale, if there are too many failures from the same stable.

(xi) An astute competitor has more of an opportunity of fouling the test with relatively small additional expenditures, for example with a price deal, than would be the case nationally.

(xii) Costs are high and, in a number of instances, impossible to cost with any degree of accuracy. Management time at varying levels may be heavily involved on occasion, for example.

(xiii) Finally, however carefully one measures and controls results, it does not always follow that a test market success will be a national success.

What to Test

There are an almost endless number of individual elements of a total marketing operation that can be tested and multiples and variables of them.

– Alternative marketing strategies;
– Pricing strategies, prices and margins;
– The product, its make up, positioning, concept, name;
– Packaging, eye appeal, protection, usefulness;
– Communication in all its facets;
– Sales promotions of all sorts;
– Selling and saleability;
– Distribution, extent, speed, staying power.

In a sense, it is more practical to test a number of things than simply one, although the ability to single out each element in relation to its market performance is vital. There are also many methods of carrying out a test so that each element can be checked. Therefore, a test programme is generally the order of the day, rather than simply one test market. And since it is usually sensible to test more than one mix, it follows that one should consider more than one test area. Indeed, three is probably a more sensible figure, two for test variants, and the other as a control area.

As a continuum of this thought, it can happen that one carries out a national distribution, using individual areas for testing variants of the marketing mix, and 'the rest of GB' as the control area. Obviously this can only be carried out when one is sure that the product itself is right. It happened at the relaunch of Bandaid by Johnson & Johnson some years ago. The product had been on the market in the UK for many years without conspicuous success. After much product research and some basic changes to elements such as adhesion, the product was considered the best of its type on the market and relaunched nationally. However, variations of two different advertising themes, two different weights of media expenditure

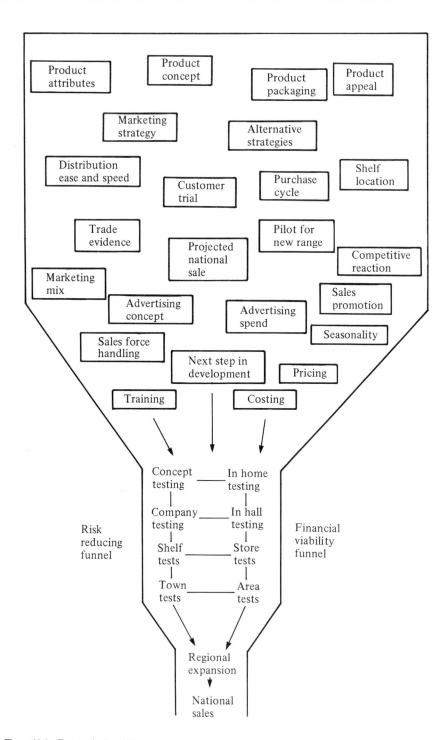

Figure 11.1 Test marketing. What to test – how to test

and two different types of advertising medium were tested in different areas and compared with 'the rest of GB'. Within these, different promotional activities were undertaken such as shelf appeal of the new packaging with merchandisers and special display drives and a competition.

Methods

Of the many methods and variations of method, perhaps six are more widely used than others.

Concept testing

How does the potential customer see the product and who are the potential customers who might be attracted to a particular concept? A chicken and egg situation to begin with for a new product type! As a first step it is probably sensible to set down possible concepts based on personal feelings, in terms of-

Structure – sight, size, feel, smell colour etc.;

Function – what it does and how it performs;

Worth – value for money, price, economy, profligacy;

Image – prestige, relevance, in keeping with type of person.

These concepts may then be tried out in Group Discussions but it must be remembered that such Groups can only throw up hypotheses for later validation. However, they can be most helpful in guiding one in waters that are relatively uncharted. Groups of between some eight or twelve people of particular demographic profile believed to be most relevant, led by a psychologist or trained researcher, set to discuss the product, can assist in arriving at relevant concepts related to most likely people. Since this cannot happen without some idea of the product to be discussed, this should be available. If not ready it is possible for a series of rough advertisements, based on the possible concepts, to be a substitute, although not such a good substitute.

From these Group findings it is now possible to carry out research, house to house for consumer goods and services, and to decision makers in companies and other organizations for industrial products and services. Again, product or rough advertisements, or perhaps description cards, are shown to respondents and then by means of a questionnaire, part of which will probably involve open ended questions, the respondents' views and their 'intention to buy' are recorded. The advent of cable television in the UK, will enable a good deal of initial reaction to advertising concepts, to be checked by telephone, as in the US.

Concept testing reflects attitudes in a very nebulous situation, since no-one can really visualise a product which currently does not exist on the market. And attitudes do not necessarily mean purchase at a later date. However, it goes a long way to helping the Product Manager decide on the next step, or a return to the drawing board.

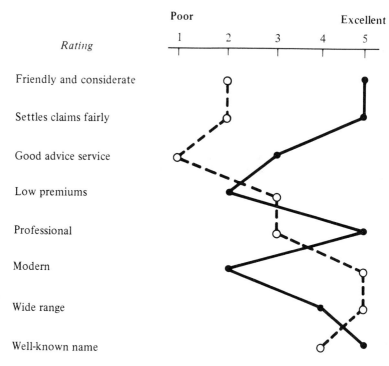

Figure 11.2 Comparison of two companies based on research questionnaire. Concept testing. Profile analysis – insurance

In home tests and in company tests

By placing the product in its usage position and watching usages and attitudes, a great deal of help in refining the product, its packaging, its positioning, what products or actions it replaces, can be obtained. The customer profile having been decided, at least for the test, a structured sample can be drawn, perhaps by telephone, and willing co-operation established.

Questions are asked of the respondent about his actions in the particular field under review, given the product for a reasonable time period to try and then questioned closely again as to his reactions, usage, attitude now, how this has changed things, and what future intentions might be.

After analysing all the data, it sometimes is the case that further questions need asking. Respondents can be contacted again to elucidate the extra point and the same sort of action can be taken if any refining of the product is necessary. This is a very useful method of learning action at the user end.

In hall/central location tests

Such locations, where a number of potential customers can be exposed to a greater array of explanatory and selling aids, brings the test one step nearer the end market place, although it is still an essentially false situation.

As for In Home tests, people of the right type are inveigled into a hall or some other venue that can cope with a relatively large number of people, perfectly willingly of course, and questioned as to their current experience, attitude, and habits to and with the sort of product category under test. They may then sample or use several products of similar type available in the hall and be questioned again as to their preferences, criticisms, and comments.

For some products in the consumer world, the respondents may be housewives, and after their initial questioning they may be given some token money and asked to go into the 'shop' next door and actually buy whichever brand or type of product they wish within a defined category. The token money is not quite enough to pay the full price asked, so that the repondent must pay a small amount and thus be faced with an actual purchase decision. The 'shop' is as near to the real thing as possible but not open to the general public.

For other products such as vacuum cleaners or home computers, where explanation and demonstration is required, this is available. A purchase is not, of course, solicited!

In store

In store tests are very closely relating to the 'real thing'. It requires product to be available in its packaging for sale at the anticipated price. From the consumer end everything is 'real' except for the influence of advertising. In terms of gaining distribution there is little relevant testing since the trader has agreed to allow his store to be used for the purpose and, most probably, the product is on sale or return so that he cannot lose. It follows that the trader must have had a reasonably positive attitude to the product or he would not have allowed his store to be used for a product that might harm his image. But this is of minimum import at this time.

The real value is the rate of sale of the test product against any competing products, or substitute products, involving customer reactions on elements of the marketing mix such as:
   – Shelf appeal;
   – Relationship with different products;
   – Ideal position in relation to traffic flow;
   – Number of facings most appropriate;

- Price;
- Container;
- Product variant, of size, shape, colour etc.;
- Repeat purchase pattern i.e.possible customer buying cycle;
- Brand switching data, who loses, who gains.

Choice of store type, size, location, customer profile and attitude of the manager or owner, are of prime importance. If possible, one needs half a dozen or so stores that are as representative of that trade as possible.

A variation of the store test which can be carried out for some consumer products, is a very similar operation on travelling vans. These go around a suburban or rural area with a 'shop' image and sell on the door step. Because they are on regular journey routes they can not only generate useful selling information but, because they are selling to the end consumer, can obtain questionnaire data regarding attitudes and usage habits as well.

Any store or van test enables different elements, such as price, or container, or pack design, to be tested with variations, by having one type of product in one or two stores, for example, and variations in others. Continual measurement of sales on a much more frequent basis than normal will be necessary to really 'fine tune' such a test.

Area tests

With all the limitations set out earlier in this chapter, area market tests are as near to the 'real thing' as one can possibly get and, as such, are invaluable both for checking, refining, and removing teething problems, and for proving the whole operation as a viable future project for the company. Or the reverse. As has been said before, perhaps two thirds of products which reach test market, go no further. And this can be of the utmost value in saving further company financial waste, no matter how disappointing it may be.

(i) Areas can be towns, Registrar General's areas, television areas, company sales areas, agricultural areas, university towns, and a host of other variants depending on the tests to be made and the number of options required. A test area for an electric cooker may have to be an electricity board region, since distribution must be obtained through electricity showrooms. For an agricultural service it might require the whole of East Anglia. For a new paving machine it might be sensible to use a local authority area. For a new drug with several uses, physicians wherever located may be used or simply one regional hospital management area.

(ii) Whichever areas are used they should be as representative of the total country as it is possible to find, accepting that it will never be a true sample of the whole. The ideal area will be as similar to the total market as possible in:

- Demographic profile;

- Distribution outlets;
- Media availability;

and be of such a nature that:

- It is isolated from 'imports and exports' from other areas (well nigh impossible but too much interference from 'outside' can nullify measurement);
- Can be measured in terms of sales, audits, research data;
- It is large enough for meaningful measurement but not so large that too many people will be upset if failure results;
- There are no 'skewing' factors such as a large ethnic minority, dependence of population on one major employer, a competitor's home base, general dislike of the product category, etc.;
- As nearly as possible, it has average sales for the product category or, if for a new category, the basis of forecasting is similar; e.g. a representative number of car owners, or medium size companies, or multiple branches etc.

(iii) The number of areas chosen will depend on the number of different elements to be tested but it is usually sensible if one wants to test, say, two different types of packaging, to use a small test such as a store test for that purpose, rather than an area. Area tests should generally be considered for testing a total strategy involving all the marketing mix as one composite whole. As such, it may be sensible to test two dissimilar strategies, providing that they are sufficiently different for any difference in sales to be attributed to that reason. For instance, it might have been sensible if the launch of soya bean as meat substitute had been accompanied by a parallel test for using the product as a useful addition for hungry mouths. With hindsight, the former did not appear to work whereas the latter has to some extent. Unfortunately a number of years has elapsed in the interim with the removal of many products from the market place.

For product categories already on the market, the test of a variation to a product, or the introduction of a competing product, one is not testing a totally new marketing strategy. In such cases a geographical area test is still testing the totality of the marketing mix but as a variation only. This is equally valid as a use of an area test but now one must ensure that a similarly profiled area is used as a 'control', where everything else is happening the same as for the test area, except for the new variation.

Regional tests

There are some occasions when it is necessary to launch immediately into a larger area, which, at the risk of seeming pedantic, may justly warrant the description of a geographical region rather than an area. The problem of manufacturing sufficient quantity of product to make machinery purchase or raw material costs sensible, may require sales volume which would not be forthcoming from a small area, for example; or the distribution problems created by multiples' demands; or the necessity of pre-empting competitive action; or simply the necessity of generating sufficient cash flow.

Timing

In essence, the duration in test must be both flexible and long enough to achieve the objectives. Flexible, because it is a test which, by its very nature, assumes that one cannot possibly know the outcome with certainty. The Product Manager responsible must be able to extend the allotted time in test if something is not clear cut and requires further time to evaluate and not have to adhere rigidly to a set time table. It is very seldom that a test time table can be shortened since, in practice, the tendency is to allow too short a time. Long enough to achieve objectives because, as has been stated earlier, the reasons for testing can be many and varied.

There are a number of constraints which will assist in setting the probable duration in the first place.

Seasonality

Since it is obvious that a test outside the main selling season of the year cannot be considered as very valuable, any product tested in a seasonal market must be ready to sell in at the correct time and the test should last as long as the season. Antifreeze, which tends to be sold as soon as the first frost of the winter has appeared, since everyone who needs it must have it by then, is dead to all intents and purposes six weeks later. The season for Jaffa grapefruit tends to be from November through to April, when Outspan takes over for the other half year. Consequently any test for Jaffa must be ready for that six months' period. Any element of the test not completed by April must wait until the next November.

Although the 'shoulders' of the holiday season have widened out considerably from the three main summer months, many services find great difficulty in obtaining decisions from all the necessary decision makers during those three months. And although the decision to buy a summer package tour has become rather later due to the current depression, still the package tour operators must catch the pre-Christmas market or their summer holiday test may be negated. So that the three factors of start date of the season, start date for attracting customers or of selling in, and duration of the season, will all influence the timing and duration of a test.

Distribution

Time must be allowed for distribution to build up before the test can become

really effective. This of course depends on such factors as:
- The deployment of existing sales persons;
- Whether outside sales persons are used to augment or be totally responsible for initial distribution;
- The extent to which head office merchandise committees, buyers, stock controllers, and so on, give listing, computer numbers, orders, instructions to warehouses and branches and physically deliver out to the branches;
- The time taken to achieve full distribution through primary distributors, such as wholesalers or builders merchants or timber yards and the like;
- The effectiveness of promotional activity in creating a demand;
- The offensive activities of major competitors.

Purchase cycle

For repeat purchase products, there will eventually be a reasonably regular rhythm to purchase. For many consumer products that cycle may be about six weeks. Until that cycle has had a chance to build up and settle down, one cannot be sure of the future. And this period tends to take much longer than Product Managers often think. As the graph below shows, it is seldom less than eight months and much more likely to be twelve months. According to one American report, their median duration for testing consumer products is some ten months. How often does a test last as long as that in the UK?

When a consumer product is launched, consumer trial is the first consideration. As people try the product, more and more as time goes on, one hopes, they will say one of three things:

'I like it, I will continue to buy when I am ready.'
'I do not like it, I will not buy it again.'
'It is not too bad, maybe I will buy again sometime.'

This continues until virtually everyone who is going to, has tried the product and come to one of the three conclusions. The sales curve starts to flatten out. The 'maybes' and 'will nots' fall out so that the sales curve turns down. Some of the 'maybes' come back into the market so that the product recovers somewhat until the curve settles down on a 'going' basis. This 'complicated' curve, virtually two S's back to back, is reasonably typical for this type of product. And what is important is that the peak may take some eight months to achieve for a six week purchase cycle product, and perhaps twelve months before it settles down to a going level.

Until the consumer has had several purchases one can never be sure that he or she will stay with the product. A vital requirement is a 'brand switching' survey from time to time, perhaps six weekly, to see how many people are staying with the product and by how much the growth curve is due to new people. Too many new people in relation to stayers and one soon runs out of new people. Of course, the ability of people who want to try or repeat, rests on their ability to find the product so that distribution and its maintenance are vital.

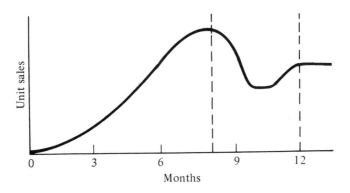

Figure 11.3

This type of a sales picture can also apply to semi-industrial products such as spare parts for agricultural machinery, animal feed stuffs, 'original equipment' for new car models and the like. However, it is of primary concern to consumer products with a reasonably high rate of turnover. And for these, it is little use expecting retailers to substitute for the manufacturer with their own tests. Certainly some, such as Boots do have their own testing programme, but in general they will not wait for a year before coming to a conclusion.

Message build up

All methods of communication, but in particular media advertising, have a build up effect and time must be allowed for this to occur in order to maximise sales effort. This threshold of advertising effectiveness will depend on weight of advertising, concentration of both media and message, competitive advertising, whether the product comes readily to mind or whether it is innovative, whether it is difficult to grasp or easy, whether it appeals to a very specialist minority or to the majority, and so on. As has been said in the chapter on communication, the second advertisement of a campaign may have maximum effect, but in general it is repetition within reason to the same people, the 'opportunities to see' that are crucial.

Market share stability

In theory, once a brand or product has settled down to a relatively stable market share, it follows that one can appraise success or otherwise. However, this depends very much on the stability of purchasers for repeat purchase products and on other elements such as product innovation, seasonality, and position on the product life cycle for maintenance of that brand share. Market share stability by itself cannot be accepted as definitive.

Evaluation

The measurement of factors related to the objectives desired, must be the criterion. In the end, the only factor that is really crucial is profitable sale. However the ability to take business from competition, or to substitute successfully for one's own declining product, or to expand distribution of a range through the addition of another item in it, or the ability to expand a whole market sector, and many other objectives, may be of prime importance.

The question of deciding what *is* success and what *is* failure must be tackled. If one sets a goal of gaining a 10% share of an existing growth market and all one achieves is 8%, to what extent is that failure? In just the same way as one should set parameters for product forecasts, one should set criteria for success or failure within parameters for test market results. Or if one achieves a 10% share as laid down for success at the beginning, but the net sales value is lower than expected, so that financially results are less than hoped for, can one still claim success?

Almost always, a number of criteria need laying down as the basis for success, before the test market commences. And these will then decide the measurement data required. They can range across a wide spectrum:
- Store audits;
- Consumer or customer audits;
- Usage and attitude studies;
- Brand switching exercises;
- Attitude shifts;
- Purchase cycles;
- Brand share studies;
- Distribution;
- Physical sales;
- Financial performance;
- Orders to calls;
- Cannibalisation;
- Effect on competition;
- Displays obtained;
- Effect on total market.

Measurement must be started before the test commences so that one has a datum against which to relate information during the test. If the product remains in the test area after the test has finished, then measurement should continue after the official test has been completed. And if one has a control area in which every other market factor is as near to the test as possible, except for the product or marketing factor under test, then measurement will similarly be required in that area. One then has seven possible relationships.

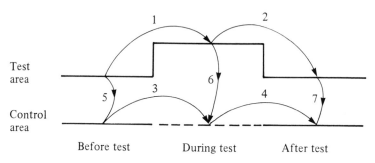

Figure 11.4

Modelling

A great deal of mystique appears to have grown up about model building. At its most simplistic, it is only a logical, disciplined way of putting 'A' before 'B' before 'C' so that one marketing factor leads to another, in a pattern which can be used to predicate the same sequence in a new set of circumstances. The fact that the computer can aid us in arriving at a forecast is a side issue. A sequence of events may be as follows:

If a new product is launched into an existing market which:
    Is growing at 5% p.a.;
    Contains three major brands which together have 60% share;
    Sterling distribution in grocers of the total market is 90%;
    Home penetration is 75%;
    Purchase cycle of 6 weeks;
And our product, in the first 3 months achieves:
    Sterling distribution of 30%;
    Home trial by 40% of target audience;
    Repeat purchase by 60% of first time purchasers;
    A brand share of 12%;
    With an A & P expenditure of 15% of total market expenditure;
We shall achieve in 12 months:

A brand share of 18%;
Of a total market which has expanded by 8%;
But if we only achieve 20% sterling distribution in the first three months, with everything else the same, we shall achieve a brand share of 14% in Year 1. Or, if we halve our A & P expenditure we shall only achieve a brand share of 8% in Year 1. Or any other variant.

This model will, of course, be based on past experience ; on many past experiences. It can gradually be built up based on a mixture of past data and mathematical probabilities and common sense, with preferably a liberal dose of the latter.

Increasingly, Product Managers have access to their own 'hands on' computers and marketing models, such as the above, are becoming easily available or can be created. Whilst to create a new model may cost a substantial sum of money, the savings that may be made by judicial use of the model before and during the launch can also be substantial. It is important that, since most markets are fluid from time to time, every opportunity is taken of up–dating the model so that reliance can continue to be placed on it. The model builder will need to work closely with the Product Manager in the initial formulation, since the Product Manager should be the one with the 'feel' of the inter–relationships between different marketing factors.

12 Communication

Understanding

'I know you believe you understand what you think I said, but I am not sure you realise that what you heard is not what I meant.' The art of communication does not come readily to most people. To communicate so that others understand the intent of the message is doubly difficult when talking to people from overseas, whether one is in the UK or overseas. Many people of the world take off their hats when entering a place of worship, some put hats on, others take off their shoes. Each regards his or her action as normal and the others as quaint. Cultures, languages, habits, environment, all require a deep understanding from the communicator if his message is to be properly understood.

Method

The communication method for delivery of the message may be one, or a series, or a host of available options. The company letterhead, the commissionaire's livery, an exhibition stand, direct mail letters, demon-strations, conferences, learned papers. Three are perhaps most widely used : salesmen and women, which is not the subject of this chapter ; media advertising, which involves most organizations to a greater or lesser extent ; and direct mail, which is especially pertinent in industrial and service markets. Stress in this chapter is laid on these last two with concentration on the Product Manager's role in initiating and controlling his communication campaign, rather than on the merits or demerits of particular media.

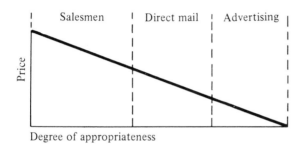

Figure 12.1

Choice of Method

Complexity

Often, the more expensive a product, the more complex it is to explain and the fewer customers it has, the more will personal selling be required. Conversely, the cheaper the product, the more simple it is, the more potential customers there are, the more can media advertising be cost affective.

Media advertising cannot communicate a complicated message, nor pinpoint with any degree of accuracy relatively few customers without considerable wastage. Direct mail can develop a theme and, with a good mailing list, pinpoint potential customers. It lies somewhere between personal selling and media advertising on these factors.

Market penetration

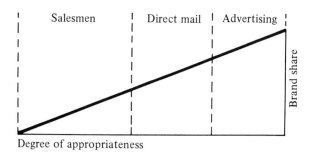

Figure 12.2

The more important the sales volume is, the deeper the penetration of the market and the higher the brand share requirement, the more will media advertising be required. Conversely, if only a small market share is necessary, a few salesmen may be able to obtain all the sales required. Again, direct mail may be able to achieve a strategy which lies somewhere in between.

Response and saturation

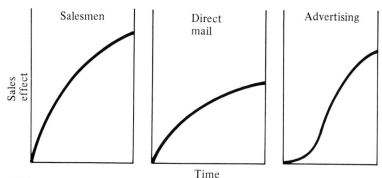

Figure 12.3

Employing sales persons, or extra sales persons, can have an immediate effect on sales, assuming that saturation point has not been reached. In fact, the saturation point for increasing sales through employment of extra sales persons is very high, probably higher than any normal organization can afford.

Advertising seldom creates immediate sales results unless perhaps, Harrods advertise the commencement of their sale or something similar.

More often, advertising has a build–up effect and the saturation point at which advertising ceases to 'pull' is high, often higher than the advertiser believes to be the case. However, there is some evidence that, at least for some products, it is the first advertisement that creates interest and demand with the remainder of the campaign having less impact.

Direct mail can have an immediate effect, although repetition will build up awareness and action. However, the saturation point is relatively low for the same product.

Summary

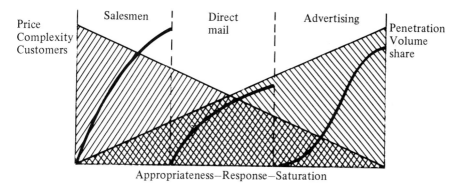

Figure 12.4

As examples, if one were selling a nuclear power station, which is a complicated, very expensive product with only one customer, which does not rely on sales volume or brand share, and which takes a very long time to mature, advertising or direct mail are not likely to be important communication vehicles. On the other hand, to sell pins or pencils requires only a simple message, there are very many customers, it is not an expensive or an important purchase, volume of sales is important and perhaps brand share, so that media advertising could be effective. To sell management systems or factory insurance requires pin pointing decision makers in fairly specialised capacities where direct mail could be very cost effective, although no doubt requiring a personal follow up.

Reaction to Advertising

To change or not to change

As in all things to do with marketing, we must start from the customer, not consider first what our advertising can do to our chosen audience, but what they may do with our advertising. Advertising is an extremely complex process. Different campaigns act and obtain reaction in very different ways.

Whilst we may like to think that customers and decision makers are all rational, interested, orderly individuals, this is very far from being the case. In practise, we are all submitted to a battery of messages every day, hundreds of them – on ball point pens, on 'T' shirts, on race tracks, shop windows, television, 'free' newspapers, and the rest. Some we may react to consciously if we are sufficiently interested in the product, others may add a further fleeting impression to our subconscious, and still others pass us by completely. The message may, consciously or subconsciously, help us to continue with a certain product or brand name. This is the easiest decision for us to take rather than to have to make a conscious decision to change. Or it might be sufficiently strong for our conscious mind to decide to make a change. Or it might simply be an addition to all the previous influences derived from all sorts of sources, friends, remembrance of a physical sighting, or perhaps an unrealised source, which represents the final input to cause us to change.

People often appear to act irrationally but, in their view, they are by no means being irrational. With few exceptions, they are not really agonising over a decision, as the advertiser often is. Frequently their interest is minimal. Inertia may be caused by the comfort of the familiar, even with a realisation of a superior product elsewhere. Habits can be strong.

Related decisions

Often a decision on one purchase cannot be made without creating a whole range of other decisions. The purchase of a fridge freezer where none was owned before, will create decisions concerning the best use of kitchen space and changes in types of food bought. The purchase of a computer will affect virtually every office system. Potential customers sometimes have little time and even less interest to appraise superior options, on the basis that what they have is perfectly acceptable and that the 'best' is constantly changing and that, anyway, they are 'different' from other companies or individuals.

Selective perception

Potential customers may read into an advertisement something that reflects their basic conception, rather than the meaning intended. The sophisticated controls of the latest washing machine will not make washing easier, but more complicated. The chemical additive to the water supply will pollute rather than purify. This theory of 'Selective Perception' implies an acceptance only of the acceptable.

An amateurish written sign for 'Fresh Farm Eggs' in a rural setting, is probably quite acceptable to most of us, but a similar sign in the same location saying 'Flying Training School' would probably conjure up the impression of a couple of 'stringbags' and you take your life in your hands! An advertiser goes against accepted conventions at his peril.

Cognitive dissonance

Where an expressed idea is violently at odds with an established perception then the dissonance created causes a complete rejection of the idea – 'Cognitive dissonance'. For example, after a very important or expensive purchase such as a car, the customer is desperate for reassurance that he has made a wise purchase. If he sees an advertisement for his model he may be reassured to the extent that any adverse criticism by, for instance, a motoring correspondent, will be rejected by him. But if the door has fallen off or the starter motor failed, he will have such a dissonance with the advertisement, that he will react against his car marque, accept the newspaper criticism, and become the worst advertisement for that car that the supplier could wish not to have.

Effect of attitude on buying behaviour

For many years researchers have debated to what extent this is so. Fairly obviously for some purchase decisions, the right attitude is all important. To buy travel insurance when one is going on holiday, one must feel that insuring against risk is a good thing. But that attitude may have been partially generated by the attitude of a friend who did not believe in insurance and lost all his luggage. Conversely, it does not always follow that a change of attitude will lead to a change in buying behaviour. And, for a product which represents a new concept, there may be no attitude at all. However, for most products and services, some sort of an attitude does already exist and such attitudes can affect the perception of advertising, as well as the eventual buying decision.

An existing *attitude* of mind can affect our *perception* of a product . as seen through the advertisement, which can create a *desire* for that product which eventually leads to a *purchase*. But these four factors do not necessarily work in that order and many other factors can provide an input at each stage.

Rational appraisal

We all have many decisions to make every day of our lives, some of no importance and others of major importance, from going to the doctor to going to lunch. Not all of these can or will be made with the same attention to detail, of gathering all the options, of rational appraisal. Those which significantly affect us personally, whether as a business person or as a domestic consumer, we will do our best to appraise sensibly – sensibly in our terms. The rest of our decisions may result from habit, or the easiest and quickest resolution, based on our broad opinion, resulting from a host of unrelated influences over time.

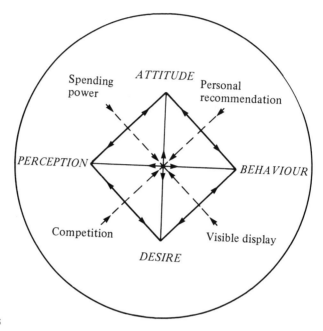

Figure 12.5

Concentration of Effort

With such a complex, often irrational and therefore largely unpredictable reaction to advertising, how can the Product Manager decide on the 'best' advertising for his product in his market circumstances? Surely there must be some guidelines. Those that follow are intended as a guide – no more. They must be seen in the light of the multitude of different reactions that advertising might generate.

Objectives

First of course, set objectives. What is the purpose of the advertising, what is it designed to do? These are many:
- Obtain new customers;
- Obtain trial;
- Get existing customers to buy more, or more frequently;
- Retain existing customers by increasing brand loyalty;
- Obtain enquiries;

- Open doors for salesmen;
- Educate and inform;
- Support traders;
- Change opinions or strengthen them;
- Ensure awareness by opinion formers and decision makers;

and so on.

Conscious awareness

Among the welter of advertisements to which we are all subjected each day, there are perhaps three main reasons why our chosen audience might *not* be interested.

(i) *The subject is not of any interest.*   An advertisement for a Mozart concert at the Town Hall will not be read by those not interested in classical music, as a general rule. In consequence, we must clearly define the type of person we wish to influence, as explained later under 'Advertising Strategy', and try to 'flag' them in our advertisement.

(ii) *There is insufficient weight*   to break through the barrier of conscious-ness; through the many messages all clamouring for our attention. Conse-quently, the media schedule must be concentrated.

(iii) *The message has no impact.*   Even though we may be in the market and can hear the message, there is nothing in it to arouse our interest or desire. Impact is both difficult to define and varies with recipient. It represents a combination of personally influencing factors. The advertising campaign must contain that all important 'idea', that single motivating factor that is likely to cause most of the designated recipients to react favourably. Consequently, the message should be concentrated, simple, and represent a customer benefit.

Message Presentation

Advertising cannot be placed in watertight compartments. However, in order to explain the principle ways in which the message may be presented to the prospect, it may be helpful initially to do so. But it must be stressed that agencies today tend to search for the all important 'idea' rather than rationalise any particular type of approach. There are several different, underlying, basic approaches, but perhaps three are most widely used. Historically, 'News in the product', as originally propounded by J. Walter Thompson, can be said to have initiated modern creative approaches. Over the years, because of the recognised importance of creating a product difference, this has tended to develop into a 'Unique selling proposition'.

Unique Selling Proposition (USP)

Customers remember only one thing from an advertisement. One may give a dozen reasons why the product should appeal but customers will remember one. This may be any single one, a distillation of them all, or a composite of several. If one USP is available, something that no–one else can say or is saying, then this should be single mindedly attacked to the exclusion of everything else, says the theory.

It goes without saying that the chosen feature should be of substantial interest to the chosen customer. For example, Stolyshnaya vodka is the only Russian vodka on the UK market, all the rest are made in 'Varrington' or elsewhere. Or the distinctive nature of a piece of Barbara Hepworth sculpture, exciting the comment, 'Ah! A womb with a view'.

It follows that if one is featuring a specific unique reason for purchase, one must say it in a forthright, imperative, almost dogmatic manner. 'Guinness is good for you', although that has not been said for many years. 'A glass and a half of full cream milk in every half pound bar' for Cadburys. It will be seen that the distinctive feature is not necessarily one that competitors could not also claim. It is simply that strong usage over time creates the uniqueness as perceived to belong to one product. If Mackesons stout advertised that product as 'Good for you' most people would immediately associate it with Guinness rather than Mackesons. This USP approach to the end customer often gives rise to the descriptive phrase of 'hard sell' although one is selling equally hard with the other two approaches.

Brand image

David Ogilvy, that doyen of advertising, is believed to have articulated the belief that, in today's very competitive world, very few products indeed can claim anything sufficiently unique to really separate themselves from their neighbours. And in any case, 'It is the total personality of a brand, rather than any trivial product difference, which decides its ultimate position in the market'. In the factory, cosmetics are manufactured; in the shop they sell hope. To create an image requires the product to be invested with an aura, a mood with which the chosen audience can identify. The snobbery within most of us makes After Eight Mints correct for the dinner table. The fact that every confectionery manufacturer could make a similar product does not affect Rowntrees' product one iota.

Martineau, a motivational researcher describes an image as 'The total set of attitudes, the halo of psychological meanings, the assertion of feelings, the indelibly written aesthetic messages over and above the physical qualities', a description which itself, creates an image of the writer! Shoes are not bought to keep the feet dry but to feel smart, to look good. However, Ogilvy went on to say that imagery was not enough. By itself it was too nebulous, too intangible. To it should be attributed one or two facts about the product. As long as they are relevant, it is not too important what they are. It is simply that customers need something tangible with which to justify their purchase decision, to themselves, as well as to others.

The copywriter who described a lovely girl as-

> So sweet her frame, so exquisitely fine,
> She seemed a statue by a hand divine,
> Her faultless form the hero's bosom fires
> The more he looks, the more he still admires.'

– knew all there was about imagery. In fact it was Ovid describing the feelings of Perseus as he zoomed past the rock to which Andromeda was chained!

Realism

This approach is based on overtly recognising that the customer is likely to be a reasonably intelligent human being and telling him or her the truth; sometimes called the 'Honest Joe' approach. It involves a down-to-earth, factual presentation full of 'reasons why'. A classic example, often quoted is that of Avis, the car hire company who basically said that they knew they were number two in the brand share league but that meant that they would try harder than the brand leader, Hertz, so give the Avis the business for a better deal. Or the newly appointed Honorary Physician to the Queen, who entered his university lecture room next morning to find a message on the notice board which read, 'Congratulations – God save the Queen!'

The admixture

These three basic approaches can usually be singled out from any major advertising campaign and certainly Product Managers should objectively be able to agree the best approach to take in their own circumstances. However, it was said earlier that one cannot put advertising into watertight compartments and this is so. For instance, any USP approach will inevitably create an image of the product after a few exposures, as will a realistic approach. The use of an image which involves one or two 'nuts and bolts' will often be indistinguishable from realism in the consumer's mind. For example, the Cadbury's 'glass and a half' which implies goodness is combined with 'chunkiness' to illustrate good value for money. This is both 'image' with a specific to back it up and 'realism' within a longer term image.

But since an advertisement should be simply and easily understood, any dilution of the basic approach chosen, is likely to detract from clarity and result in an advertisement that is 'muddy around the edges'; all too often evident unfortunately, especially in technical publications.

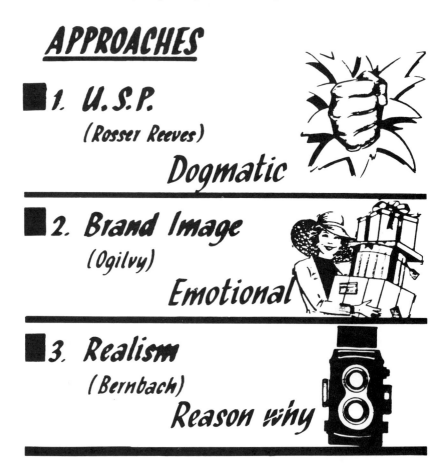

APPROACHES

1. U.S.P.
(Rosser Reeves)
Dogmatic

2. Brand Image
(Ogilvy)
Emotional

3. Realism
(Bernbach)
Reason why

Figure 12.6

Some Creative Do's and Don't's

- 'White' space in an advertisement is as important as 'black'.
- Do not crowd available space.
- Frequent changes of type *face* can inhibit readability.
- The audience should be more interested in the message than the advertiser. The advertiser's name 'big and bold' at the top can be a sure 'putter-off'.
- Advertising that wins awards may not win hearts or minds.

- Simplicity means understandability.
- It is easier to read an advertisement from top to bottom and left to right, as for a book. If the reader's eye is required to travel a different way, there needs to be a good reason.
- Visual and copy should be in harmony.
- A good *Idea* must form the basis of a good advertisement.
- Committees can criticise an advertisement – they *cannot* create one.
- Repeat a good advertisement until there is clear evidence that it no longer 'pulls'; the advertiser's familiarity is no guide.
- Do not copy.
- Remember that advertising is controlled by legislation, codes of practice *and* public opinion.
- Be happy to claim responsibility for the advertisement.
- Test reaction of chosen audience.

The Media Plan

Each of the very many forms of media available in this country for communicating to a particular group of people, possesses its own peculiarities. Each will have a readership or viewing profile by type of person and by geographical coverage. The best media mix will be that which gives the greatest coverage of the chosen audience, the highest number of times at the least cost. The aim should be concentration of effort in order to build sufficient 'Opportunities to see' (OTS's) at the lowest 'Cost per thousand' (CPT). As a general rule it is far better to have six advertisements in one publication than one advertisement in six publications. However, some recent work on television commercials suggests that two exposures in one week may be more cost effective than one or four (MacDonald of BMRB). The eventual media mix chosen will be based on:
- The audience profile;
- The budget;
- Marketing requirements such as dates, time periods, geographical areas, any relationship to other events;
- Creative requirements such as size, shape, use of colour, message, image;
- Competitive actions.
From these deliberations a media plan or schedule with detailed recommendations should be prepared which will include such elements as:
- Publications or other media forms to be utilised;
- Coverage of target audience for each and in total;
- OTS's for each and cumulative;
- Start date, frequency, and duration of campaign in each and in total with forward booking and cancellation dates;

- Type and size, or time length with details of colour, mono, etc.;
- Detailed costs of media and production, together with any research costs specifically related to media effectiveness;
- Control methods related to objectives set.

Application to Industrial and Service Products

It really must be accepted by Product Managers in these types of market, no matter how specialised their products might be, that the basic disciplines of advertising apply every bit as much to such products. There are numerous examples of such application from companies as diverse as Sulzer, the world market leader in large marine diesel engines; the Resistant Materials division of Carborundum with their brand 'Fiberfrax' insulation material; British & General Tube as an old established steel stockist; and perhaps more readily known, the campaign by Eton Yale for their fork lift trucks with the headline 'What Idiot designed this load of rubbish!'

If, in this chapter, there are more references to consumer products, it is simply that they are usually more widely known and, of course, there is much more advertising carried on for such products. Perhaps the most significant difference in industrial advertising, concerns the choice of media and the conspicuous lack of advertising data over much of the available field.

The Advertising Strategy

Just as one requires a Marketing Strategy to define and control a marketing operation, so an Advertising Strategy is required to ensure understanding of and commitment to a course of action which can be of enormous benefit to a product and which certainly costs a great deal of money. For the larger companies with an advertising agency to create and place advertisements, an advertising strategy forms the basis of their relationship with each other as far as the actual advertising is concerned. For the smaller companies with much less money to spend and who are tempted to 'go it alone' it helps to ensure a framework which generates consistency in approach, when personal subjective likes and dislikes might lead to scrappy, incoherent, and inconsistent advertising.

There are many variations practised by advertisers and agencies. Sometimes an 'Account Brief' originated by the advertiser, although often written by the agency, may be used. From this may stem an 'Advertising Plan'. Sometimes the nomenclature is a 'Copy Strategy' although the strategy covers much more than simply the copy or words used. Whatever the title and whatever its content, some written discipline is very necessary for two organisations, advertiser and agency, to agree on the basic advertising policy to be employed. The Advertising Strategy should stem directly from the

Marketing Strategy and is almost invariably the result of agonising appraisals of market motivations, competitive positions and claims, deep analysis of market trends and hours of discussions concerning possible approaches. Advertising is a business, not a game. There are many different ideas as to the necessary contents of an Advertising Strategy, but the following are virtually 'musts'.

Audience

Who do we want to communicate with? What sort of people are they? A clear description of the 'prime customer profile' as described in the Marketing Strategy but amplified with some advertising factors, such as 'bald, fat and forty with a birdlike mind, darting in many directions at once, a tendency towards a coronary, avid reader of comics, motivated by the latest pub story'! Bearing in mind that one does not talk to a fifty year old in the same way as a fifteen year old, or a male the same as a female, or someone at the top of the tree in the same way as a peasant, the normal standard profile breakdowns will also be added.

Objectives

What do *we* want *them* to do? As explained above this can range across a wide spectrum, from 'To open a new current account' to 'Maintain loyalty to continued purchase' or 'To purchase an electric shaver for first time shavers'. Any objective should be capable of measurement to ensure that it is or is not achieved.

Customer benefit

No matter what we want our prime audience to do, they are only interested in 'what is in it for them'. We have to articulate this in their terms – the Promise. 'To present the face and people of the bank in warm human terms' so that they will know that they will receive sympathetic and understanding treatment! 'That the vodka will create a climate of social pleasure, free of inhibitions'! 'That the fork lift truck is so designed as to minimise maintenance problems'.

Approach

How do we talk to our chosen audience? Do we wish to tell them straight out in no uncertain terms that our product is the only one with right handed threads, that there is no other to touch it. Shall we punch this at them in an imperious way? Or shall we be mild and gentle, appeal to their senses, to their emotions? Or have we got the ten most important factors required in a new car and suggest that the customer compare us with our competitors on these counts?

Method

Which will be the prime communication vehicle for delivering the message to the chosen audience? National press or television; commercial radio or specialist publications; direct mail or posters, and so on. This will encompass the general media policy including national or regional coverage and including particularly appropriate seasons or times.

Promotion

This is not a 'must' but there may be a policy for or against supporting specific sales promotion with media advertising. It is generally wise to accept that one cannot carry out 'theme' advertising and promotional advertising in the same advertisement. A promotional advertisement should set out to sell the promotion and not the product.

Client–Agency

It will be obvious that once the Advertising Strategy is agreed after a great deal of discussion, it can form the basis of the working relationship with the agency or with creative 'hot shops', media brokers, or one's own creative department. There are of course, pros and cons for using a full service agency, a more narrowly specialist agency, or doing it oneself. Usually this reflects a company viewpoint and Product Managers are expected to conform. It might, however, be profitable to consider for a moment the major reasons for using a separate advertising agency.

Why use an agency?

(i) *Skill* The Product Manager is usually not trained in copywriting, visualising, printing, media planning, and buying, film production, and the host of other specialisms that should be found in an advertising agency.

(ii) *Cost* If he costed out the time spent struggling to produce and place selling advertisements, it would probably be substantially more than any fee that an agency would charge.

The same two factors apply also to a company having their own advertising department. It is doubtful if they could attract the best talents, or keep them fully occupied.

That is not to say that a largish company should not have its own Advertising Manager if it wishes to. Any agency would welcome having a like minded person at the client end.

(iii) *Growth* An agency has an in-built momentum as a spur to growth. The only way this can happen is if its clients also expand so that the impetus can be a useful addition to the client's own growth.

(iv) *Services* Many ancilliary services such as research, merchandising, sales promotion, as well as access to a wider range of information services is available through an agency.

(v) *Objectivity* Whilst agencies have their own internal politics, they are not the clients'. The agency can often be more objective and less concerned with past political thinking than their clients.

(vi) *Originality* This is the agency's stock-in-trade. The prime essential in a good advertising campaign is a good idea. This type of original thinking can be applied in many directions to the benefit of the client.

(vii) *Customer knowledge* Perhaps one should hesitate to say it, but sometimes agencies know more about their customers' motivations and actions than their clients, simply because they are talking to those same customers on behalf of several clients with different products.

If a company wishes to appoint or change an advertising agency, the Institute of Practioners in Advertising have an excellent booklet suggesting how to go about it to the best effect and are only too pleased to assist.

How to get the best from an agency

(i) *Have a very clear written understanding* with the agency. The standard contract needs amplifying with details as to who pays for what; when accounts are rendered: what is included in the fee or commission and what is not. There is nothing more calculated to raise hackles than for the Product Manager to be charged for something that he did not expect.

(ii) *Information flow* Keep the agency well informed. Expect them to be interested in all aspects of the business. Advertising must be profitable and therefore measurable. It affects all departments of the company directly or indirectly. Virtually every piece of information the agency has is confidential to its clients. Agency personnel are probably more conscious of confidentiality than company personnel.

(iii) *Brief well* A clear and comprehensive brief as to what is expected by Product Management will save many arguments and misunderstandings.

(iv) *Ensure agreed advertising strategy* Probably the agency will originate this but it is the Product Manager's strategy and must be agreed by both parties, *and adhered to.* 'Bad' clients move the goal posts during the game. 'Bad' agencies change the strategy to fit a creative, but irrelevant idea!

(v) *Reporting* Ensure regular reports of such factors as ratings, OTSs, CPTs, poor reproductions, expenditure against budget, etc.

(vi) *Mutual respect.* Recognise that each has different lives and approaches. Trust and understanding can pay dividends.

(vii) *Different levels of contact* from time to time are advantageous. Whilst the Account Executive is the proper representative of the agency and the normal line of communication, meetings with Account Supervisors or Directors or other titles, can be most useful.

(viii) *Allow time* Agencies are always up against dead lines. Try to allow a reasonable time for the best results. Panics may be the order of the day but they seldom result in the best answers.

(ix) *Research* Advertising research is essential but to carry out sufficient research to enable advertising to be originated on good information, before anyone puts pen to paper, is even more important. It can save many thousands of pounds. Further, £1000–worth of expenditure before shooting a £50,000 television film for a £1 million campaign is worth any amount of research carried out after the money has been spent. Try the simple test of substituting your competitor's name for your own in the advertisement. If it could work equally well then there is something wrong.

Check List

- Is there one main message, clearly stated, which differentiates your product from its competitors?
- Does the advertisement clearly 'flag' your chosen audience?
- Is the message likely to get instant interest from that audience?
- What action comes across as being required of the reader?
- Do copy and visual clearly complement each other?

– Is message, style of presentation of that message, layout, choice of typeface, medium used, and position within the chosen media, all harmonised within the same image?

– Is there sufficient weight of advertising to create impact?

Finally, is the advertising achieving the desired results? 'Last night we advertised for a night watchman. This morning we were robbed!'

Direct Mail

Direct mail is very widely used as a means of marketing communication especially in industrial and service organisations. As a medium, it can be highly effective in terms of both resultant action and cost, but a great deal of money can also be wasted on it. It cannot be overstressed that direct mail is a means of communication very similar to advertising. Indeed, it is a special type of advertising and many of the same principles should apply. To begin with, let us be clear as to what we mean by Direct Mail for some people wrongly use the term Direct Marketing, of which it is only a part.

Direct marketing embraces:

(i) Direct response advertising, where the recipient is persuaded to send for the advertised product by mail – as with Scotcade or one of the many book clubs of W.H.Smith.

(ii) Mail order catalogues, where individuals order through an agent, as with Littlewoods or Freemans.

(iii) Telephone selling – such as Lyons Maid or the Arthur Murray School of Dancing.

(iv) Direct mail. A communication of any sort direct to an individual. In the UK perhaps *Readers Digest* and *Time Life* spring most readily to mind.

Marketing integration

A direct mail 'shot' may require brochures, price lists, response cards or other pieces of literature, but for maximum impact it *should* include a letter. The literature is impersonal, general, factual. The letter makes it personal, particular, appealing. And the essence of a direct mail shot is that of a personal communication. The total shot must create an image consistent with the objective *and* reflect the organisation. It should lock into the overall marketing campaign and not be treated as a separate entity.

Clearly defined objectives

To whom is the direct mail shot directed? What sort of person is he or she?

Clear definition of recipient is vital in order to decide how to talk to such a person. One would not write in the same vein to a 50 year old as one would an 18 year old, for example; or to a business man in the same vein as a housewife.

Why is the communication being made – at all? at this time? in this way? What is its purpose? There must be some offer to be made of benefit to the recipient. This should be *one* offer, not several. The one offer may have several variations but to make two or several different offers in the same mail shot will confuse and have less impact than single-mindedly talking about one. Whilst joint mailings or joint distribution with other direct mail offers is less costly, it can also be less effective through diffusion of attention, where concentration is preferable.

Objectives may range from specific sale of a product; to a show of interest for later commitment to a sale; to opening doors for salesmen; to enticing people to an exhibition, or seminar, or special display; to announcement of new inventions or products; to seeking information; to giving information; and very many more. The one objective for the direct mail shot should be clearly defined and written down, so that everyone concerned is clear and so that later measurement of the effectiveness or otherwise can be based on clearly understood criteria.

Means of delivery

Whilst direct mail, as its name implies, is usually sent through the post, there are a number of alternative vehicles by which it can be delivered:
(i) As an insert in a magazine or other publication. Whilst this might reach specific individuals, such as *Marketing* reaching specific people engaged in marketing; or *Angling Times* reaching fishermen, it is obviously not as personal as directly to an individual through the mail.
(ii) Inserted in newspapers, perhaps by CTN's, consequently very localised and not directly personal.
(iii) Via and with other companies' direct mail shots, for example to Harrod's card holders. Almost certainly, this would be as a result of a joint promotion, tailor-made, with Harrod's.
(iv) Delivered by hand by door to door distribution agencies such as Circular Distributors Ltd., or by the Post Office's postmen, perhaps using ACORN area classifications.
(v) Sent with other deliveries to companies or distribution outlets.
(vi) Picked up by customers at point of sale.
(vii) Delivered by salesmen in person – expensive unless as part of their normal selling pattern.
Each of these alternatives to direct mail, except perhaps the last, reduces the personal nature of the communication and is, therefore, more suitable for

general notification purposes, or promotional incentives, such as competition prizes, premium offers, coupons and the like.

Choice of mailing list

A list of names and addresses can be obtained for almost any special interest group – from abattoir equipment suppliers to zinc workers; from accountants to zip fastener manufacturers; from anglers to adherents of the faith of Zoroaster. Access to such lists can be obtained:

- Through reputable direct mail houses;
- From not so reputable direct mail houses;
- Often bought from individuals or organisations who have no further use for them; such as an importer of plastic ducks from Hong Kong who has sold his mind benders, and now wishes to get the last drop of cash from his investment by selling the list, sometimes to several people;
- Perfectly reputable individuals or businesses who have specifically set out to compile lists, often of a fairly narrow sector of the business world or domestic community;
- By building one's own list.

Most lists originate from directories or professional registers or electoral rolls, which are always out of date before they are printed, at least to a certain extent. By frequent usage or specific desk research, such lists can be updated fairly regularly, if they are regularly required. Lists very infrequently used will not be so up to date. The process of regularly 'cleaning' lists is essential for maximum cost effectiveness and this applies equally to one's own list. Companies with own lists tend to add new names whenever possible, but seldom weed out lapsed potential – the gone-aways, cannot be founds, died – so that cost per enquiry or sale tends to climb higher and higher. People and organisations change names, change addresses, change jobs, change interests, go out of business, more frequently than is often realised, and new ones are born or created. Constant attention to the make up of a direct mail list is vital to cost effectiveness.

In terms of costing before the event, an allowance of up to 10% 'Gone aways' should be allowed for, depending on previous experience of the list. It is to be hoped that the actual will be nearer 1 or 2%.

Writing the letter

This is a specialist job. The direct mail letter is a very special type of advertisement which must conform to the laws of advertising to be effective. Yet it has a major difference from most advertising in that it is directed at one person at a time. Advertising too is directed at one person but in the context of appealing to many people at the same time. It is *not* the same as writing a sales letter to a sales force, where the writer often has authority over them, but it *is* writing a letter that *sells* – whether immediately or longer term, whether a product or a concept.

A professional direct mail writer, employed by a reputable direct mail house, or as a freelance, will almost always write a more effective letter than someone not trained as a copywriter or letter writer. The writer must:-

(i) *Clearly establish the offer*   to be made, the profile of the recipient and the objectives it is hoped to achieve in specific terms, remembering that 'What's in it for me?' is likely to be the reaction of the recipient.

(ii) *Decide on the overall approach* – hard hitting, punchy, factual, emotive, image creating, subjective, concentrating on one aspect alone or several, using humour or keeping serious, requiring immediate action or longer term. The approach must have a relationship with any other form of communication from the same company to the recipient – be within the corporate or brand image and also relate to the offer being made and the type of person the recipient is. Whatever is said and however it is said, the recipient will usually retain one image and one overall fact only, which will be an individual distillation of everything in the letter.

(iii) *Consider the length of the letter*,   whether there is space or time to build up a story or whether the salient point must register immediately. Generally brevity, with easily read paragraphs, is to be preferred. Elaboration can sometimes be included in enclosures, leaflets, brochures, lists, and so on.

(iv) Go through A I D A – attention, interest, desire, and action. As with the headline and visual of an advertisement, the *attention* of the recipient must be gained in almost the first eye blink, or he is lost. The opening sentence is as important as the headline of an advertisement. It is so important that possibly two alternatives should be written and each tested to see which pulls best. But immediately the recipient who is attracted to continue reading because his interest has been aroused must have that *interest* retained and elaborated on, so that a *desire* for the *action* required of him or her is generated. The end result should usually be a commitment to action. In consequence, the action required must be clear and unequivocal. The finish, as the opening, should be relevant, crisp and clear. The opening and closing are vital – *so* is the piece in the middle.

(v) *Consider the letter head*   – should it be the firm's normal heading or is that too austere, or not newsworthy enough? Should there be a specially designed head?

(vi) *Consider the envelope.* Should this be plain white, or buff, or other colour? Should there be a message, with or without a visual, some incentive to open rather than reject? For promotional literature to domestic consumers this might be desirable; for business purposes to top management, probably not; to middle management, perhaps. Should the address be typed or printed straight on to the envelope or an address label fixed – preferably not the latter.

(vii) *Consider a reply paid card,* or freepost, or other printed response – keep it simple, easy to complete and easy to post.

(viii) Decide whether the envelope and letter should be *personally addressed* and personalised in its contents and, if so, by what method. There are many ways of achieving this, some more obvious than others, but it is expensive. Can the extra expense be justified? To a businessman:

(a) How many will be addressed with the wrong title, or initials, or letters after the name?

(b) How many will no longer be with that company, or no longer performing the same function?

(c) Of the remainder, are they really unaware that it is one of many identical letters? Will they give you full marks for spending more money on them, or will they wonder how elastic are your budgets?

To a domestic consumer, personalising may result in 5–10% greater response, or it may not, or, even if it does, the extra may still not be cost effective. Conflicting reports of *extra* response due to personalising require this to be a subject of testing in specific instances.

(ix) *Create understandable 'keying'* of any expected response – reply to Box No, or to Mr H.J. Smith, or to Harry Smith, etc.

(x) *Finally, always use good English.* Slang words or phrases *may* create a more relaxed 'I understand you' reaction, but they may also jar and create as much illwill as goodwill. Like humour, slang is a very tricky subject to use.

Testing

There are a number of possibilities to be tested:-

(i) Before proceeding with a costly operation, we may want to test:
- the cleanliness of the list itself;
- the opening paragraph or sentence alternatives;
- that the letter is in fact communicating what we want communicated;
- if the reply paid card is understandable;

   – what the response rate may be; no point in receiving a flood of replies
     that we cannot action within a reasonable time;
   – the total cost likely per response.
(ii) Afterwards we may want to know:
   – how many replies were received specifically in answer to our mail
     shot;
   – whether any change in the recipient's future action is contemplated;
   – if there is any change in the recipient's image of you, any attitude
     shift;
   – what was the actual cost per sale, or new distributor, or . . . or. . . .
Strictly, any testing must be made on a representative and statistically
significant sample of the mailing list. Confidence levels will depend on this
and mathematical models will be employed, particularly where multi-
variant testing is involved. Research professionals should be used for this
purpose, as well as for research into attitudes or attitude shifts, compre-
hension and other behavioural factors.

However, considerable problems arise with relatively small lists in
creating statistically significant samples and the cost of research professionals cannot be justified for every mail shot. So sensible compromises must
be reached. Often it is enough to know whether there is a reasonable
preference for, or against, one element, or whether it falls into that grey area
where no one knows the answer.

To test two alternative opening sentences on, say, 100 of the mailing list,
chosen at random, will usually give a fairly clear picture of the 'best' and also
some sort of idea of the likely response rate, even though one recognises the
risk that a particular batch of 100 may be unrepresentative of the
whole.

Measurement

To measure response may not be as simple as measuring the number of reply
cards received. Breakdowns by area, by type of respondent, by time, by type
of action, and so on may be necessary. This may require briefing telephonists
for monitoring response calls, or depots, or branch offices, or other
departments within the company. Yardsticks, based on objectives, need to
be established. Is a 1/2% response rate good or bad? No one knows. For
specific mail shots in specific circumstances, 1/2% may well be considered
good, with 2 or 3% very good and 10% a miracle, but it depends on the
audience, the time, the competition, and the impact and relevance of the
mail shot. Each response rate should be measured so that, gradually, a bank
of knowledge is built up and measurement can become increasingly a true
reflection of the effectiveness of direct mail.

Follow-up

Often, particularly when one is not well known by the recipients, it is sensible not to rely on one single direct mail shot alone. Just as one would not expect too much from one direct mail shot unless the offer is extremely powerful. A follow-up can often gain an increasingly economic response since the ditherers, or those previously not convinced, are given another boost. Further, repetition for an unknown organisation can, at times, engender confidence.

The law

Suffice it to say that any public communication is controlled by many different acts of Parliament and codes of practice,
- *Liability* such as copyright, dishonesty, libel, infringement of trade marks.
- *Responsibilities* engendered by trade descriptions, lotteries and amusements, food and drugs, hire purchase and consumer credit, racial and sexual discrimination, weights and measures.

There can only be one possible recommendation – clear every direct mail shot with a solicitor or legal man of some sort. Perhaps the requirements for advertising might sensibly embrace the many restrictions that surround direct mail, that it should be

LEGAL
HONEST
DECENT and
TRUTHFUL.

Logical Progression

To list the Product Manager's activities in originating, executing, and controlling the communications mix, one must accept that there will be substantial differences of detail within each company and organisation. The broad sweep however, in all probability, will not differ too much.
  (i) Decide on the objectives required of the total communications programme;
 (ii) Define the customer benefit;
(iii) Originate the theme and style of approach;
 (iv) Describe the prime audience;
  (v) Itemise all possible communication options in terms of practical application within the budget;
 (vi) Choose the 'mix' most appropriate;
(vii) Cost the necessary concentration required in each medium to achieve the requisite objectives of OTS and CPT;

(viii) Relate to total marketing budget and adjust as necessary;
 (ix) Create advertising; obtain necessary copy and legal clearences;
  (x) Commission production – artwork, blocks, films, etc.;
 (xi) Book space and time;
(xii) Monitor advertising exposure; continuously analyse results in terms
      of audience action, costs, and sales.

13   Sales Promotion

Incentives to greater efforts – Short term appeal – Customer reaction – Setting objectives – Choice of method – Promotional plan – Measurement – Promotional types – Merchandising – and the trader – Public relations – The idea – Sponsorship – Legality

Incentives to Greater Efforts

Ever since the day that Adam was given one apple free, since the travelling salesman in old England gave a free toothpick with his elixir of life, to the present day when the world is full of such aids to sale, from the MCC paying extra bonuses for extra runs to £5 off a pair of Hush Puppies, the emotive consequence of providing incentives to greater achievement has been recognised as a powerful force.

Whilst, without question, a considerably greater volume of promotions is run for consumer goods, from both consumer goods manufacturers and services to consumers in the domestic sense, they are equally applicable to industrial suppliers. However, in this chapter more weight is given to consumer markets since they also include middle men in the shape of retailers and wholesalers and distributors.

In total, sales promotion is big business. No-one knows for certain how much money is spent on this aspect of marketing activity, partially because special promotional discounts cannot be audited with any degree of accuracy, but it is probably more than is spent on all aspects of media advertising; some estimates go as high as four times as much. Whatever the sum, does it work? 'Yes', if it is a good promotion and 'No' if it is a bad one. An obvious answer but so seldom do those responsible for promoting measure the effectiveness of their efforts. Knowledge of what is a winner and what a loser, at least in that grey area in the middle, one would have thought vital with such a costly facet of the total budget. A promotion with a good idea, well thought through, designed to achieve a specific objective, well executed, will work. There are innumerable examples of well documented success stories. Equally, there are many not-so-well documented failures. Success might be epitomised perhaps by the fact that it is those shops with the brightest promotional scene that gain the customers. After all, we all like a bargain.

It is doubtful if the Birmingham garage which had a sign up saying 'We operate a staff incentive scheme on these premises. If at first you don't succeed, you're fired,' got any worthwhile extra effort.

Short Term Appeal

Essentially any single promotion has a short life. In the retail business, two weeks if one is lucky. From the consumer standpoint, longer commitment may be obtained through a save-up scheme. Four packet tops for a £1 voucher, cards in packets of tea, attachment to a forthcoming attraction such as the World Cup in soccer or a royal wedding, and media advertising of the promotion might prolong it, as well as adding considerably to the cost. However, rather the same as for media advertising, there are so many promotions happening in most markets at any one point in time that the initial impetus is difficult to sustain. It is doubtful, for example, if an end of year bonus to a trader to achieve a certain turnover is really an incentive until the last month of the period.

Consequently, Product Managers would do well to assume that their promotions have most effect at and shortly after launch, and that, if the objective is to retain loyalty, any longer term promotion will need an injection from time to time.

It should not be forgotten that promoting in general for a product or brand, can have a long term affect on the *image* of that brand. To take an extreme example, a brand which is constantly promoting on price is likely to become thought of as a cut price product. This has happened with 'white' goods in total; for example, washing machines, refrigerators, and the like.

Customer Reaction

It is interesting to recognise that, as individuals, we probably think of promotions as 'gimmicks', at which we rather turn up our noses. Yet, as marketeers we think of them as important parts of the marketing mix. And as recipients of next year's diary, or a Bémrose calendar, or a Honeywell paper weight containing a microchip, we can feel rather pleased with life. These differing attitudes straddle all socio-economic groupings. The up-market holiday maker taking a Swans (Hellenic) cruise down the Nile, is very happy to be given a free overnight bag with 'Swan' emblazoned on it, which he will carry well after the trip is finished. In just the same way the football fan going to Spain with Sportsworld was happy to be given a 'T' Shirt and become a similar advertising site!

There has been evidence from reports by Taylor Nelson and Associates and others, that consumers who are housewives not only actively distrust promotions, particularly 'reduced price packs', but tend to feel that they would prefer the price to be reduced properly, rather than have all the 'gimmicks' that abound on their normal shopping occasions. This is a natural public reaction but does not apply to promotions that *they* find interesting or to products that give *them* satisfaction. It is probably the case that if a fast-moving consumer product had absolutely no promotional activity through-out the year, the ability to reduce the price of one pack would be much less than one penny; and volume of sale would almost certainly drop so that such a move might be self defeating. One of the reasons for an apparent innate suspicion of many promotions is the promotor's problem of cost. The amount affordable for a 'free give-away' or an 'on pack premium' and other forms, is often small per unit. A cheap product allied to one's own can demean our product. There is no doubt that the real value of such items has increased over the years but 'the fast buck from a plastic duck' image dies hard.

Another reason is that customers are perfectly well aware that someone has to pay for all the promotions to which they are subjected and that that someone is them. Customers are not morons, as David Ogilvy says, 'They are your wives!' A similar reaction is noticed towards packaging. Whilst customers want and need good packaging there is a belief that there is a great deal of excess packaging which pushes the price up. All these price problems are, of course, more acutely noticeable in periods of depression of the economy.

Yet another reason has been the nature of the sales promotion scene which has spawned many individuals and organisations only concerned with a transient profit. Fortunately, the Institute of Sales Promotion has done wonders in straightening, policing and guiding a fast-becoming-healthy and important industry. Its Code of Practice, membership qualifications, annual awards schemes and the rest are valuable additions to the marketing discipline.

For Product Managers, therefore, a crucial requirement is to ensure that any promotion is in keeping with the image of their product. The product must come first. The middle aged woman entering a store, was greeted by the department manager with the news that, as the millionth customer, she had won a holiday for two in Florida. 'Thank you,' she said, 'But you will have to wait till I have been to your complaints department with this pen that won't work.'

Objectives

The discipline of setting an objective first and then considering the best promotion to use in the circumstances, is an essential to cost effective sales promotion. No good the Product Manager saying to himself that since he has no more money left in his budget, yet the Sales Manager is pressuring him for some back up, then he will run a self liquidating premium because it will not cost him anything. If Maxwell House offer a garden chair worth £10, for £5 plus two labels and the offer results in 100,000 chairs 'sold' it may not have done Maxwell House any good in sales terms. They are not in business to sell garden chairs but coffee. This will only happen to any significant extent if they manage to obtain special featuring at point of sale through trade interest in the promotion. The special featuring will result in increased sales. The garden chair is simply a means to that end.

Whilst no one can pontificate and state categorically that a particular type of promotion will achieve certain specific goals, figure 13.1 showing possible objectives that certain types of promotion might achieve, is based on experience and can be used as a guide. But it must be stressed that certain products in certain situations may well react differently to others, depending on such market factors as competitive activity, the topicality of the idea, the simplicity of the promotion, the breadth of appeal, the extent to which it is supported by advertising and so on.

To the objective set, should be attached figures. Like all objectives, they are clearer, easier to measure, and less nebulous if numerate, rather than expressing what might be termed pious hopes. It should be noted that mention has been made of 'objective', singular. A common fault is to set a number of different objectives:

To combat competition;
To provide a talking point for the sales force;
To expand sales;
To exploit seasonality;
To highlight the large size;

all with one promotion. It must be obvious that no single promotional idea can possibly concentrate on all these objectives. As a spin-off, certain other effects may well stem from one promotion but if an attempt is made to design a promotion to achieve multiple objectives it will be a very scrappy

Figure 13.1. Objectives, which certain promotions *might* achieve depending on circumstances.

OBJECTIVE	Self-liquidating premiums	On-pack premiums / Gifts	In-pack premiums	With-pack premiums	Container premiums	Continuing premiums	Trading stamps, gift coupons, vouchers	Competitions	Personalities	Couponing	Sampling	Reduced price packs	Banded packs	Related items
Launch or re-launch						X	X	X	X	X	X	X		
Induce trial							X	X	X	X	X	X	X	
Existing product — new usage					X	X	X	X	X	X	X	X		X
Gain new users				X	X	X	X	X	X	X	X	X	X	X
Retain existing users				X	X				X	X				
Increase frequency of purchase				X	X									
Upgrade purchase size			X	X						X		X		
Increase brand awareness							X	X						
Expand distribution						X	X	X	X	X	X	X	X	
Increase trade stocks			X							X		X	X	X
Reduce trade stocks									X					X
Expand sales — off season					X			X	X	X	X	X	X	
Activate slow moving lines								X	X	X	X	X	X	
Gain special featuring in store	X	X	X	X		X				X	X	X	X	
Increase shelf facings		X	X										X	X

operation with no single-mindedness of purpose and, very probably, difficult to explain clearly and simply.

Promotional Plan

It will be useful if the Product Manager has headings for the various elements of each promotion that he is likely to run. This will act as both a reminder of points to cover and as a brief for others involved. Headings might include:

  (i) Product – size, flavour, variant to be specially featured;

  (ii) Area – of geographical coverage;

  (iii) Customers – i.e.trade elements to be covered;

  (iv) Timing – start and stop dates of each element, such as literature distribution, advertising, sales notification etc.;

  (v) Sales force – requirements such as which divisions of the company, commando sales hiring, merchandisers;

  (vi) Agents – involvement of advertising agency, sales promotion house, direct mail, handling house, distribution company, etc.;

  (vii) Consumers – profile of prime audience participation required;

  (viii) Objectives – hopefully, only one;

  (ix) Promotion Description – type such as coupon, free give-away, etc.;

  (x) Budget – in total and by broad breakdowns;

  (xi) Measurement – methods, criteria, judgement as to success or failure;

  (xii) Special requirements – from Production, Distribution, Sales, Research, Packaging, Printing, etc.

Not only will such a systematic planning operation keep the Product Manager on the right track, but many others who will be affected as well. Further the all too prevalent scrabbling for time – so many details to tie up by yesterday – will perhaps be eased somewhat. And of course it almost forces one to make some effort at measurement followed by analysis after the event.

Measurement

The belief that one can never separate the effects of one promotion from all the manifold marketing activities which in total impinge on selling influences, whilst obviously having a grain of truth in it (perhaps more than a grain sometimes), should never result in the totally negative attitude that any attempt at measurement is worthless. In Appendix I to this chapter is a 58 point check list. No one is expected to check 58 points for every promotion of course, but if the Product Manager cannot find two or three key indicators from that list which are particularly relevant, then there must be something wrong.

The problem of measurement is no more or no less acute for sales promotion than for advertising, display, merchandising, sales persons, packaging, eye appeal and all the labyrinthine channels to effective marketing that would put Knossos in the shade. Just as for any action, one should measure and record before, during and after the event. One should test where necessary, at varying levels, from individual stores, to test towns, regions, roll out areas, to national. To be able to test in a location which can be compared with a control location where the promotion does not occur, is one useful way of excluding other factors. However, test marketing is important enough to warrant its own chapter in this book (Chapter 11).

The only real measurement is cost effective sales increases but nothing can be quite as simple as that. For instance there are many occasions where maintaining sales can represent a considerable success story; when fending off a new entrant to the market, for example. Further, short term gains made at the expense of mortgaging the future sales pattern may not be considered too successful. Nor may the staggering response to a free lighter offered by John Player. Instead of the 'few thousand' expected, two and a quarter millions were demanded. They cost £1 each!

Promotional Types

This book is not the place for an examination of the many different types of promotion available. There are many excellent books on the subject. Ogilvy & Mather produce a first class *Guide to Consumer Promotions*, for example. However, in Appendix II of this chapter is a relatively brief resumé of the advantages and disadvantages of the various types of promotion, originated by Tony Yeshin (Managing Director of Stowcastle Promotions Ltd.), who has tremendous experience in this field.

The promotional scene, like any other, changes from time to time. Sometimes one type of promotion is in fashion, each has its devotees. Charities have great appeal currently. Giving away money, in the shape of reduced price packs and coupons, have represented some 60% of all promotions over the last few years of depression, as measured by MPI Ltd. In the United States, travel is currently reported to represent over 11% of total incentives, 23% of sales incentives and 33% of dealer incentives. No doubt the pendulum will swing sooner or later.

Merchandising and the Trader

From the standpoint of many retailers the word 'merchandising' embraces *all* activities at point of sale designed to actively sell goods at maximum profit. This starts with the range of merchandise, goes through stock control, location of departments and product groups, space allocation, traffic flows, pricing, mark up, and finishes with promotion and special display. The last two, promotion and display, whilst of major importance to the trader, are by no means his only consideration. Further, in terms of profit, however measured, he does not gain in the long run if he sells more of one brand and less of another. For other retailers, however, the word merchandising only applies to the merchandise.

The sales promotor would do well to remember that the retailer's prime ways of expanding his business are to:

– Attract more people;
– To buy more;
– More frequently;
– Of products with a higher mark up:

and that profit to him, which may be measured in many different ways from 'wall square meterage' to 'linear footage' is a composite of mark-up times stock turn, not mark-up by itself. A 100% mark-up on a product with a stock turn of once a year, does not rate alongside a product with a 20% mark-up and 16 times a year stock turn.

All these factors create a demand by retail multiples, for 'tailor made' promotions. Those which no one else will be running at the same time. This can cause substantial problems for the Product Manager if he has no system for coping. A bank of promotions, well thought out, with cut and dried components such as competition prizes, literature, method of execution and costs, which Key Account Sales Managers can unveil to the multiple buyer or Merchandising Committee, will save many headaches. They will probably be related to order size and need to be freshened from time to time. Such a system needs only the button pressed for everything to be automatically executed for that one customer.

Whether or not the promotion is tailor made for a multiple, or more widespread for all and sundry, merchandising in manufacturer's terms, that is obtaining special displays and effects, and ensuring stock availability at the differing points of sale, is crucial to the proper execution of the promotion. And whether that is carried out by own salesmen or women or by specialist merchandisers, it needs to be done.

A substantial number of individual purchases of repeat purchase products are made as a result of delayed decision making. The consumer may have a sort of loyalty to a particular brand but if that loyalty is not very strong and if differences between it and competing products are marginal, the consumer may, at point of sale, be persuaded to buy an alternative on that one occasion, if something attractive applies to that acceptable alternative.

Public Relations

PR is part of the total promotion of products and services. It tends to be treated as a separate entity because there are specific skills, particularly related to a journalistic approach, that may be needed but more importantly, because this is the only aspect of marketing which really cannot be measured in sales terms. Generally it must be taken on trust. It may work or it may not. No-one ever really knows. Perhaps that is a bold statement. Certainly, PR people genuinely believe that it is measurable – in terms of column centimetres of editorial, in terms of attendance at demonstrations, in terms of publicity for special occasions. Their task is to influence people's minds – in the right way, of course.

First define the 'public' to be addressed; the financial community, one's employees, people living in the vicinity of one's manufacturing plants, and so on. Then decide what is required of them; to keep share prices up, to engender a feeling of 'belonging', to be able to obtain staff easily. Now, find ways and means of attracting their interest and getting the message across. These may range from a hot air balloon, to a 'Royal' opening, to a personal 'give away'. The petrochemicals division of ICI was giving away collectable 'logic games' long before the Rubik Cube made its appearance.

With some reservations, Product Managers are well advised to take PR on trust and make what use they can of it, providing they can afford it. But there are two other aspects. First Product Publicity, as distinct from Public Relations, is probably more pertinent to the Product Manager. PR might be considered more of a corporate venture in some instances. To produce a helpful booklet on the positioning in store of, say, salad varieties based on original research, may be more helpful to a brand than to sponsor a London taxicab for charity. The second aspect is that sometimes, a PR executive may spend more of his time keeping information *out* of circulation, than in trying to obtain publicity for it, with advantage to the company.

The Idea

One comes back time and again to the fact that in any aspect of promotion, including media advertising, the all important requirement at all times is an idea which has impact; usually this means originality and, since there are very few new things in this world, the originality can be expressed in the treatment of the idea.

Jack Barclay Motors, selling Rolls Royces in Berkeley Square, could still find a talked-about incentive to Rolls purchasers who had everything, by presenting a large bouquet of flowers to the wife (girl friend?) of the buyer. Texaco can still get mileage from a hackneyed conversion table by offering a metric conversion table from gallons to litres on a special Parker pen; who make such a business from business gifts that they have a special Business Gifts Manager. Slimbridge, as part of the World Wildlife Fund, originated a novel sponsorship scheme by getting enthusiasts to sponsor a Bewick Swan –

not just any swan but a named Bewick, the longest known having journeyed from Siberia every winter for 22 years.

Sponsorship

Perhaps the least said about such a controversial subject the better. There is an excellent book written by Victor Head of the Commercial Union Insurance Company on this subject. He quite honestly says that it is no good marketing people looking to prove the effectiveness of sponsoring by normal sales means. The approach must be that each company or organisation must, quite altruistically, recognise that it owes the community something for its wellbeing and not expect a quid pro quo from sponsorship, even though this may well transpire.

It is an interesting consideration that the vast majority of sponsoring revolves around only two facets of our life – sport and culture. Without sponsors, there would probably be no Wimbledon for tennis lovers. The fact that Robinson's man, who makes sure that the bottles of squash are always turned to face the cameras, probably gets more out of it than Slazengers (as part of Dunlop) get out of sponsoring John McEnroe; is neither here nor there!

Legality

It is doubtful if any Product Manager *cannot* plead ignorance of the law as it applies to promotional activity. Even lawyers and the courts are not clear on many facets. The Trade Description Act, The Price Marking (Bargain Offers) Order, the Merchandise Marks Act, and a host of others, have thrown up such a volume of case law that the only clear advice that can be given to Product Managers is to check every promotion with the company's legal advisers. Even then one court in the land might convict where another might aquit. What, for example, is a test of skill, such a vital legal requirement for a competition? How can one be sure with any price comparison that a particular price has prevailed in the locality in the time period stated? Is the avoidance of any proof of purchase sufficient to enable one to run what might otherwise be a lottery?

To further complicate the scene, the European Community has been trying to harmonise sales promotion law across the Community for a long time. Occasional pieces fall into place but if the whole of the UK promotional legislation had to conform with that of the EEC, life would be substantially different. No more garden chairs with Maxwell House coffee for example, only items with a relationship to coffee; no more Spot the Ball competitions, and so on.

It is suggested that Product Managers should not rely wholly on outside sales promotion houses, of whatever calibre, for legal clearance. Of course they are careful and have their own legal advisers; at least, some do. Even so, if a Product Manager's promotion is illegal it will be his company that will suffer.

Appendix I: Promotional Techniques and their Application

A. YESHIN

1 *REDUCED PRICE OFFERS*

Sometimes referred to as R.P.O's or price packs. Consists of a specific price reduction communicated on-pack, typically 3p off regular price. Value of offer differs according to Brand need/competitive environment.

Advantages
(a) Speed of implementation – promotion can be offered within days, and can be introduced without prior testing.
(b) Trade likes price reductions. Represents immediate offer of increased value to consumer.
(c) Promotion has universal appeal – everyone likes money.
(d) Inherent advantage of 'tried and tested' format with readily anticipated results. Impact of money-off can be directly predicted in terms of volume delivery.
(e) Available to all manufacturers/Brands since there are no economies of scale.

Disadvantages
(a) High cost – every pack sold contains promotional offer.
(b) Easily matched – competition can respond rapidly with similar or greater offer.
(c) Danger of price war – retaliation can create environment for price war between Brands.
(d) Undistinctive format – not a 'unique' promotion – everyone can offer money-off.
(e) Impact on imagery – if over-used may denigrate brand image and undermine product quality story.

2 *COUPON OFFERS*

Can be communicated in a variety of different ways. Most common is on-pack coupon (sometimes called reverse label coupon). Also via door-to-door delivery, freesheet insertions (eg shopping), or in the media. Consists of a money off coupon redeemed against subsequent purchase of Brand.

Advantages
(a) On-pack coupons almost as effective as 'money off' but at considerably lower cost.
(b) Effective method of inducing product sampling, particularly amongst new users.
(c) On-pack coupon requires minimal setting up costs.
(d) Media couponing can be targetted to specific consumer groups by appropriate selection of media.
(e) Door-to-door couponing offers regional facilities for promotion.

Disadvantages
(a) Some parts of the retail trade do not like handling coupons.
(b) Dangers of misredemption (but should not be overstated).
(c) No display advantages – difficult to display coupon offer.
(d) High establishment cost associated with door-to-door couponing.
(e) Considerable wastage.

3 BONUS PACKS

Alternative expression of money-off. Consumer receives extra product free, eg 25% extra free.

Advantages
(a) Often represents cost saving – product cheaper than cash offer.
(b) Has high perceived value to consumer.
(c) Can be used to trade up consumer to larger size.
(d) Offers advantage of on-shelf impact.
Disadvantages
(a) Requires amendment to packaging requirements. Not available to all Brands, and may incur substantial extra costs if only for a small run.
(b) Presents some shelving difficulties to trade.

4 MULTI-PACKS

Similar to Bonus Packs, but without major packaging changes. Offers 2 or more packs of product banded together at reduced price, e.g. 3 for the price of 2.

Advantages
(a) Available to brands where packaging limitations preclude bonus pack offer.

(b) Requires no amendment to basic packaging.
(c) Offers consumer high perceived value.
(d) Promotes multi-purchase by consumer and, hence, short-term loyalty to brand.

Disadvantages
(a) Some danger of shelving difficulties.
(b) May be costly to mount. Banding packs may be labour intensive.
(c) Requires considerable lead-time.

5 *FREE GIFTS*

Any item of merchandise given away freely with purchase of Brand at time of purchase. Distinct forms – on-pack; in-pack; with pack; and the pack.

Advantages
(a) Free gift offers have immediacy of impact.
(b) Can extend Brand appeal by associating gift with product usage e.g. Free spoon with Coffee.
(c) Adds value to Brand.
(d) If collectable item may induce loyalty over extended period.
(e) May be highly distinctive.

Disadvantages
(a) Difficulty of locating good free gift items. NB: quality of free gift should be as good as that of Brand.
(b) May adversely affect imagery of Brand.
(c) Potentially expensive.
(d) On-pack gifts liable to pilferage.
(e) In-pack gifts require special packing facilities.
(f) With-pack gifts highly subject to pilferage and not liked by trade.

6 *FREE MAIL-INS*   *Te above*

Consumer invited to send proofs of purchase to handling house in exchange for free gift.

Advantages
(a) Value of offer can be enhanced since gift occasioned by multiple purchases of Brand.
(b) May provide distinctive offer.
(c) Many consumers may collect labels for redemption but not redeem.
(d) 'Collectable' items may assist to build loyalty to Brand.

Disadvantages
(a) As with free gifts, difficulties of locating good premium items.
(b) Additional costs of postage and packing.
(c) Relatively low appeal to trade.
(d) Lacks immediacy – not available at time of purchase.
(e) Difficult to assess redemption levels.
NB: Prior testing of free gift items for acceptability and to assess likely redemption levels important.

7 SELF-LIQUIDATING OFFERS

Brand offers 'gift' to consumer at cost, e.g. Ovenware, normally £4.95, Yours For Only £2.75 plus proof of purchase.

Advantages
(a) Minimal cost to Brand since consumer bears total cost of item.
(b) Creates apparent value offer without associated costs.
(c) Can be used to generate display if item attractive to retail trade.
(d) Merchandise can be used as 'stock loader' to trade.

Disadvantages
(a) Mostly unable to generate trade enthusiasm for promotion.
(b) Minimal consumer redemptions.
(c) Danger of being left with surplus stocks if commitment to merchandise exceeds consumer/trade requirements.

9 PERSONALITY PROMOTION

Brand 'personalities' used to tour an area, focus interest on the Brand and reward consumers with proof of purchase after answering a 'skill' question. Requirement to call on 1 in 1000 homes. Little used today, but popular in mid–1960's e.g. Miss Camay, White Tide Man, etc.

Advantages
(a) Generates trade excitement.
(b) Can achieve significant impact on consumer sales.
(c) High visibility of promotion format (can be enhanced with media support).
(d) Does not require special packaging and is effective against current stocks in trade.

Disadvantages
(a) Labour intensive, hence high promotion cost – prohibitive to all except major Brands.

(b) Relatively difficult to organise.

(c) Promotion format over-used in 1960's and lost 'originality'.

(d) Majority of consumers never see personality, leading to high level of consumer scepticism.

HOWEVER, can be used effectively on a one-by-one store basis. Often only effective means of sampling new product to consumer.

9 *CONTESTS/COMPETITIONS*

Competition format in which consumer offered chance to win (major) prizes in return for proofs of purchase and completed entry form. NB: Requirements of Betting, Gaming and Lotteries Act – Determination of prize winners *MUST* be the result of the exercise of *SKILL*.

Advantages

(a) Relatively low cost.

(b) Can be set up speedily.

(c) Offers opportunity for impactful display.

(d) Creates aura of major activity.

Disadvantages

(a) Lacks immediacy.

(b) Often generates only low level of consumer participation.

(c) Enthusiasm of consumer/trade determined by scale and nature of prizes.

(d) Need for skill element acts as deterrent to entry.

NB: Game Promotions may offer appearance of lottery but really be dependent on exercise of skill, however, often more appealing to consumer, e.g. Matching Halves style of promotion.

10 *OTHER ACTIVITIES*

Charity Promotions
Brand offers to make donation to charitable body in return for consumer sending-in proof of purchase. e.g. Ski Stoke Mandeville Appeal.

Advantages

(a) Opportunity to associate 'emotive' charity with Brand.

(b) Enhancement of Brand imagery.

(c) Can have major impact on consumer sales.

(d) Potentially attractive to consumer 'groups' e.g. Schools, Scouts, Guides, other organisations etc.

(e) Can create major display and PR opportunity.

Disadvantages
(a) Often difficult to find charity with necessary broad appeal.
(b) Inherent risk of Brand being perceived as exploiting charity for commercial ends.
(c) Can be time consuming to establish and run effectively.

Sponsorship
Manufacturer or Brand 'adopts' sporting or arts event(s). Event re-named to associate Brand e.g. John Player Grand Prix, Texaco Cup etc.

Advantages
(a) Potential of Brand name association with major consumer interest activity.
(b) Consequent PR spin-off potential.
(c) Venue for trade 'entertainment'.

Disadvantages
(a) Usually requires high level of investment.
(b) Minimum consumer association of brand name with the event.
(c) No real evidence of consumer sales impact.

Appendix II: Sales Promotion Evaluation

Measurement criteria

A. EX-FACTORY SALES
   1. Weekly if possible
   2. by size (flavour, perfume, etc.), by area, by outlet type with particular emphasis on special promotion packs
   3. in units and sterling
   4. for previous 'X' weeks, during promotion, for 'Y' weeks after
   5. also for the same periods as in 4 for the year before.

B. CONSUMER SALES
   6. Weekly if possible, otherwise monthly. Two-monthly is too long.
   7. By size, area and outlet type singling out any special promotional pack
   8. in units and sterling
   9. for previous 'X' weeks or months, during promotion and for 'Y' weeks or months afterwards

10. also for the same periods as in 9 for the year before.

C. BRAND SHARES
11. of one's own brand compared with
12. competitors' shares in relation to
13. the total market
14. for the time span mentioned above and with the same period the year before.

D. DISTRIBUTION
15. of one's own brand and
16. competitors and of the
17. total product category
18. by shop and sterling
19. for the period of measurement above
20. compared with the same period a year ago.

E. OUT-OF-STOCK
21. of one's own brand and
22. competitors and of the
23. total product category
24. by shop and sterling
25. for the period of measurement above
26. compared with the same period a year ago.

F. DISPLAY
27. Number of own brand *special* product features achieved, by type of outlet.
28. Number of pieces of point-of-sale material *erected*, by type of material if useful, by type of outlet.
29. Average length of time each in-store display lasted, if possible.
30. Number of product displays and point-of-sale material erected each week of the promotion if possible.
31. Number of competitive displays at time of promotion.

G. CONSUMER ACTION
32. Number of buyers of own brand and competition, by age, class, sex, etc.
33. for the period of measurement and
34. compared with same period previous year.
35. Frequency of purchase, compared with competition and past history.
36. Quantity purchased – heavy, medium and light users.
37. Source of purchase compared with competition and past history.

38. Perhaps method of use, if a different method from normal is being promoted.
39. Perhaps image questions, such as changes in 'liking' or 'intention to buy' etc.

H. PROMOTIONAL DETAIL
40. Number of premium item applications, or
41. premium items sold into trade or given to them or distributed with pack.
42. Number of samples distributed or applied for.
43. Number of competition entry forms received and number of entry lines.
44. Number of demonstrations.
45. Number of 'personality' calls made.
46. Number of coupons issued and redeemed (with estimate of mis-redemption).
47. Number of gift vouchers issued and redeemed.
48. Number of collectors' cards issued and number of albums requested or purchased.

I. COST FACTORS
49. Hire of extra salesman or merchandisers or demonstrators or personality girls.
50. Promotional media advertising, consumer and trade, including production costs, if *extra* to theme advertising budget.
51. Special promotional display material, not forgetting artwork, blocks, dispatch, etc.
52. Collateral material such as printing of leaflets, coupons, catalogues, special promotion packs, salesmen's presenters.
53. Premium items, competition prizes, judges' fees.
54. Outside service fees, consultants, handling houses, direct mail houses.
55. Special packaging, labelling, postage.
56. Extra administration and handling costs.
57. Extra production costs.
58. Trade handling allowances, extra discounts.

14   The Future

*Forces of change – The economy – World
view – Moral attitudes – Concentration of
buying power – Flexibility – Planning and
execution – Job satisfaction*

The 21st century just about to dawn may seem, from our present viewpoint
sixteen years before the event, to presage a time of ferment, of total
unpredictability. Dynamic changes are afoot in every conceivable field – in
space, under the oceans, in communication, in travel. Vast movements are
taking place in social attitudes and actions, in learning, in human
awareness, in relations between nations and in political allegiances.

If we had looked at our present 20th century, sixteen years before it
dawned, in that period of peace and tranquility, it is doubtful if we would
have envisaged the colossal changes wrought by man in our time. Now, two
world wars later and with three millions unemployed, what is our attitude
to the changes in communication, in travel, in social structures, and in the
myriad other outlets of man's ingenuity ?

Looking back, the 19th century of the Victorians may seem to us to have
been one of stability and security, of tremendous advances in technology
and wealth. But to many, it was not so. The land was literally being torn
apart, great gouging canals and disfiguring railways, pithead slagheaps,
flooded valleys for the black satanic mills, scarring quarries for great

buildings, exploitation of labour, for some near-starvation.

Marketing in this country is only just twentyfour years of age from its advent around 1960. Can the last two centuries tell us anything worthwhile ? At least, the cynic might say, we cannot possibly do worse in the 21st century. Poor consolation really. We must do better and we can. We can for many reasons, not least the greater human consciousness of us all. In the business world, which has a tremendous effect upon the affairs of man, we can because the profession of marketing, for the very first time in the history of any business discipline, puts the customer first. Or that is what we preach.

The Forces of Change

No doubt each decade is thought of as one of change, but all the evidence points to the '80s as being one where continuous and dramatic change is normal with no oases of stability at which to draw breath. This headlong rush into the future will bring many traumas for Product Managers in its train. Mistakes will be made and lessons learned. Some will benefit, others, alas, will not.

The Economy

What fundamental market changes may affect their role ? The painfully slow and painfully hurting transition of our economy from many of the basic traditional industries, and from the many services that fed them and fed on them, towards the more dynamic, complex, and scientifically demanding industries and services, illustrates two basic requirements of Product Managers in the future.

(i) First, the ability not only to think 'wider than the box', to be aware of outside influences, but to exert the management skills and authority that ensure that something is done about them. Not to be imbued with top management thinking and the inevitable politics that follow to such an extent that the Product Manager is simply a 'Yes' man or women. So many of our ills would not have happened as severely as they have, if managements had seen the light and taken avoiding action in time. Marketing is the limb of the company that can ensure that action is taken.

(ii) Secondly, Product Managers must be more professional and dynamic. Academics and politicians alike appear at long last to have seen the red light from schooling and training that bears little relevance to the business world. Dare one hope that businessmen in the '80s may become the elite of the country. Slowly the message seems to be going home that the country prospers in direct relation to the business we·conduct. Slowly the mention of profit becomes less of a morally emotive issue. Slowly, although hopefully with gathering momentum, industrial managements themselves are becoming marketing oriented. No matter how professional and dedicated the Product Manager may be, if top management is not of similar outlook little will happen.

World View

As one element towards greater professionalism, Product Managers of the future must be increasingly 'citizens of the world'. Whatever happens at GATT conferences and the like, overseas competitors in our markets can and often do reflect customer and consumer intentions to obtain good value for money, *in their terms*. To Buy British is only relevant if the product is as acceptable in customer values as other products and services available. In fact, it might be advantageous for every Product Manager to attend a course on overseas market influences, once in a while. Even to attend a course on exporting from these shores might have a salutary effect in opening eyes wider than before.

Moral Attitudes

Customers are better educated to events which affect their daily lives and have very much greater protection from wrongdoers, in the commercial sense, than ever before. This may be an irritant in some cases but, since we are all customers, the generality of protection of individuals and companies should be welcomed. Not only must the Product Manager be aware of legal and quasi-legal requirements to a greater extent, therefore, but, as an arbiter of moral decisions, he must in addition be seen to be 'whiter than white'.

Concentrated Buying Power

The continual concentration of buying power into fewer and more powerful hands can lead to a lessening of competitive choice and an increase of dictation which can only be detrimental to the end customer. This must be fought hard but at the same time, Product Managers' actions are inevitably going to be more and more coloured by the few customers who are so important to his company operations. As a dichotomy, this scene is not new and in many companies, administrative changes in marketing departments have been made to accommodate that prime importance of key accounts. Kellogg has appointed 'Category Managers' to its marketing department to create closer links with its trade customers. This is an inheritance from the United States and is a variation of Product Manager insofar as a Category Manager is also responsible for the output of one factory, since factories in that company tend to produce separate categories of product.

Flexibility

Marketing has grown at different paces and in different ways over the last twenty years from its inception in this country. Sensibly it has melded its methods and responsibilities to suit different industries. Requirements in heavy industrial companies are different in detail from those in specialist veterinary product companies, or service organisations, or fast moving consumer goods industries. The latter has been in the forefront of development since marketing began and sophisticated techniques have generally originated there. Might this have some lessons for the future ?

Planning and Execution

Since the practice, as well as the practitioners, of marketing is growing and since, at least for some purposes, there is a continually greater need for strong liaison between marketing and sales (indeed sales forces are increasingly coming under the direction at top management level of Marketing Directors) might there be a thought for the future of Product Management, of a basis of operation ?

Some Product Managers are ideally suited to a close role with sales departments. They may be extrovert, very interested in the 'sharp end' and perhaps less comfortable with the numbers game of computer modelling, of research, of planning in any sophisticated way. Indeed, they may have been salesman or women at some time in their recent past. Whilst other Product Managers, equally good and professional, are much more interested in the planning operation, in the reasons why, in the 'back room'. In a sense, both aspects are vital in the well rounded marketing person but they tend to represent opposites. Whilst within a marketing department it is possible to have both, within one person it seldom is. In a nutshell, there may be a difference between the thinker and the doer.

Could one envisage marketing developing into two distinct branches ? The Planning Branch on the one hand and the Executive Branch on the other. The idea may immediately conjure up the difference between a service department and a 'proper' marketing department. But the possibility outlined above is more fundamental than that. Certainly the Planning Branch would incorporate analyses, research, economic trends, forward planning in the market sense, and so on, but to plan without the responsibility of execution and control makes little sense and certainly gives little personal satisfaction. The Planning Branch might still have profit responsibility for the products concerned. The Executive Branch would be responsible for achieving the sales targets by providing all the total marketing direction related to customers. The manager would be a combination of Marketing and Sales Manager but with a much wider role than Sales Management. Key Accounts Sales persons would still be required but they are, in any case, business negotiators requiring a marketing input.

So perhaps one may see 'Product Manager-Planning' and 'Product Manager-Executive' in the future. But whatever the structure and whatever the title, Product Managers will need to be better at reading the future, better at practical planning, better at gaining tactical advantage, and better at suiting the product to the chosen market segment, than ever before.

Job Satisfaction

They will require deeper and more regular personal training, more continuous awareness of fundamentals affecting market conditions, greater flexibility, greater sophistication in marketing techniques, a bolder attitude to entrepreneurial possibilities, more detailed market sector exploitation and an ability to sell himself to everyone connected with the implementation of marketing plans. Altogether a daunting, fascinating, dynamic, and demanding role. Perhaps lying on a sunny beach in Samoa, as Gaugin did, would be easier. But the questing, thrusting, human mind of the good marketing person would soon reassert itself, and pride, both personal and national, would spur us on to accept one of the most challenging and necesssary roles in business – that of Product Manager.

Index